WHAT'S LEFT?

What's Left?

THE ECOLE NORMALE SUPÉRIEURE

AND THE RIGHT

DIANE RUBENSTEIN

THE UNIVERSITY OF WISCONSIN PRESS

The University of Wisconsin Press
114 North Murray Street
Madison, Wisconsin 53715

3 Henrietta Street
London WC2E 8LU, England

5   4   3   2   1

Printed in the United States of America

Permissions have been given to reproduce quotations from the following sources: *The Structuralists from Marx to Lévi-Strauss*, Jacques Lacan, 1966, Anchor Press; *Fascist Intellectual: Drieu La Rochelle*, Robert Soucy, 1979, The University of California Press, copyright © 1979 The Regents of The University of California; *Margins of Philosophy*, Jacques Derrida, translated, with additional notes, by Alan Bass, 1982, The University of Chicago Press, copyright © 1982 by The University of Chicago; *Sade, Fourier, Loyola*, Roland Barthes, translated by Richard Miller, 1976, Hill and Wang, a division of Farrar, Straus and Giroux, Inc., copyright © 1976 by Farrar, Straus and Giroux, Inc.; *Force of Circumstance*, Simone de Beauvoir, 1965, Editions Gallimard; *Politiques de La Philosophie: Châtelet, Derrida, Foucault, Lyotard, Serres*, edited by Dominique Grisoni, 1976, Éditions Bernard Grasset, copyright © Éditions Grasset & Fasquelle, Paris, 1976; *Moses and Monotheism*, Sigmund Freud, translated by Katherine Jones, 1939, Alfred A. Knopf, Inc., copyright © 1939 by Alfred A. Knopf, Inc., and renewed by Ernst L. Freud and Anna Freud; *I, Pierre Riviere, Having Slaughtered My Mother, My Sister, and My Brother: A Case of Parricide in the Nineteenth Century*, 1982, The University of Nebraska Press; *Teachers, Writers, Celebrities*, Régis Debray, 1981, New Left Books; *Sense and Non-Sense*, Maurice Merleau-Ponty, translated by Herbert L. Pon Dreyfus and Patricia Allen Dreyfus, 1964, Northwestern University Press, copyright © 1964 by Northwestern University Press; *Power/Knowledge: Selected Interviews & Other Writings, 1972–1977*, 1981, Pantheon Books; *Elites in French Society*, Ezra Suleiman, 1978, Princeton University Press.

Library of Congress-in-Publication Data
Rubenstein, Diane, 1953–
    What's left?: the Ecole Normale Supérieure and the right /
Diane Rubenstein.
    232 pp.   cm.
Includes bibliographical references and index.
    1. France—Intellectual life—20th century.   2. France—Intellectual life—20th
century—Historiography.
3. Intellectuals—France—Political activity—History—20th century.
4. Ecole normale supérieure (France)—History—20th century.
5. Conservatism—France—History—20th century.   6. Politics
and literature—France—History—20th century.
7. Education, Higher—Social aspects—France—History—20th century.
I. Title. DC33.7.R78   1990
944.081'5'008631—dc20   90-12644
ISBN 0-299-12560-2   CIP
ISBN 0-299-12564-5 (paper)

To Philip

CONTENTS

ACKNOWLEDGMENTS

This study of the Ecole Normale Supérieure's institutional authority would not have been possible were it not for many institutions and "authorities," most important, the ENS. I wish to express my profound gratitude to M. Humbert, director of the ENS, for the aid and authorizations I was given which greatly facilitated my research. For three years, 1979–1982, the ENS was a spiritual home. My debt to the library and to its alumni are enormous. I wish to thank Messieurs Etienne Balibar, Georges Canguilhem, Jacques Derrida, Claude Jamet, Thierry Maulnier, Henri Quéffelec, and Jacques Soustelle for granting me interviews. In particular, I should like to thank Messieurs Maurice Bardèche and Georges Lefranc who were especially helpful in providing me with introductions and unpublished manuscripts in addition to their invaluable recollections. Jean François Sirinelli (whose *doctorat d'état* on the *khâgnes* of the twenties and thirties was recently published) was exceptionally generous with both suggestions and contacts. Cohorts of these *normaliens* also provided recollections and introductions for which I am extremely grateful. Pierre Andreu was especially helpful in both regards. M. Jean Drieu La Rochelle was unusually generous with his brother's manuscripts and his personal reminiscences. Me. Jacques Isorni was an invaluable witness for my reconstruction of the postwar trials.

I was able to carry out this research owing to the generous grants of the Yale Concilium on International Studies and the French-American Foundation's Chateaubriand Grant. A Taft Summer Research Fellowship from the University of Cincinnati enabled me to see the Déat manuscript at the Bibliothèque Nationale and conduct interviews in the summer of 1984. Grants from the Wisconsin Alumni Research Fund allowed for revision of the manuscript and additional research in 1987–88. For all of these grants, I am extremely grateful.

I also acknowledge the help and cooperation of the staffs of the Archives Nationales, the Bibliothèque Historique de la Ville de Paris, the Centre du Documentation Juive Contemporaine, and the Bibliothèque Nationale. The Maison des Sciences de l'Homme provided a very congenial environment for the examination of secondary source material.

This book began as a Ph.D. thesis under the direction of Professor Juan J. Linz at Yale University. I have benefited greatly since then

Acknowledgments

by discussions with and readings of the manuscript by David Apter, David Cameron, James Scott, and Juan Linz. I have also benefited from Pierre Bourdieu's reading of my Ph.D. thesis and in particular his suggestions for Chapters 3 and 6. I would like especially to thank two of my colleagues at the University of Wisconsin at Madison, Professors Murray Edelman and Elaine Marks, for their astute comments and encouragement. Tom Keenan was a scrupulous reader of the manuscript. It was a continual pleasure to work with my editor, Gordon Lester-Massman.

I cannot underestimate my personal and intellectual debt to Professor Juan Linz for originally suggesting a study of French intellectuals and for his vigorous encouragement and continual support. His innumerable valuable suggestions greatly improved upon earlier versions. From Professor Linz I have gained insight into comparative research and an appreciation of sociological analysis.

It gives me great pleasure to affectionately acknowledge the constant support, encouragement, and insights of my parents, Gilbert and Natalie Rubenstein, and my husband, Philip Protter, whom I met at the Ecole Normale.

CAVEAT LECTOR

This is a book about the politics of writing in France. But it is also, perhaps due to the circumstances of its own writing, a book about the politics of writing in America. In other words the thematic concerns of the book treat pedagogical and literary institutions in France. The methodological concerns address a polemic about the way a study about intellectuals is to proceed and the applicability of that French import—deconstruction—to empirical investigations within the human sciences.

It may be somewhat appropriate to describe a book written within the context of a diacritical notion of language to say what it is *not*. This is a book about the politics of writing. It is not a treatment of what is traditionally called political or ideological writing. Its primary focus is not on a specific content or thematic register per se (i.e., French fascism, nationalism) but rather on the signifying forms (texts, institutions) that produce a political subject or agent. Specifically, it addresses the philosophic question of agency and the relation of this problem of agency to educational institutions in France. Moreover, although this examination of intellectuals, ideology, and power proceeds at times by the conceptual machinery of literary theory—poststructuralism, semiotics, deconstruction—this book is neither an apology for nor a pedagogical treatment of any one of these theories. The tone of this book is thus not prescriptive but descriptive (theoretical and constantive). It is not an impassioned appeal to give up empirical social science nor to advocate "deconstruction" for all of the social sciences. It does not attempt to convince, or even to persuade—which is to say that this is, above all, a written book. It is not conversational. A "deconstructive" book is like the psychoanalytic situation. Take it, it says, or leave it. It is not a dialogue as much as it is eavesdropping.

What follows then in these next few pages is what is called in French an *avertissement* or warning. Our attempt is not to translate the untranslatable difference between the French and American approaches to the study of intellectuals, culture, and power but to adumbrate the effects of this dislocation.

The most important difference of this book is in its treatment of ideology, intellectuals, and deconstruction.

Ideology

The notion of ideology deployed in this book may appear unusual to some readers. For it is not ideology as an assortment of *isms*—conservatism, liberalism, royalism, nationalism, or fascism—that is the primary concern. In other words, I do not treat ideology as some sort of transcendental signified, an assemblage of official pronouncements, explicit assertions, and discourses. Rather the notion of ideology invoked is a *gnostic* one; ideology is something hidden. The rightist discourse is thus to be found where it seems not to be: in the trivial, marginal or, worse yet, in the seemingly neutral institutional mechanisms (such as the *concours d'entrée*). This does not mean that one ignores the public discourses, the rituals, gestures, and costumes; rather it necessitates that they be read backward, as emblems.

Roland Barthes once defined ideology as that which goes without saying.[1] This examination of *normalien* ideology attempts to say precisely that which goes without saying, which means it will at times appear trivial or frivolous or banal to those readers who see ideology as a set of stable signifieds, that is, who see ideology only where ideology says it is.

Intellectuals

The discussion of intellectuals is also a rejection of the two traditional treatments. It is a challenge to the liberal humanist tradition familiar to readers of Julien Benda and Raymond Aron. The intellectual presented here is disinterested or *dégagée*. But it is also a challenge to the conventional notion of the engaged or committed philosopher exemplified by the work of Sartre and Paul Nizan. For Sartre the intellectual was not just committed, he was a writer of the left. (This is why Sartre was so disturbed by Drieu.) However opposed these two treatments of intellectuals may seem, we should take note of the similarities. Both of these views have in common an ethics of intellectual life. Both sets of works are works of moral prescription. What recent French writing on intellectuals (such as Foucault, Deleuze, Derrida, Lyotard) lacks—if you will—is a missionary position. Régis Debray supplies the following maxim: "Act in such a way that the maxim of your actions can never be construed as a general law."[2]

This difference in tone is related to two ancillary concerns. It parallels the philosophic rejection of essentialism and logocentrism. An intellectual for Foucault can never be a representing consciousness. "A theorising intellectual, for us, is no longer a subject—a representing and representative consciousness."[3] Moreover, there is a displacement of the question of agency (i.e., the "responsibility" of the intellectual) to the site of contestation (schools, institutions, disciplines). The question of the intellectual is less a question of will or choice than an effect of geography: his place in a university, publishing or media site of power, legitimation, hegemony. Theory is no longer totalizing; it is regional.

This, it should be noted in passing, is in keeping with a shift away from a description of the signifier to a description of the signifier's place. The signifier is seen strategically as that which occupies a place. Foucault focuses on the regional constraints upon writing; Derrida situates texts. The geographic effect is especially pronounced in Foucault's work. Here, the text is a place among places where strategies of control in society are conducted. Discourse for Foucault, as Said noted, works at the level of the base and not of the superstructure.[4]

This emphasis on the signifier's place and a movement away from the subject should not be read as an apolitical aestheticism. Following Jameson and Said, there is an ethical imperative at work beneath the focus on textuality. And it should be noted that even this displacement recalls the earlier traditions of writing on intellectuals for it maintains Sartre's privileging of writing and philosophy while it retains the ethical imperative, albeit seen in reference to the signifier and no longer to the subject's consciousness.

The reformulation of the question of intellectuals takes various guises which share a politicization of pedagogy.[5] Some recent examples include Michèle Le Doeuff's examination of the discourse of philosophy and her concern for institutional barriers which prevent philosophy from being the true object of its own inquiry. Régis Debray's work focuses on political discipline in a Kantian sense: "the determination of limits placed on the use of a faculty." Derrida's examination of the teaching apparatus can also be seen in this French neo-Kantian light. Barthes's examination of teachers as intellectuals makes use of the psychoanalytic model, while Bourdieu uses this reformulation of teachers as intellectuals to turn educational theory into social theory. All these authors recall Gramsci in that they regard pedagogic activity as having an inherently political quality. Yet there is a crucial difference: there are no claims of agency. What we have here, paradoxically, are transformative intellectuals without hope of emancipation!

Yet this only underlines a salient difference in the French approach to intellectuals. Where the traditional view of emancipatory intellectuals focuses on possibility, the French focus is on the impossible. Debray writes: "A critique of political reason tells me what I can not do but under no circumstances what I should not do. It spells out the impossible, not what is wished for or detested. Whoever may search through it for a sketchy stand, not to speak of a line, will thereby risk a radical misreading."[6]

Deconstruction

It should be stated from the outset: deconstruction is not to be considered here as a methodology. But then what is deconstructive about the book if it neither produces a pedagogic treatment of deconstruction nor advances it as a method? The book shares with deconstructive works a certain notion of the text as well as conception of what is meant by reading. The notion of reading makes it impossible to reduce deconstruction to a method; the notion of text makes it impossible to reduce it to "discourse analysis."

Reading is understood in the Demanian sense.[7] It is not a means to an end, a means that should upon its arrival become transparent and meaningless. Reading is not a mere intervention like some computation in an algebraic proof. Reading is being attentive to the rhetorical complexities in a text. Deconstruction would then take into account the problematic of the phenomenalism of reading—in this case, the reading of the rhetoric of an establishment (the Ecole Normale Supérieure). Understood this way deconstruction is also a *phronesis*, a way of acting in the world which simply can't be reduced to a method one can pick up or abandon at will. This conception of deconstruction as a *phronesis* without emancipatory claims has made it particularly repugnant to social theorists who persist in restricting deconstruction to a *technè*.

The notion of text deployed here is a cryptic and gnostic one. The text is something that hides something. The attitude taken is one of a hermeneutics of suspicion which follows both Foucault's and Derrida's position on textuality. As Said so brilliantly resumes the now canonical opposition: Foucault resemantizes texts. He affiliates them with institutions, academies, disciplines. Derrida's approach is to dedefine and displace them. Derrida's textual practice is both rigorous and eccentric; Foucault's is protracted and systematic.[8] This book deploys both of these textual modes.

This heterogeneous approach underscores the second point about textuality: the text is not a stable and fixed entity, something that is synonymous with the book. The Derridean concept of the text is a generalized one. Heterogeneous in nature, the text is seen as a field of forces, differential and open. This is why, as Derrida stated recently, deconstructive readings and writings are not concerned just with library books. Nor can they be reduced to discourse analyses. "They are also active interventions, in particular political and institutional interventions that transform contexts without limiting themselves to theoretical or constantive utterances even though they must produce such utterances."[9] The heterogeneity of the text will call for a heterogeneity of approaches—at times discourse analysis, at times analyses of institutions, rites, and myths, at times empirical sociology.

What follows then is a reading of the Ecole Normale as a text. We are reading an institution which is also a reading institution concerned with a politics of writing.

Whoever said it would be normal!

WHAT'S LEFT?

1 INTRODUCTION

*I will speak, therefore, of a letter . . . And I must state here
and now that today's discourse will be less a justification
of, and even less an apology for, this silent lapse in
spelling, than a kind of insistent intensification of its
play . . . And I insist upon the word* faisceau *(sheaf,
bundle) for two reasons. On the one hand, I will not be
concerned, as I might have been, with describing a history
and narrating its stages, text by text, context by
context . . . On the other hand, the word* faisceau *seems
to mark more appropriately that the assemblage to be
proposed has the complex structure of a weaving, an
interlacing which permits the different threads and
different lines of meaning—or of force—to go off again in
different directions, just as it is always ready to tie itself up
with others.*

—J. Derrida, "Différance"

For a work concerned with the impossibility of considering institutional politics without reference to a textual script,
the origin of the Ecole Normale Supérieure is most auspicious. Indeed, the origin of the ENS can be traced to a violation of orthography
and a deeply felt republican animus. Nor are these two concerns—
political position and the act of writing—disjoint. For Joseph Lakanal, who founded the ENS in 1794 ("par decret du 9 Brumaire an III")[1]
as a "republican" institution, also chose to signal his separation from
his "royalist brothers" through changing the spelling of his name to
"Lacanal."[2]

And these twin concerns, the intermingling (or, more accurately,
the *faisceau*, or "bundling")[3] of the militant republicanism of the ENS,
heralded in the change of a letter (*k* to *c*) which must be read or written
(and not merely spoken), parallels our itinerary as well. Our examination of the ENS seeks to trace a link between power, political position,
and writing, as well as the repression of this link. In other words,
our reexamination of the right at the ENS seeks not only to displace
the dominant view of the ENS as a leftist institution, but, more important, to demonstrate the inextricability (*faisceau*) of this stereotype
from a view of politics as speech or behavior. Indeed, this predomi-

3

nant equation of politics with speech (and its corollary that writing is secondary) is an ironic reversal of the founder's intentions. For Lakanal, political position clearly could not be sufficiently inferred from political behavior. The change of a letter was a necessary feature of his republicanism. Or, Lakanal's republicanism took two forms of expression: a change in spelling and the founding of an institution to train a corps of loyal teachers. Our discussion of the ENS will therefore illuminate the politics of the ENS in the spirit of the founder's original intentions.

The priority of writing is a consistent theme which will also serve to explain the importance of rightist *normaliens* well beyond their actual numbers as well as highlight the specificity of the ENS as an institution devoted to the dissemination of cultural values. In other words, our reinscription of writing within politics will parallel our reinscription of the right within the ENS political tradition.

"Queen of the Academic System"

From the outset, as a logician, with his usual lucidity and precision, Napoleon decreed that special schools would be strictly professional and practical schools. "Make me regents," he said one day of the Ecole Normale, "and not littérateurs, sensitive souls or scholars."
—Hippolyte Taine

The Ecole Normale Supérieure, like its *confrère*, the Ecole Polytechnique, was created during the Convention. The ENS was at first only an *"école normale primaire"*; it was not until 1808 that it received its actual mission. In 1845, it received its title: Ecole Normale Supérieure.[4] The ENS was housed in the buildings of the Collège du Plessis (rue St. Jacques) before it moved to its current site at the rue d'Ulm in 1847. Robert Brasillach describes its location, set off by trees, a "rectangle of buildings surrounding a courtyard of trees decorated with a pond and lawns." To the south is the rue Claude Bernard, to the north is the rue des Feuillantines, and it is also bounded by the rue Lhomond close to an annex of the Ecole Polytechnique.[5] Until 1903, when the ENS merged with the University of Paris, this insular universe lodged all *normaliens*. Students were allowed to live outside of the school only after the 1903 reforms.

But the 1903 reforms changed more than the dormitory regulations. The *concours d'entrée* which admitted students into the ENS was no longer a separate one from that of the *bourses de licence*. Yet this should

Table 1. Comparative Institutions of Higher Education

| | Grandes Ecoles | | Université de Paris |
	ENS	Polytechnique	Sorbonne
Date founded	1794; Convention reestablished 1808	1794; Convention reestablished 1808	1253; suppressed 1792; reestablished 1808
Founder	Joseph Lakanal, politician	Gaspard Monge (comte de Peluse), mathematician; Lazare Carnot, engineer	Robert de Sorbonne, chaplain of Louis IX
Mission	Provide a teaching corps for secondary education	Formation of a corps of officers and engineers	Instruction in theology, letters, and science
Ministry	Ministère de l'Instruction Publique et des Beaux Arts	Ministère de l'Intérieure/Guerre	Académie de Paris
Admission	*Concours*	*Concours*	Baccalauréat degree
Duration	3–4 years for *license* and *agrégation*	2 years	—
Residence	Before 1903, dormitory only; after 1903, either dormitory or *externe*	*Externe* (no dorms)	*Externe* (no dorms)

not trivialize the arduous nature of the *concours*. Brasillach recounts that the subject matter covered was vast—roughly equivalent to two *baccalauréats*, but in greater depth.[6] Indeed, it would be difficult to overestimate the importance of the *concours*. For the goal of the ENS went beyond its initial mission of training lycée teachers. Philippe Ariès notes that the main purpose was to create an elite. In other words, the *concours* insures that one develops a culture *before* one acquires a profession. Ariès resumes the importance of the *concours* in creating "ascribed achievement": "The *grandes écoles,* where one entered by competitive examination, which became more and more difficult, established within the powerful but fluid divisions of society, a new social category, defined at once by its small size and its merit. It carried a name, the 'elite.'"[7] Suleiman situates the ENS in opposition to the university which declined in the nineteenth century in direct proportion to Napoleon's realization of the strategic place of the *grandes écoles*. Yet among the *grandes écoles*, the ENS has a peculiar status. "Queen of the academic system," she has provoked ambivalent responses.[8] For although the ENS is a *grande école* in the sense that a rigorous *concours* is required for admission, it differs from the others, such as Polytechnique, in that it isn't a vocational school in the narrow sense. The ENS has always been more renowned for its politicians, philosophers, and men of letters than for its contribution to the corps of lycée teachers.

The specificity of the ENS is perhaps best revealed in the memoirs of its students. Part of the uniqueness of the ENS is due to the legacy of the 1903 reforms. The postreforms ENS was an institution, Brasillach writes, without obligation or punishment. Conservative critics castigated the new decrees for creating a "furnished hotel," yet students reveled in this new freedom after several years of arduous preparation for the *concours*.[9] Brasillach refers to it as an asylum: "the most astounding asylum of poetic anarchy."[10] The lack of regimentation made the existence of the ENS a question of metaphysics: "That is, the Ecole Normale has as its primary virtue its non-existence, which is decidedly rare."[11] One took the same exams as Sorbonne students (*certificat de licence, diplôme d'études supérieures, agrégation*) with the same teachers. Before 1902, the ENS had autonomy: special courses and teachers. The only obligation after 1903 was to take the exams at the year's end. Failure at the licence level would entail suspension until this exam was successfully passed. The only other requirement was preparation for military service, and one finds ample evidence in the ENS disciplinary files that there was much student protest against this constraint. Expulsion was the sole punishment, and it was rarely inflicted. Nor was class attendance mandatory. Rather a principle of tact obtained. If one's absences were ostentatious, perhaps "the director would diffidently proffer his comments, which would never be accompanied by any effective penalty."[12] If there were no rules, there were, indeed, customs. A morning bell rang at seven-thirty to signify breakfast. However, three quarters of the students didn't partake of this repast: "Besides, the coffee was dreadful—we preferred, generally, bistros . . . and we got up at eight, nine, or at eleven A.M." A life without regulations was not without rituals: a noon lunch, dinner at seven, white wine on Fridays.[13]

Creature comforts increased during M. Vessiot's tenure as director of the school. (He was a "*scientifique*" in distinction to most of the other directors such as Lavisse, Lanson, Bouglé, Carcopino.) Napkins and glasses appeared. Rumor suggested that M. Herriot's intervention was the cause of this beneficence. The money which augmented the *normalien* living standard was taken from the budget of the Jardin des Plantes. When Herriot discovered that the monkeys were to have their budget increased, he protested: "What about the *normaliens*?" After the laughter died down, the money intended for the monkeys went to Ulm.[14] Although the ENS parallels Erving Goffman's total institutions, the low living standard and "physical contamination" described by both Goffman and Orwell in his boarding school recollections were not the case at Ulm during this period.[15] Déat's memoirs, however, attest to a more Spartan regime in the immediate post–World War I period.[16]

Although there were little external constraints, life within Ulm attested to a well-structured hierarchy. The first year, six students shared a room on the ground floor; the second year, there were three or four to a room on the first floor; and in the third year, the "elect" were only two or three to a room located on the second floor, called the "*palais.*"[17] The lack of a central core of courses and teachers led to a displacement of the ENS focus: the library, the refectory, and the tennis court increased in significance. "Le tennis, la bibliothèque . . . ainsi s'organise la vie."[18] In addition, Bouglé's Centre de Documentation Sociale was a center for serious discussions and for the perusing of learned journals. A room on the ground floor was a haven for newspaper reading.

Yet one can argue that there is a method in this apparent anarchy. For the relative freedom of the ENS allowed for autodidacticism. Indeed, the importance of the library in this system, especially a library with the unusual feature of open stacks, can not be overestimated. The library is consistently mentioned in *normalien* memoirs as well as by those *normaliens* interviewed. Former students who do not attend any of the special functions of the ENS return to use the library. One might see in this system a perfect mode of creating an elite intelligentsia, which would mediate the Scylla of autodidacticism (through the rigid selection process of the *concours*, which functions as a "quality control" mechanism) and the Charybdis of a rigid specialized curriculum (which might squelch the spontaneity or creativity of this elite.)

If our discussion has focused on the similarities and the differences between the ENS and the other *grandes écoles*, the ENS can also be situated in a process of displacement. Foucault describes the continual deferral of the "secret" of philosophic initiation: "The secret knowledge promised was always postponed to a later date."[19] From primary school to the lycée to the "*classe de philo*" (in the last year of lycée) to finally higher education, of which the "holy of holies" was the ENS.

This displacement, deferral, relay is a key notion in our analysis of the Ecole Normale Supérieure. For an analysis of the ENS and the right is a heterodox focus and as such shares an affinity with what has been called "deconstruction." Jeffrey Mehlman, author of a volume on a closely related subject, *Legacies of Anti-Semitism in France*, defined those key features which tie his work, as well as my study, to "that general interpretative effort" known as deconstruction: "The discovery and valorization of the marginal . . . its intricate displacement to a strategic near center from which a chiasmic shift in the values of a corpus may be effected strike me as among the most difficult and rewarding gestures that reading at present allows."[20] Moreover, my analysis of the ENS parallels Mehlman's readings of Blanchot, Leon Bloy, and Giraudoux in that the marginal ideas that are displaced to near center are not just eccentric (for Mehlman, it is anti-Semitism; in my own case, it is the right); they are taboo as well. What Mehlman writes about anti-Semitism can be echoed for the right as well: "Anti-Semitism, by dint of Europe's recent history, is one of the few taboo regions of speculation in our secularized democracies. Here then lies a margin one can pretend to displace only at some risk."[21]

In addition, my study harbors other uncanny similarities to Mehlman's book. Both are not dependent upon what he calls "intentionality"; rather, both question the "sustaining effects of a cultural milieu" which appears to Mehlman anti-Jewish and for my own work, rightist. "It is as though only the slightest displacement were necessary within the designation of the French monument to reveal therein a drama of Jewish exclusion," Mehlman writes.[22] What I have also attempted is such a displacement within the monument of one of France's most elite educational institutions.

With this broad theoretic schema in mind, we will now turn to a chapter-by-chapter overview. Chapter 2, "What's Left? The Ecole Normale Supérieure and the Right," situates the study of the ENS in light of poststructuralist theory, much of it produced by former students of the ENS. Reexaminations of three concepts central to the study of intellectuals—author, writing, university—are detailed. Our presentation is outlined in relation to Lévi-Strauss's notion of *bricolage*, which is employed to trace the displacement of authority as both a political and a textual principle. In addition, deconstruction has always concerned itself with the institutional constraints upon discourse: the question of how and where a discourse takes place. Indeed, what does it mean for a discourse to take place (*avoir lieu*)? Moreover deconstruction, in contrast to hermeneutics, takes as its object monological institutions (academies, law), as opposed to dialogical situations.

Chapter 3, "Le Cru et l'Écrit" ("The Crude and the Cryptic," apologies to Lévi-Strauss), considers the interrelations between institution and myth. I attempt to remedy a double absence: the neglect of the right within any institutional analysis or empirical sociology and the lack of any elaboration of the mythic function of the ENS. I show that the leftist caricature of the ENS both is inaccurate and represses the role of writing in political behavior. Several distinct generations of rightist *normaliens* are described as well as the similarity of both rightist and leftist *scolarité* until the moment of the *agrégation* and *débouchement*. If sociological variables fail to explain the differences between right and left, a focus on writing reveals a salient difference: writing is seen as a supplement for leftists (political parties have priority) although it is prior for rightists. Moreover, an analysis of the mythic function of the ENS shows that the importance of the polarity is in the opposition not between right and left, but between *rite* and *what's left* out in any institutional approach: myth. In other words, we examine the power of acts of institution to both resist and recuperate political difference from within; the only significant difference is between insider-outsider (and not communist-fascist). I examine two instituting rites: the *canular* (hazing initiation) and the *concours d'entrée* (the state exam which affords entry into the ENS) via two concepts of Pierre Bourdieu, the "amnesia of genesis" and *habitus*, respectively.

Chapter 4, "The Return of the Repressed: The ENS and the Right," combines the double absences of the third chapter; the repression of the school's rightist students as well as the mythic status of its rites of institution necessitates a reinscription of the right within the rites, especially the *concours d'entrée*, which is subjected to a detailed analysis. An institutional discourse is outlined in a way similar to that of Derrida's reading of Rousseau, in which texts are shown to function against their own explicit assertions, "not just by creating ambiguities, but by inscribing a systematic other message behind or through what's being said."[23] Or, in other words, however much the ENS celebrates illustrious *normaliens* of the left, it does so in a language (as seen in the *necrologies* and distribution of literary prizes) that reinforces notions of superiority, exclusivity, hierarchy that bear a startling similarity to analogous notions on the right. Moreover, a seemingly neutral institutional mechanism such as the *concours d'entrée* parallels certain rightist thematics: it is an act of investiture that turns history into nature as well as an expression of the horror of mediocrity, to cite just two examples. The "discourse of importance" so admirably produced by the ENS (and elegantly described by its student, Bourdieu) not only underscores rightist themes but masks differences between right and left.[24] An examination of the *canular* and the family romance it engenders in the form of a *normalien patrimoine* reveals that the masses are to be excluded from a specific thematic register as well as from the form of language which clothes this theme. The separation of ordinary language from scientific language will be seen as a reinforcing mechanism for elite self-perception and politics and will be considered in our next chapter.

Chapter 5, "Language and Authority," outlines the *mise en forme* (verbal formulations) of elite discourse. If our focus until now has been on repression, then this *mise en forme* will be seen as the *Aufhebung* of repression. The ENS will thus be seen as the standard for all elite discourse in France. We examine the rightist ideology as that signifying form through which this standard is realized. Transgression is to be understood less as the expression of a contrary content than as the use of inferior codes which break a linguistic contract. The ENS is seen as a privileged first site of what Bourdieu calls "practice," and it is here that social difference is translated into verbal distinction. Following Barthes, we examine "professors as agents of the sentence" and "encratic language (language of power) as a language of repetition."[25] In addition to repetition we examine various figures such as neologisms and alliteration which further delineate ordinary from elite speech. Moreover, neologisms are seen as attempts at euphemization (or compromise formation) which mythologize difference. We conclude with an examination of how the binary opposition articulates difference. Here a *mise en forme* is seen as, above all, a challenge (*mise en garde*).[26] Relations of oppositions inherent in the binary opposition always relate to the opposition between different social groups. Relevant binaries concern the sacred-profane, high-low, and inclusion-exclusion. In addition, in the case of the ENS elite discourse, we witness the transformation of pejoratives into superlatives. For example, facility and leisure are transubstantiated into aristocratic virtues when they take *normaliens* as their object.

Chapter 6, "The ENS and the Scene of Writing," analyzes the relation between writing and politics in its *performative* dimension. Our previous chapter having looked at the codes of discourse, we will now examine writing as a practice. Indeed, the traditional divorce of writing from politics underlines the denigration of culture as "just one type of signifying practice." It is contended that thought and authority intersect in the scene of writing, that is in literary networks. The ENS will be seen as a *"pépinière"* (nursery) to publishing circles. Moreover, it is a paradoxical *pépinière* as extremist journals fare better with *normaliens* than more moderate ones. The tendency toward extremism will be one focus as will the uneasy demarcation of right and left within these circles. Indeed, the scene of writing in the thirties will be read as a successive deconstruction of three sets of binary oppositions: right-left, young-old, and political-aesthetic. The literary politics of *normaliens* will be seen as a miniature of the complex alignments that characterized the Occupation. *Normalien* traditions of pacificism and socialism will be reinscribed in the historical conjuncture known as Vichy. The importance of school ties in political itineraries will be underscored by the case of Déat. Moreover, certain institutional themes—camaraderie, the *"équipe"*—will "explain" Brasillach's and Déat's participation in *Je Suis Partout* and *L'Oeuvre*, respectively. Both of these journals will be seen as a journalistic recreation of a *normalien* experience. (This will parallel our earlier discussions in Chapters 3 and 4.) Yet this foray into the "performative" will recuperate that fundamental undecidability of our title, "What's left?" For the *normalien* literary networks are most marked by an absence or inexplicability of political alignment in relation to any clearly defined boundaries. All difference can be recuperated within *normalien* myths and institutional discourse.

Chapter 7, "The Postwar Trials: Words and Deeds," brings our narrative development of a literary signature and of the connection between writing and politics to its end in the confrontation between textuality and criminality, or between literary and legal authority. In the trials of collaborationist *normaliens*, we witness the author as the victim of his own writing. For either one views the trial sentencing as arbitrary, or the trials underline the political importance of the bearers of the word. The trials judge the ENS as a licensee and regulator of discourse and are both a judgment on and a protection of an educational system that ritualizes speech. In many ways, they function as the *last word*: the last word as value, the last words, literally, of the book.

2 WHAT'S LEFT?

THE ECOLE NORMALE SUPÉRIEURE

AND THE RIGHT

To deny a people the man whom it praises as the greatest of its sons is not a deed to be undertaken lightheartedly— especially by one belonging to that people. No consideration, however, will move me to set aside truth in favour of supposed national interests. Moreover, the elucidation of the mere facts of the problem may be expected to deepen our insight into the situation with which they are concerned.
—Freud, *Moses and Monotheism*

For many readers even remotely conversant with the Ecole Normale Supérieure, situating it with relation to the right would appear every bit as scandalous as Freud's declaration that Moses was an Egyptian.[1] For the political tradition of the ENS is founded on the participation of its greatest sons on the left: Jean Jaurès, Léon Blum, Lucien Herr. To argue that both the rightist milieu and its renegade students (Robert Brasillach, Marcel Déat) are equally typical, or indeed, in some respects, prototypical, may well provoke. However, I hope that this disorientation will also "deepen our insight"; for the leftist stereotype of the ENS has obscured our vision. The traditional view would favor left over right, political parties over literary participation, voice over text, when in fact there is much evidence to the contrary (not least the postwar trials of intellectuals). More important, this image of the school seriously circumscribes its institutional importance at the same time that it reduces the notion of political praxis to parliamentary behaviorism. Just as I argue that the power of the ENS cannot be reduced to narrow political criteria (e.g., party membership), so too I will argue against the denigration of "symbolic" politics vis-à-vis politico-administrative concerns. Indeed, our displacement

13

What's Left? The Ecole Normale Supérieure and the Right

of the ENS away from the left serves to undo that binary opposition as well.

Freud's proclamation that "Moses was an Egyptian" did not just substitute one illusion for another. Rather this utterance raised as many problems as it answered. And so our displacement of the focus on the ENS from left to right raises questions uncannily akin to those of Freud: "In what exactly consists the intrinsic nature of a tradition, and in what resides its peculiar power . . . from what sources [do] certain ideas . . . derive the power with which they subjugate individuals and peoples . . ."[2]

Let us begin our rightist reinscription of the ENS with a comparison to Freud's rewriting of the Moses story. Freud wonders why commentators have preferred to assume that the woman who fished Moses out of the water knew complex Hebrew etymology rather than recognize that Moses was a common Egyptian name. Moreover, even those few interpreters who did realize the Egyptian origin of this name refused to make the obvious inference from the "name to the race." To Freud's amazement, "nothing further was deduced from it."[3] So too one invokes tortuous rationalizations to explain away the presence of rightist *normaliens,* or one refuses to draw any further deductions. In other words the presence of rightist *normaliens* is either ignored or seen as an aberration. Moreover, in the case of the ENS, there is a striking pattern of denegation at work. We have a leftist history of the school, *De Jaurès à Léon Blum: L'Ecole Normale et la Politique,* written by an active participant in Valois's prefascist Faisceau who also served as Déat's editor (Hubert Bourgin). The only extant mythology of the school, *Rue d'Ulm,* is compiled by a center-right minister: Alain Peyrefitte. In other words, those who deny most fervently that Moses was an Egyptian are themselves Egyptians.

One witnesses a frantic attempt to contain rightist politics to a few aberrant youth who are contiguous to the 1928 promotion. One ignores the postwar sentencing of illustrious *normaliens:* André Guérin, Robert Brasillach, Claude Jamet. At the same time one forgets the political careers of Marcel Déat and Pierre Pucheu. The "riddle" of the ENS is *not* how a few rightist *normaliens* can be explained away, but rather, how both right and left positions can be recuperated within the institutional logic and discourse of the Ecole Normale.

Indeed, the assumptions upon which one grounds any leftist appraisal are problematic. Why does parliamentary participation assume such importance at precisely that moment marked by an intellectual critique of parliamentarianism? Why does the ENS prefer to see leftist-oriented students as its mirror image when many of these students became politically active only after their stay at the ENS and a career in teaching? Moreover, why do we favor the politically nonsynchronous when we ignore the politically synchronous: namely, that rightist students were active at the school? The radical rightist journal, *Revue Française*, we will see, was composed in the dormitory lodgings (*turne*) of Brasillach and Thierry Maulnier.[4] In addition, leftist students delay their political activism and dilute their extramural *normalien* contacts by their careers in teaching which often require a first post in the provinces. In contrast to this pattern, rightists make different career choices which enable them to stay in Paris and more easily partake of the old school tie.

On a more general level we might also ask why the thematic confluence between the ENS and the right is consistently ignored, as is the presence of anti-Semitism and the political role of an elitist, exclusionary discourse. One of the purposes behind a radical displacement of the ENS to the right is to underline this tie between the principles of linguistic and political authority. For that very literary signature that is the norm/value of ENS institutional praxis becomes the legal norm/standard of the postwar trial sentencing. Or if, as Bourdieu states, the goal of *normalien* pedagogy is to "speak like a book," then *normaliens* are doubly victims of their sentence.

But this reorientation of the ENS bears yet another structural similarity to Freud's rewriting of Moses, that of theory. For both can be seen as *deconstructive*[5] works, and as such they share the starting point of *difference*. Again Freud speaks to us:

> I had hoped the suggestion that Moses was an Egyptian would prove enlightening and stimulating in many different respects. But our first deduction of this suggestion—that the new religion he gave the Jews was his own, the Egyptian one—has foundered on the *difference*—nay, the striking contrast—between the two religions.[6]

In a deconstructive text, Barbara Johnson writes, the "starting point is thus not a point, but a difference." Deconstruction, she reminds us, is not an act of "textual vandalism." Alternative readings are motivated not by "random doubt or generalized skepticism, but by careful teasing out of warring forces *within the text itself*."[7] What is destroyed in a deconstructive reading is for Johnson the "claim to a univocal domination of one mode of signifying over another."[8] Our deconstruction of the ENS will turn on its leftist caricature and its rightist subtext. Our initial question, "What's left (out)?" will resume this tension. For

What's Left? The Ecole Normale Supérieure and the Right

I am not saying that the Ecole Normale Supérieure is a rightist institution, but rather that the exclusion of the right underlies what is central
to the ENS: the inextricable tie between writing and politics, the insistence of the literary signature within political/legal authority. The
exclusion of the right is not just wrong or empirically inaccurate; it is
symptomatic. Again, this is not an attempt to set the record straight as
in the correction of a mistake, but a meditation upon an error, which
reflects a constitutive blindness.[9]

Deconstruction in its *etymon* implies an undoing, a reading backward from what appears natural (or in our case, *normal*) to the ground
of that system's possibility. The Ecole Normale will thus be seen as
an object or set of discursive practices which focuses on the left and
political parties and which ignores both the presence of the *right* and
the constitutive role of *writing* in its *rites* of institution. Like all good
deconstructive points of departure, it is "necessarily blind to itself."
Moreover, as in all good deconstructive texts, discrepancies will be
produced by a *double-edged word*, or, in Derrida's words, a "hinge
[*"brisure"*] that both articulates and breaks open the explicit statement
being made."[10] We will isolate two types of "hinges": those that turn
on the play between author and authority point to the second type
of "hinge" based on *homonymy*. Author-authority articulates the tie
between writing and politics, which is made through a connection
between the *right* and *writing*. In addition, the transubstantiation of
institutional practices (either the meritorious underpinnings of the
state examination known as the *concours d'entrée* or the *canular* which
heralds passage into the ENS) into *rites* will also articulate the link
between rightist and *normalien* discourses. There are thus two types
of slippage or displacement: between authority as a textual and as a
political concept and a homonymic displacement evinced in the play
between "rite," "right," and "write." It must be reiterated that this
slippage is not invoked to signal an equation of the ENS and the right.
Rather these homonyms suggest that an ignorance of the role of the
right in the school is also, and more importantly, a blindness to the role
of writing in political behavior and to the role of rites in perpetuating
myth and in institutionalizing charisma.

Johnson tells us that deconstruction is a process of textual work,
"a certain strategy of writing"; thus our examination may appear to
be a remystification of the ENS, whereas it really hopes to achieve a
demystification through making connections that even self-conscious
normaliens fail to make. Debray begins his *Critique of Political Reason*
with precisely the sort of questioning as is performed by our deconstruction of the ENS: "It never occurred to me to establish any relation

16

What's Left? The Ecole Normale Supérieure and the Right

between the two *norms:* between study at the school and experience on the streets, between *textual exegesis* and a look at the newspapers."[11] With our reinscription of the right within the ENS political tradition, we will also reinscribe writing within politics, ideology within institutions, and at the same time, develop a methodology (or, principles of a reading) for the study of intellectuals.

Our analysis of the ENS will bear a striking similarity to what Lévi-Strauss calls *bricolage;* the *bricoleur* is a tinkerer, "someone who uses the means at hand, that is, the instruments he finds at his disposition around him . . . which had not been especially conceived with an eye to the operation for which they are to be used."[12] But a theoretical risk ensues once we realize that *bricolage* functions as both a form of discourse and its critique. We will be borrowing analytic tools which have been typically deployed in literary or philosophic criticism. Our critique of the ENS as *bricolage* is thus "mythopoetic"; it also runs the risk of insularity as its instrument of analysis can also serve as its own metacritique. In other words, we run the risk that our own explication of myth will itself become yet another form of myth. But it could not be otherwise.

With these caveats in mind, we can begin our discussion of the theoretic concepts produced and employed in our deconstruction of the ENS. Moreover, this rewriting is actively informed (or deformed) by current poststructuralist thought, much of it produced by former students of the ENS: Derrida (promotion 1952), Bourdieu (promotion 1951), Foucault (promotion 1946), and Debray (promotion 1960). From Derrida we have "borrowed" a critique of the binary opposition as well as the general inspiration for a deconstructive reading. Derrida provides us with a critique of logocentrism which proceeds through an undoing of a binary opposition central to our concerns as well. Just as Derrida demonstrated that the privileging of speech over writing was based on a metaphysical bias toward presence, so too we will see in the leftist tradition a no less meta-physical priority of political participation (i.e., *party* participation) over writing. Both our rereading of the traditional picture of the ENS and Derrida's (*Grammatology*) analysis of the privileging of voice over text share the following conclusion (and reversal): writing comes first.[13] It is with reference to the written that both political party participation (one recognized form of speech) and general forms of speech are correctly situated. That writing and the written trace will have assumed priority vis-à-vis the more explicitly performative and political will be obvious in our chapter on postwar trial sentencing. Thus our reconstruction of rightist circles of the ENS parallels Derrida's deconstruction of logocentrism.

17

What's Left? The Ecole Normale Supérieure and the Right

We will borrow the notion of normalization of Foucault and Bourdieu. Normalization is to be understood as the way a dominant ideology seeks to coerce without resorting to direct repression.[14] Moreover, both theorists stress the social conditions of the production of discourse which "produces" its authors as much as it is produced by them. The writings of Roland Barthes demonstrate that even within linguistic play—sentence mastery and manipulation—are revealed traces of prior political domination.[15] Régis Debray's work shows us that the notion of authority derives from the study of the concrete conditions of hegemony. Moreover, he states that even elitist titles can serve a social function, for "snobbery is as precious as a compass in the woods."[16]

Let us now examine three key notions that have remained relatively unproblematic for American analysts of intellectuals, but which have been a consistent focus among poststructuralists. These notions are crucial for our examination of the ENS as well. We shall designate these terms as *author, writing,* and *university*. Each will be briefly outlined in turn. The university as an institution is that which sets itself apart. Thus it is part of an implicitly political situation. As an instance of exclusion it produces, in turn, concomitant theoretical exclusions: university is habitually reduced to a "locus," author to a "subject" or "person," writing to a "work." These notions—university, author, writing—underline the philosophic problems of the literature on intellectuals: The "author" is the intentional, unproblematic subject (or agency) who produces a work. "Writing" is viewed equally facilely as either a neutral act connoted by a verb or as the well-bounded work produced. "University" signifies a precise place, an institution whose norms are decidedly value neutral. In all three cases there is no problem either political or philosophical in linking a determinate subject with an equally determinable predicate.

Author/"Author function"

Michel Foucault, in a seminal essay, "What is an Author?" questions that seemingly innocent term that is so casually manipulated in studies of intellectuals. What he designates as a specificity of the "author function" will prove crucial to our analysis of the literary signature (and the ENS as arbiter/standard of such a signature) and the interrelation of political and textual authority. The author's name, Foucault reminds us, is not solely a function of civil status, nor is it fictional; but it is "constituted at the breach among discontinuities which give rise to new types of discourse." Therefore, the author is above all else a social function, "concerned with the existence, circulation and operation of certain discourses within society."[17] Not all written texts have authors (e.g., contracts have underwriters); thus the presence of an author's name connotes a certain type of discourse, deemed worthy of memory. Most interesting for our purposes (especially with reference to the postwar trials) is Foucault's statement that authors were assigned to texts/speeches only when the author was subject to a penal code. Legal authority and literary/textual authority are necessarily linked through reference to a juridical code. Moreover, Foucault demonstrates that the author is not linked to his text by creative inspiration or other romantic conceptions of genius (what can be denoted as a form of "linguistic voluntarism") but is rather "interpolated" through a series of complex and precise procedures. We need only look at two: the *concours d'entrée* and the *canular*, which will be analyzed in Chapters 3 and 4. In short, the author is no free subject; he emerges merely as a function of discourse. The presence of an author's name signifies that the discourse produced is a determinate product of social relations, deemed worthy of memory and connoting a certain privileged status or distinction, deserving of a commensurate reception.

In addition, an essay of Derrida's on the teaching of philosophy, given at the Ecole Normale, underlines the separation of the author function from that of pedagogy. It is teaching which most ably resembles Nietzsche's "Eternal Return."[18] Authorship, however, is involved with the production of discourse. Derrida recounts an anecdote in which these dual tendencies are all the more poignant as they are embodied by the same person: himself. Derrida refers to this tension between his institutional role as a *répétiteur* and his writings, or between his teaching (*enseignement*) and his published texts, as a "dissociative fiction." "I pretend as if this work (i.e., his published works) did not exist." This binary logic does not escape his students. One of his students recounts: "I decided not to read you in order to work without bias and to simplify our relationship." He will read the texts of Derrida as author only when he is beyond the *agrégation* (Derrida as teacher). Another student will tell him (after he has completed his studies) that he prefers certain of his texts, but he does this only to underline the fact that he now reads him. "You know, what I have just said, is above all to show you that now I read you."[19] I recount these anecdotes, as does Derrida, to underline the specificity of the author function.[20]

Thus the notion of "authority" evinced in poststructuralist preoccu-

19

What's Left? The Ecole Normale Supérieure and the Right

pations serves as a critique of the transcendental-idealist underpinnings of the study of intellectuals at the same time as it reinscribes the social conditions of the production of the discourse.

Writing

> *How often we now hear in conversations, at least in more or less intellectual circles: "What is he doing?" "He's writing."*
> —Roland Barthes, "To Write: An Intransitive Verb?"

If our overview of the concept of the author has underlined the social nature of discourse, our considerations of "writing" provide a link between intellectuals and politics. Those uninitiated to structuralist/poststructuralist preoccupations may well wonder how such a "simple" notion as writing is problematic. We will see not only that writing poses a problem in any analytic study of intellectuals and political power (i.e., it can not merely be seen as a neutral instrument) but, most important, that it is a privileged notion as well. On a philosophical level, Derrida's reconsideration of Western metaphysics has involved a detailed reexamination of the concept of writing. Indeed, Derrida shows how metaphysics is *constituted* by the exclusion of writing from its concept of language. If we now read Jameson's reexamination of Derrida,[21] we see that what is being discussed under the sign of metaphysics is really ethics. I should like to pose the problem of writing paraphrasing both Derrida and Jameson: ethics/politics is constituted by the exclusion of writing from the concept of political praxis.

Régis Debray traces the intersection of politics and writing to the figure of the scribe. Focusing on scribes allows Debray to pose two sorts of questions: (1) "What must symbolic activity be like in order for it to have an influence on the materiality of social relationships in a secular republic such as ours?" (2) "What must society be in order to be, yesterday as well as today, in organic need of special corps of indicators of meaning?"[22] Debray's "genealogy" of intellectuals reveals the connections between intellectuals and politics, between writing and power; both sets of connections are themselves marked by repression. For the absence of the intellectual from Marx's field of study is the "obverse of the absence of the party of parliament, of all the mechanisms of representative democracy."[23] Indeed, rightist and liberal as well as Marxist depictions of intellectuals pose stark binary oppositions: mind against matter, value versus need, culture against interest, and as we will see in the history of the ENS, writing against political parties. What is interesting is not just this tendency to binary logic, but rather the denigration of mind, value, culture, and writing in relation to matter, need, interest, and political parties, especially in the case of intellectuals.

Intellectual and state power are not opposed terms; intellectual power is not a lesser form of state power. Rather both forms meet and are constituted in writing. Students of national integration have long been aware of the importance of writing in the centralization and the unification of nascent nations. The anthropologist knows that states without writing are seen as "other." Moreover, writing does not appear where there is not even a germ of the state. (The inverse of this isn't true, however.) There are societies without writing just as there are societies with forms of political organization other than the state, but it is definitely with the "man who writes" that the scandal arrives.[24]

If the scribe/intellectual has been denigrated vis-à-vis the politician/ ruler, he has been revered above the technocrat. Both metallurgy and writing share the same origin, yet the technician of fire "beneficent and cursed" is expulsed while the technician of signs "ambiguous but consecrated" is untouchable and adorable. This corresponds to the preeminence of verbal over motor activity and symbolic over technical orders. "By vocation and by nature, the scribe is on the side of Gods and leaders, not artisans and technicians."

The instrumentality of writing is less important than its symbolic aspect. Moreover, writing isn't a neutral term; inscription is also prescription: "Writing commands. Tyranny of the letter."[25] Two tablets of law, ten commandments. Yet there is an important distinction: He who engraves is not he who dictates, whether God, emperor, or the sun. If Constantine is the "Oedipus of the political unconscious"—sovereign, warrior, theologian—then "the scribe also hates his shadow."[26] And this ambivalence is due, perhaps, to the necessarily dual posture of the scribe. For repression of the link between power and writing also serves as his protection: "To what do the makers of words owe their life and living? To the fact that the others have never taken them at their own word."[27] The postwar trials of intellectuals will show the tenuous (indeed, dangerous) ground of the intellectual taken at his word.

But writing may also share a profound structural affinity with social group formation. For both groups and writing are constituted in reference to what is missing or *absent*. (Writing is assumed to be that trace of a prior moment of linguistic plenitude, namely, speech.) One of the main purposes of our reexamination of writing is to develop a notion

21

What's Left? The Ecole Normale Supérieure and the Right

of politics other than the dominant one of speech. This is attempted through the adumbration of a concept of writing in which writing is seen as both political (i.e., not a neutral instrument) and prior. We will see that the ENS is an institution only in reference to a script; that the classification, formation, participation, and judgment of its students are dictated by submission to a written code, legal or textual. Moreover, we will see that "the procedures which place individuals in a field of surveillance also situate them in a network of *writing*." [28]

Just as our revision of the author function attacked the notion of the author as a free subject, so too our analysis of writing necessitates revision of the traditional view of *write (écrire)* as an active verb. Roland Barthes suggested that *écrire/to write* be treated as a middle verb (which would take *être/to be* instead of *avoir/to have* as its auxiliary). The specification of *écrire* as a middle verb is perfect for our purposes as it is a diminution of that type of free subjectivity that would allow for the interruption of action due to the speaker's initiative and exemplified by a separated past. A middle verb has an *integrant* past which cannot be delivered by the simple initiative of the speaker. And this form does not lead to simple passivity either—"*on m'écrit*," "I have been written," "somebody wrote me" are not possible transformations of "*je suis écrit*." The middle verb *to write/écrire* will thus serve as our model for the peculiar status of the intellectuals we are studying as well as the institutional discourse of the ENS which both "produces" them and is produced by them. "In the modern verb of middle voice *to write*, however, the subject is immediately contemporary with the writing, being effected and affected by it." [29] Moreover, this revision entails a concomitant transformation of the locus in which writing and reading take place.

University

> *Today, how could we not speak of the university?*
> —J. Derrida, "The Principle of Reason: The University in the Eyes of Its Pupils"

> *What's more public, in principle, more demonstrable than (a) teaching?*
> —J. Derrida, "Où commence et comment finit un corps enseignant"

Derrida's initial pun—"in the *eyes* of its *pupils*" [30]—and the reversal which contributes much of its humor underline the impossibility of dissociating work from a reflection on the political and

institutional conditions of that work. Just as we have seen the impossibility of the author's externality to his text and the analogous
impossibility of *écrire* as an active verb, so too the reflection on the
university is no longer an external complement to the university. This
is signaled by another play on the word *faculty* which in the case of the
university invokes the teaching body, but also the capacity for sight/
insight: "What can the university's body see or not see of its own destination, of that view of which it stands its ground? Is the university
the master of its own ground? Is the university the master of its own
diaphragm?"[31]

The strategic importance of separating the university from the rest
of society parallels the separation of mind-matter, culture-interest,
value-need that we saw in our earlier section on writing. The university will thus have its own view, but we will see that it is a view to
which it is necessarily blind (read value free). Or the faculty (teachers) will not use the faculty (sight) to see the relation between the
university and the conception of work or the presence (intrusion) in
the university of forces apparently external to it (press, foundations,
academies, media). As Derrida has remarked in another context, "The
inside is the outside," yet there is a willful attempt to separate the
university from what surrounds it.[32] This is made easier in the United
States where boundaries of many universities seem clear. James Siegel
writes:

> Many American universities were founded outside cities, often
> in places that evoke the admiration of European visitors for their
> beauty and sometimes their surprise as well that one would
> think of having a university in such an environment. The at
> tempt to separate the university from the rest of society con
> tinues even where the city has caught up to the university as,
> for instance, in the case of Harvard.[33]

The boundaries of the American university are clear—what is excluded from it is evinced in the town/gown polarity in evidence at Yale
or elsewhere. The presence of the ENS in the center of a city will necessitate an act of institution to separate the institution from its physical
surrounds (we will see this to be one of the key features of the *canu-
lar*) at the same time that this physical location will provide much of
what we consider to be the institution's view. Two students as divergent "politically" as Brasillach and J.-P. Sartre will both celebrate the
strategic location of the ENS and herald it with snapshots taken from
the rooftop (or, in the language of *archicubes*, the *palais*). Just as Jimmy
Cagney (quite mistakenly) feels in *White Heat* that he is "on top of the

23

What's Left? The Ecole Normale Supérieure and the Right

world, Ma," the *normalien* photos on the rooftops of Paris signal the internalized belief that they too are of the elect.

But the relationship of the university to its location (and view) is also one of *metonymy* (contiguity, proximity). Both Derrida's and James Siegel's analysis of Cornell show how a university's location can shape thoughts of work: "The oscillation between thoughts of suicide and thoughts of thinking and particularly of language: 'Yeah, the library is right next to the gorge.' "[34] Brasillach also concurs that the importance of the ENS is its location in the heart of the Latin Quarter and that this is what makes it more amenable to thought than the plusher accommodations of the Cité Universitaire. (This will be especially important as the period in which we are studying the ENS is marked by neither a fixed curriculum nor resident teachers.)[35]

Another way of posing the problem of the university's view is to recode it: what is the university's *position*? An examination of the position of the university shows that it, too, is no neutral term. For Derrida, all institutions imply position taking. Power is not external to the university; either it resides in an authoritative discourse of *"il faut"* which surveys every lesson, or it naturalizes the conditions of the production of discourse and produces a "neutrality effect."

> when I say, according to an extremely trivial slogan, that power controls the teaching apparatus, this is *not* to place power outside the pedagogical state nor to give rise to thoughts or dreams of teaching without power. . . . This would be an idealist or liberal representation which comforts itself with a teaching corps blind to power: that to which it is submitted, to which it is disposed, in the name of which it denounces power![36]

Normaliens, it will be argued, are themselves not immune from the semiotics of the *"rapport pédagogique."*[37] The teacher/writer both delivers and is constituted in signs. This will be explored in greater detail in our discussion of language and authority.[38]

The teacher who is blind to the university's power recuperates the visionary position of the "eye of its pupils." The vision of the university is based on the dual tension inherent in its missionary position: "Is the task of the university to reproduce professional competence by preparing professors for pedagogy and research who have respect for a certain code?" Or, "does the university have as its essential mission that of producing professional competence, which may sometimes be external to the university?" One of our principal concerns will be the possibility of thought to remain a solely *intra-institutional* event. The displacement of our focus on the ENS toward the right will help to

24

What's Left? The Ecole Normale Supérieure and the Right

show that the "university reflects society only in giving it a chance for reflection, that is *dissociation*." [39] Moreover, our examination of the social circles around publishing networks as well as our analysis of the transcripts of the postwar trials reveals that it is not only within the university that the "university style" dominates. The university may well be a philosophy in construction, as Derrida would have it, but we will analyze the political implications and ramifications of the *normalien* philosophy in construction, nowhere more apparent than in its supposedly neutral institutional features.

It is not an accident that Derrida's work (both theoretical and political) has shifted its focus from writing/metaphysics to the university. For both the university and writing can be included within the logic of the "supplement." [40] Like writing and the author function, the university lacks the autonomy to constitute its own principle of unity. Just as the author is constituted by his oeuvre, and the verb *to write/écrire* is seen as a middle verb whose contemporaneity destroys the subject-object distinction, so too, "during more than eight centuries, 'university' has been the name given by a society to a sort of *supplementary* body that at one and the same time it wanted *to project outside itself* and keep jealously to itself, *to emancipate and to control. On this double basis the university was supposed to represent society*" (italics mine). [41]

Our reading of the Ecole Normale Supérieure will be analogous to Derrida's considerations on the university. We will be examining the ENS through the eyes of its pupils and inquiring about the vision of this institution. To paraphrase Derrida, we will be asking: "The ENS with a view to what?" "What is the ENS view and how is this transmitted in an institutional discourse?" We will examine the mark or trace the ENS leaves on its students and the text these actors impose on the world. The ENS in short will be seen as a *script*. And its students are contemporaneous with the process of writing.

If we have begun this introduction with the figure of Moses, we will end with a consideration equally biblical, that of judgment. It has (always already) been the book that served as mediation in our analysis.

> Between the too warm flesh of the literal event and the cold skin of the concept runs meaning. That is how it enters the book.
> Everything enters into it, transpires in the book. That is why the book is never finite. It always remains suffering and vigilant. [42]

"What's left?"

In opposition to traditional empirical sociologists, we have supposed that *Being* was a grammar. And so our analysis of the ENS

25

What's Left? The Ecole Normale Supérieure and the Right

is, quite literally, *by the book*. Intellectual formation, discursive practices, literary engagements, courtroom verdicts achieve their ultimate meaning in the book, according to a written script:

> Being is a grammar, and . . . the world in all its parts is a cryptogram to be constituted or reconstituted through poetic inscription or deciphering; that the book is original and that everything belongs to the book before being and in order to come into the world; that anything can be born only by approaching the book, can die only by failing in sight of the book, and that always the impossible shore of the book is first.[43]

If Genesis (and Moses) was our beginning, Samuel and judgment is our end.

3 LE CRU ET L'ECRIT

Normaliens, like wine, are classified by year and region of origin. There can be little doubt that in France *normalien* is an *appellation* extremely *contrôlée.* And, as with wines, there is relative agreement about the *meilleurs crus.* For the left, 1924: Jean-Paul Sartre, Paul Nizan, Raymond Aron, Daniel Lagache, Georges Canguilhem, Georges Lefranc. And for the right, 1928: Robert Brasillach, Maurice Bardèche, Thierry Maulnier, Georges Pelorson. As *normaliens* leave the *cuvée* of rue d'Ulm (replete with its *"cuve,"* the "bassin d'Ernest")[1] they are *débouchés* (uncorked) to careers in journalism, teaching, and politics.[2] Like wines, *normaliens* are often described with a small handful of adjectives attesting to their *goût* (taste): *vigoreux, fine, distinction, netteté* (clarity), *délicieux, du cru.* Indeed, in the universe where knowledge (*savoir*) is equated with having taste (*avoir du goût*), the parallels with a discourse of viniculture are startling.[3] And yet this symptomatic semblance with wine illustrates the double nature of the Ecole Normale Supérieure, as both institution and myth, the six o'clock apéritif and the *concours d'entreé.*

Extant literature on the ENS has (albeit unself-consciously) reproduced this double vision. Work on the Ecole consists mainly of personal "souvenirs" of *anciens élèves* (old boys),[4] useful primarily as exampla of the various myths of being a *normalien,* whereas the paucity of scholarly literature underlines the relation of the ENS with the left (its parties and deputies).[5] While the institutional literature largely ignores or fails to integrate the contributions and presence of rightist *normaliens,* the lack of an elaborated theory of the mythic function of the ENS neglects a crucial moment in elite formation.

I will begin our discussion of the ENS with an institutional approach, that of Ezra Suleiman's *Elites in French Society.* Suleiman speaks of a "critical spirit that generally placed the school in radical opposition to all non-leftist governments." A political history would be adumbrated as follows: The twenties were years of leftist socialism and pacifism; the thirties and forties were marked by Marxist-Leninism and Stalinism.[6] Recent history can look to the Maoist and Trotskyist students of Althusser (while, concurrently, on a formalist level, commentators such as Charles Lemert situate the "textual empiricism" of Althusser as yet another derivation of the *normalien* "fashion").[7] However, Suleiman does caution: "But although Normale is firmly associated with the Left, one must not forget that it has also produced illustrious men of the Right." The logical foundations of this literature is evinced in his summation:

> *Normaliens*, for example, played an important part in the politics of the Third Republic, not only because they were well-represented in the Parliament, but also because almost one-half of those who did become deputies also became ministers. It was *normaliens* like Jaurès, Blum, Painlevé and Lebrun, who directed attention to the intense political interest of the Ecole Normale Supérieure.[8]

A more nuanced and detailed version is found in Jean François Sirinelli's discussion of the original Grasset book jacket of Thibaudet's *République des Professeurs* decorated with a band exclaiming "Normale and Company." Sirinelli lists all nine *normaliens* elected or reelected in 1924 (and their promotions: from 1883 to 1910), as well as the five new *normalien* deputies included in 1928 (Léon Blum is defeated in Paris only to be elected the following year as a deputy from Narbonne). Sirinelli notes the overrepresentation of *normalien* deputies under forty years old and those with literary formation, as well as the prevailing public opinion of the ENS as a politically leftist institution. Although the number of deputies may be of slight quantitative interest, what Sirinelli underlines as important is how many *normaliens* become ministers. For example, in the first Painlevé government there were three *normalien* ministers: Painlevé (minister of war and president of the Conseil), Emile Borel (minister of the navy), Yvon Delbos (minister of technical instruction and fine arts). In his second government, in addition to Borel and Delbos, there was *normalien* Aimé Berthod.[9] Yet both Suleiman's and Sirinelli's analysis rest on assumptions which become increasingly problematic when applied to the study of rightist intellectuals.

First, there is an implicit quantitative assumption that a large number of *anciens élèves* with leftist political identification is, in itself, significant. We are not disputing the fact that there may well be numerically more famous "leftist" *normaliens*. Moreover, Sirinelli (citing Annie Kriegel)[10] argues for a "paradigmatic" form of representation à la Lukácsian typology or Weberian "ideal types" which are never solely quantitative. What is at issue is a differential focus on the rightist student as paradigmatic due to the emblematic function of publishing. For the case of a rightist intellectual elite, a large number of *normalien* alumni does not prove as important as the large diffusion (*"tirage"*) of right-wing journals, for which a "handful" of *normaliens* wrote. Indeed, Régis Debray states in *Le Pouvoir Intellectuel en France* that political combat was often displaced onto journalistic combat in which the large *tirage* of rightist journals (640,000 copies for *Gringoire*, 340,000 copies for *Candide*, as compared with 120,000 copies for *Marianne* and 100,000 for *Vendredi*) placed them in the "front lines." [11]

Moreover, a quantitative focus also obscures the powerful role of a few symbolic figures. As François Mauriac said in a postwar trial of an *ancien élève:* "Each generation becomes conscious of itself in a very small number of writers. For men of the right, Brasillach was one of these." [12] One cannot underestimate this symbolic power of the French intellectual. Debray describes the temptation to denigrate this "symbolic" power with a culinary metaphor—as "cream on the cake." But as "nouvelle cuisine" has shown, cream is no longer an ornament—"It is the cream that makes the cake edible." The correlative problem of basing a discussion of *normalien* political influence on a small number of leftist-identified students who later become deputies and ministers parallels the concern of Debray: "Can the sociology of power accept the traditional division of the political field at face value: the symbolic on one side and the political and administrative on the other?" [13] Although party identification and parliamentary participation may be suitable criteria for leftist intellectuals, the case of rightist intellectuals is more ambivalent.

René Rémond has observed that while leftist intellectuals tend toward party activism, rightists tend toward literary collaboration. In other words, leftists join parties, rightists found journals.[14] We will find that the categories of traditional political science for describing political behavior are woefully inadequate to account for an elite who sees its primary political role (and who had its primary political effect) as writers and who were quickly bored by those they saw as "ideologues." Moreover, many writers wrote for organs of parties that they never joined—Brasillach for *Action Française, Emancipation Nationale, Je Suis Partout*, without joining Maurras's Action Française or Doriot's Parti Populaire Français. (In this light, Drieu's adherence to the PPF may be an exception that proves the rule: he joined the party in a Nietzchean moment of extreme nihilism, admitting that Doriot was never to be the fascist leader of his dreams. Adherence was a form of political suicide.)[15]

Indeed, we will come to see that there is more than a little irony in the lack of a political history of rightist *normaliens* precisely because their political praxis consisted of literary production. I will aruge that it is precisely not parliamentary but literary activity that is crucial. First, it underlines the shift in importance from universities to journals during the 1920s to 1940s, what Debray calls "university cycle" 1880–1930 and "publishing cycle" 1920–1960: "The decline of the *teacher* is the rise of the *author* . . . The public counterpoint to the twilight of the University is the return of the Academy: the Dreyfus Affair in reverse."[16]

Second, we will see, paraphrasing Jacques Derrida, that whereas literary activity was a "supplement" for elites of the left, political activity was little else than literary activity for the rightist intellectual.[17] We will see in postwar trial sentencing how strictly correlated was political activity with literary activity. But if the political activism of rightist intellectuals was crystallized in the activity of writing and literary production, then the role of *normalien* culture—its emphasis on writing and speaking—cannot be overestimated. As Pierre Bourdieu has noted: "In an academic universe where the ideal is to speak like a book, the only fully legitimate discourse is that which assumes at every moment the entire context of legitimate culture and solely that culture."[18]

Commentators[19] have stressed the relationship between the "*normalien* mode" and the formation of an intellectual elite. If, as Pierre Bourdieu states in *La Reproduction*, the goal of French pedagogy is "*parler comme un livre*" (to speak like a book), the act of reading itself is not sociologically neutral. Charles Lemert explains at length:

> Reading is much more than a neutral tool of intellectual work.
> In France being well read is an *emblem*. It is a necessary and
> sometimes sufficient badge of intellectual competence. Those
> who wear it authentically are those who have distinguished
> themselves in the French schools. . . . Pupils who succeed in the
> French schools are those who have most perfectly demonstrated
> a brilliant and compelling literary and oral style—the standard
> for which is France's literary culture. In other words, the first
> condition of intellectual excellence is good speaking and good
> writing, which are inculcated by means of good reading.[20]

We will see that it is in a deconstruction of the "*parole lettrée*" (lettered speech) that discussion of the ENS's political influence would be more profitably focused. On the one hand, the ENS has to be reexamined as an object of extreme ideological lability (in the words of the illustrious *normalien* Poincaré: "The art of giving the same name to different things.")[21] On the other hand, its "emblematic" function raises interesting general questions such as the "routinization of charisma" as it relates to an intellectual elite. In many ways, "*normale*" parallels fashion ("*la mode*") in that it occupies an intermediate position between "a field which is organized for a succession" and a "field" where everyone is irreplaceable.[22] The *normalien* (and the couturier's) *griffe* (designer label) is a sign which changes the very social nature of its object. One need only think of the *concours d'entrée*: "between the last one accepted and the first one rejected the *concours* creates a difference between all and nothing and for a lifetime."[23] We will see that our initial disjuncture between myth and institution is a blind polarity: for "social magic" inheres in the *"rites d'institution"* of the Ecole.

For admission into the Ecole Normale Supérieure and the title *normalien* represent far more than a narrowly constrained instrumental diploma. The title is a "patent of nobility," a "title of nobility,"[24] the sign of a self-defining gentry. However, the status of this title is ambiguous, as it cannot be directly transmissible. The title *normalien* (like the titles of all French *grandes écoles*) operates as a guarantee, which guarantees far more than it is supposed to guarantee. Holders of this title are "called upon to really procure the attributes assigned to them by their status."[25] The market value of their title is both extremely high and extremely durable[26] and acts as a multiplier effect on all types of cultural capital through sustained exchanges between "old boys" and in the creation of a transdisciplinary solidarity. Moreover, the title possesses extreme generalizability, attaching itself to all adjectives linked to virtues and abilities.[27] This function has not gone unnoticed by non-*normaliens*, Bourdieu recounts,[28] who surround themselves with *normaliens* to bask in their reflected glow. Thus what appears to be a formally neutral procedure—the *concours*—is really a process of investiture; indeed, a tacit inscription into an order.

Righting the Leftist Depiction

> *Empirical sociology may well be a blind alley when it comes to studying the intelligentsia. But in order to find out, we have to plunge fearlessly into it. And since we have nothing to lose except time, here are some doubts, dates, and figures.*
> —Debray, *Teachers, Writers, Celebrities*

One consequence of the overidentification of the ENS with the left is the perpetuation of the myth that collaborationist writers were aberrational figures—if not wholly opportunistic, they were certainly not integrated into one of France's most elite educational institutions. Our first task is thus a political sociology of the rightist *normalien*.[29] Can we characterize the rightist *normalien* by any pattern—career or demographic? Does their *scolarité* differ from that of their leftist cohorts? How apt is the leftist caricature of Ulm when examined from the viewpoint of an empirical study?

The years 1922–28 were predominantly years of illustrious leftist *normaliens*. The 1922 promotion included Pierre Brossolette; the 1923 included Jean Cavaillès and Lévy Bruhl. We have already noted the illustrious roster of the 1924 promotion (Sartre, Nizan, Canguilhem, Lefranc,[30] Lagache). Ironically, the *concours d'entreé* of this promotion was lamented for its "inexperience and lack of philosophic originality." The 1925 promotion included Jean Hyppolite, Jacques Monod, Pierre Vilar; Merleau-Ponty was a member of the 1926 promotion. There were, however, exceptions throughout this period—Catholic *normaliens* ("*talas*") such as Guillemin flirted with the right-wing press in the thirties as did his classmate (in the 1923 promotion) Pierre Henri Simon.[31]

We witness an increasing concentration of rightist intellectuals in the years 1927–29. When one includes leftist students who later become Vichy collaborators (either out of an identification of socialism with Pétain, militant pacifism, or the mere desire to continue publishing),[32] the number of students is even more significant. In 1924, there is Raoul Audibert, co-student of Brasillach at Louis-le-Grand as is the Breton Henri Quéffelec (1929 promotion) and René Chateau, pacifist collaborator in Déat's *L'Oeuvre*.[33] But it is the 1928 roster that reveals a startling concentration of rightist *élèves:* Maurice Bardèche, Robert Brasillach, Thierry Maulnier (who was called Jacques Talagrand), Georges Pelorson (who later became a minister in the Vichy government, as well as being an important polemicist) and Claude Jamet (a student of Alain whose "left-wing collaborationism"[34] earned him a sentence of seven years' forced labor after the Liberation). The 1928 roster also boasts an equally startling exception—Simone Weil— as well as Jean Beaufret, the Heidegger scholar.[35] The 1929 promotion included René Etiemble as well as Vichyiste Maurice Gait. Georges Pompidou, 1931's most famous alumn, entered these circles when he was "*débouché*" to a lycée in Marseille and shared an apartment with rightist intellectual André Fraigneau, a friend of Maurice Bardèche.[36] Pompidou later confided that for him Brasillach represented the ideal young intellectual.

Yet one must be cautious about any facile inference from this juxtaposition of names and from a hasty diachronic analysis which would signal a shift from leftist circles to rightist circles in the late twenties. Proximity of promotion does not imply contact while at the ENS. For example, Maurice Bardèche remained unaware of Sartre's presence at the Ecole as a fourth-year *"agrégation-répétiteur,"* nor did he see much of Simone Weil after the days of the *concours d'entreé*, as she was an *externe* (i.e., she didn't reside at the school).[37] Moreover, the structure of the ENS itself mitigated easy division among right and left. Significant interaction was on the level of the *turne*, a cell grouping of five students. In this way, Claude Jamet was brought into contact with Bardèche and Brasillach, whereas his political affiliations as a student of Alain's would have normally isolated him from this group.[38]

As for the notion of a common unifying *"normalien* spirit," there is also much debate on this point. Critic A. Thibaudet has stressed the role of the ENS as a melting pot *(creuset)*.[39] If there is debate about the existence of a "common spirit," [40] and if there is no necessary assumption of contact from proximity of promotions, there is also a synchronic problem. There appears to be a time lag in fostering *normalien* networks. Often contact is made many years later that reinforces a school tie, or there may be a symbolic linkage on the totally imaginary level— e.g., Pompidou's identification with Brasillach, with whom he had no contact at the school and who represented for him an ideal of the *normalien*. An article by Jean François Sirinelli reveals another synchronic problem.[41] There is often a time lag between student and later political orientation. Sirinelli uses the example of Aron and Sartre. Aron, at ENS, was far to the left of Sartre. Pascal Ory's recent volume on Nizan reveals his flirtation with Georges Valois's Faisceau, becoming one of its first members in 1925 while a student at the Ecole.[42]

These caveats aside, a cursory glance at the rosters of the ENS in the years between 1880 and 1930 affords the following generalizations. There are several distinct rightist generations. Promotions of the late 1880s and 1890s comprised academician Abel Hermant as well as fascist ideologues such as Hubert Bourgin (a member of Valois's Faisceau and editor of Marcel Déat). During the early years of the twentieth century, Jérôme Carcopino (*secrétaire* of the Ecole under Vichy), René Gillouin, and Jean Giraudoux (minister of information and author of a virulently anti-Semitic tract *Pleins Pouvoirs*) represented the 1900, 1902, and 1903 promotions, respectively. The year 1908 saw the admission of Henri Béraud and Jean Piot (chief editor of *L'Oeuvre*). Marcel Déat (another renegade student of Alain's and collaborator on *L'Oeuvre*), Pierre Gaxotte, and André Guérin (editor of *L'Oeuvre*) attended the Ecole during the war years 1917, and 1919. (A socialist cohort, Jean Prévost, also wrote for *L'Oeuvre*.)[43] The importance of these figures will be enlarged when we consider their strong extramural contacts. The fact that there have also been *normaliens* with rightist orientation refutes the argument that it has only furnished a few aberrant intellectuals such as Brasillach. Moreover, these "prewar" rightist *normaliens* will prove important in transmitting ideology and a literary heritage to the post–World War I generation. There is also the question of nationalist-socialist figures such as the late Péguy and the Tharaud brothers (especially in their linkage to Barrès) who are later appropriated by the rightist ideological canon. In sum, the 1928 promotion does not mark an abrupt departure.

Nor can one argue that 1928 was a substandard year. Rather, critiques have focused on the 1922–24 promotions, whose students' progress was disturbed by the war and who had weak written work.[44] The weakness of the 1924 *concours;* results on the philosophy exam were especially disappointing: one half of the copies were frankly mediocre, barely attaining the level of the *bac* (70/101). Many even fell below this point, "an astounding philosophical experience." Even among the "good" papers "original philosophic style is rare." In place of the originality and individuality of other years' essays were "vague and trendy" themes. Orals were even worse! From the standpoint of aggregate numbers who presented themselves for the exam and those who were admitted, 1928 was a relatively "strong" year (14.2 percent compared with 17.3 percent in 1924 and 21.1 percent in 1926).[45]

When we turn to demographic variables, there is a relationship between provincial as opposed to Parisian origins and the rightist *normalien*. Although it was at the lycée level that the first Parisian experiences occurred for these students, yet one can make the argument that the relative autonomy and structurelessness of the ENS, after years of intense study for the *concours,* allowed for the first "real" discovery of Paris. Jean-Paul Sartre's preface to Nizan's *Aden Arabie* echoes many of the prevalent themes of Brasillach's *Notre Avant Guerre*: "For most of us, including me, the Ecole Normale was the beginning of independence."[46]

When we consider region of origin we note that leftist students reveal disproportionately greater Parisian origins compared with both rightists and the total universe of students in the promotions from 1922 to 1929. Ten out of twenty-five leftist-oriented students have Parisian origins (40 percent) as compared with 11.8 percent of rightists. Indeed, one also notes that rightists have a disproportionately lower likelihood of being born in Paris. Yet if the left is more likely to have its birthplace in Paris, the right has a higher representation in both Burgundy and the Languedoc/Roussillon regions. Rightist students appear to be more equally distributed among the Loire valley, Languedoc, and Burgundy, closely followed by the Rhone, Provence, Normandy, Lorraine, Aquitaine, Brittany, Alsace, and the overseas departments. Moreover, if one compares rightist and leftist students in the Alsace-Lorraine region, one sees that there is a far greater proportion of the right (11.8 percent as opposed to 0 percent). Similarly, one finds a greater number of rightist *normaliens* in Brittany.

Two of the regions that have a greater representation among our rightist students have a qualitative importance as well. Languedoc/ Roussillon reveals the ambiguity of Provence for this elite. Dioudonnat writes: "The mythology of the Action Française is strongly permeated with provincialism; it is the land of Maurras, which is bathed by the same waters as Brasillach's Roussillon." Yet Marseille is a constant object of critique in *Je Suis Partout*: "Marseille is unaware of the separation of 'milieu' and of politics." Moreover, two of the other regions that have a high percentage of rightists also are the subjects of a special literary treatment in *JSP*. Most other provinces appear only allusively in its pages with the exception of Normandy and Alsace. Normandy, the "green province," is depicted in golden hues by Dorsay, Drieu, and La Varende, who paint a definitive portrait of a traditionalist and literary province, with its *patronne*, Charlotte Corday. Alsatian resistance to the Front Populaire is heralded by Brasillach as a "*nouvelle* Vendée." In addition, *JSP* counted among its ranks Baron Hesso de Reinach-Hirtzbach, an Alsatian Catholic, monarchist, Maurrasian, and anti-Semite, and the author of a much cited book, *La Tragédie Destinée de l'Alsace*.[47]

"Father's occupation" has been a similarly employed variable in the comparative sociology of elites. It is here that one can see most clearly the demographic impact of the First World War. For "father deceased" was the most frequent occupation of fathers in all categories, closely followed by civil service and schoolteachers. Sirinelli's study of 250 alumni of the great lycées ("*khâgnes*") reveals that civil service comprises one half of all father's occupations, followed by teaching (35.7 percent) and farming (3 percent), compared with 50 percent, 23.3 percent, and 30 percent, respectively, for grandfather's occupation. Sirinelli confirms what has been demonstrated elsewhere by Bourdieu, Passeron, and Girard: "The Ecole Normale Supérieure constitutes therefore a passageway of social promotion for some *lycéens* of the middle classes."[48]

For the moment we will consider the question of differences between rightist- and leftist-identified students. On the left, we witness a great concentration of the liberal professions—more architects, engineers, doctors, pharmacists, and professors. Among professors' sons we note Raymond Aron, Marc Bloch, and Jean Wahl. Simone Weil and Vladimir Jankélévitch were both children of doctors. Nizan's father was an engineer. Rightist-oriented students have fathers with a somewhat higher frequency in university positions other than the professoriat (for example, in administration) and have a significantly greater likelihood of having a father who is a notary or an industrialist. There are *no* leftists with industrialists fathers. Again, one should be wary of an inference made from such a small number of cases—only two rightist-identified students have notaries for fathers. Yet only two of the 197 nonrelevant *normaliens* have fathers who are so employed, which makes this difference so startling. Moreover, as we will see in Chapter 5's discussion of publishing networks, Pierre Gaxotte and Fayard's friendship was between two notaries' sons, and, indeed, for our discussions of the importance of literary signatures, this profession is not insignificant.[49]

Just as one should underline the qualitative importance of a notary father for a literary elite (whose political practice consisted of writing), so too the incidence of fatherlessness (and its suggestive relation to authoritarianism) must be analyzed in detail. We consider these questions in Chapter 4. It should be noted that politically committed students do have a somewhat higher incidence of fatherlessness, irrespective of political position. The rightists Brasillach, Talagrand (Thierry Maulnier), and Gaxotte as well as leftists Hyppolite, Sartre, Merleau-Ponty, Monod, and Lagache are without fathers. *Normalien* mothers were most likely to be employed as schoolteachers or professors.

We will now turn away from demographic variables to consider measures of *scolarité*. Whether or not one concurs with Pierre Henri Simon's formulation, "The most important thing was to be *khâgneux*,"[50] we will begin our discussion of *scolarité* with a discussion of lycées attended. Lycée Louis-le-Grand is the most frequently attended lycée regardless of political position. Indeed, rightist students appear to be overrepresented at Louis-le-Grand. The 1928 promotion almost exclusively attended it: Brasillach, Bardèche, Thierry Maulnier, Jean Beaufret, Georges Pelorson. An earlier generation including Pierre Gaxotte, Jérôme Carcopino, and René Gillouin attended Henri IV, which was the second most frequented lycée. Giraudoux attended Lakanal; Gillouin and Jacques Soustelle attended the Lycée du Parc in Lyon, the only non-Parisian lycée to place in the top four.[51] Yet the importance of the lycée extends far beyond this quantitative focus. Sirinelli documents the strategic importance of Alain for pacifist as well as leftist students. We will see the importance of Louis-le-Grand for the rightist network because of André Bellesort. Brasillach recounts that it was during his tenure at Louis-le-Grand that he discovered the Action Française via Pierre Gaxotte.[52]

It is when we look at the contribution of the nonillustrious Parisian lycées that some differences appear. These less-prestigious lycées —Condorcet, Montaigne, Lakanal, Janson de Sailly, Carnot, Buffon, Charlemagne—contribute many leftist students. More than one third of the left are from lycées other than the top two (Louis-le-Grand and Henri IV), compared with *none* of the right. It would appear that on this variable of attendance at the prestigious lycées, the rightist student is not only nonaberrant, he is exemplary. But perhaps our most striking finding is our most obvious, namely, the dominance of Paris for our sample. Although right and left may be split between prestigious and "lesser" lycées, an overwhelming majority attend a Parisian lycée.

Both rightist and leftist *normaliens* attended the prestigious *khâgnes* of the great lycées. Let us now examine another index of *scolarité*—the *concours d'entrée*—to discern differences between right, left, and other *normaliens* in our sample. It would appear that the right is slightly less successful than the norm in passing the *concours* on the first attempt. The left is, on the other hand, slightly more successful in passing the *concours* on the first try. However, when we consider those who needed more than two attempts to pass the arduous *concours* they were the least likely to be rightist identified.[53]

If we consider the subject options chosen for the *concours d'entrée*, there are some additional differences between right and left. A large majority of all students still elect the classic formula, option 1, "Latin, Greek, Philosophy"; they comprise 69.5 percent of the total sample of promotions 1922–29 as well as 69.2 percent of rightist students, and 57.9 percent of leftists. Leftists, however, diverge from the norm in their more frequent choice of the math-science option. Many of these students went on to work closely with Léon Brunschvicq, a philosopher.[54]

Table 2 illustrates the varied and random success at the *concours* and the lack of an easy correlation between rank and future success. For many of those listed it was their second attempt.

If success at the *concours* has little predictive value, it can also appear uncorrelated with record prior to entry. Some candidates with few certificates toward the licence do extremely well, while candidates entering with a complete licence do not have markedly higher scores.[55] Nor does success at the *concours d'entrée* predict later success on the *concours d'agrégation*.

As we have noted, it was the second attempt at the *concours* for some of our sample, including Brasillach, Thierry Maulnier, Carcopino, and Pompidou, among others. Georges Pelorson passed this exam on his

Table 2. Rank Received on *Concours d'Entrée*

Right	Center/Illustrious	Left
Bardèche 13	Audibert 26	Aron 14
Brasillach 26	Beaufret 7	Marc Bloch 11
Gillouin 1	Etiemble 26	J. Bruhat 28
Giraudoux 13	Pompidou 35	J. Cavailles 7
Guillemin 29	Hyppolite 26	Nizan 23
Jamet 27	Soustelle 1	Sartre 7
P. H. Simon 2		Simone Weil 6
Thierry Maulnier 9		Pierre Vilar 6

Source: AN 61 AJ 171, 250–58

first try, yet led a far from distinguished school career and was expelled from Ulm.[56] Yet the importance of this variable might be in its subjective (psychological) effect, especially combined with later failure on the *concours d'agrégation*. Preliminary findings in a study of collaborationist intellectuals revealed a curious pattern of exam failure.[57] This is especially suggestive when combined with Mosse's findings (*Towards the Final Solution*) of a rightist elite that is insecure and ambivalent to authority.[58] For as Bouglé has noted, exams became an *"épreuve de morale"* (moral test) rather than an *"épreuve de technique"* (technical test).[59] And for many *normaliens* (more notably those on the left) this was a demoralizing experience.

Romain Rolland, writing in his *Mémoires*, speaks at length of his obligation "to *force an entry*" into the Ecole Normale: "Stiff, cogwheel examinations, the *licence ès lettres*, the *agrégation*, the cold career of teaching for which I was not suited." Fifty years after the *concours d'entrée* he was still incapable of a dispassionate appraisal:

> I will never be able to make those who have not experienced it
> sense the nightmare of the examinations which my comrades
> and I had undergone, or the omnipresent idea of the narrow
> door which had only been half-opened to us . . . on a world
> where we would be able to make a secure living without offend-
> ing our sensibilities. All of our youth was made somber under
> the black wing of this burden.[60]

His aversion to exams, inaugurated at the *concours d'entrée*, persisted throughout his career (he contracted measles between the written and the oral parts of the *concours d'agrégation*) and proved decisive in his choice of writing over teaching as a career. Yet the most significant aspect of the various *concours* might well be their symbolic function as a "rite of institution"—"the bureaucratic baptism of knowledge, the official recognition of the transubstantiation of profane knowledge into sacred knowledge"—which will be explored in a subsequent section.[61]

Indeed, examinations of school dossiers of *normaliens* reveal similar patterns for both right and left, up until the moment of the *agrégation*. They all pass the various exams for the licence, although leftists do receive slightly more *mentions*. Political differences may be translated into the choice of different teachers or thesis advisers; both Thierry Maulnier and Brasillach (as well as lycée schoolmate Quéffelec) worked with Fortunat Strowski (who wrote for right-wing journals of the thirties and forties). Simone Weil, like many leftist students (Hyppolite, Merleau-Ponty, Aron), worked with Brunschvicq on "Science et perfection chez Descartes."[62] Table 3 lists some topics chosen by our *normalien* sample.

There were indeed other considerations in the choice of both a thesis adviser and a subject for the *mémoire*. For this generation, political questions were often displaced into stylistic choices, so Brasillach's reason for working with Fortunat Strowski should not be at all surprising. Brasillach remembers: "As far as I was concerned, I proposed a study on the streets of Paris in Balzac's work to M. Fortunat Strowski who was nonchalant, indulgent, and florid, and who attracted all the eccentrics."[63] One might well argue that it was Strowski's personality —"nonchalant and indulgent"—as well as Brasillach's predelictions for whimsy (*fantaisie*) and playing the role of a *flâneur* that contributed to his choice of theme. Yet choice of texts to be explicated or thesis topics can also be illustrative of later ideological or intellectual development. Brasillach's choice of Virgil and Thierry Maulnier's choice of Nietzsche for *explication de texte* reveal a later split between the "idéologue" (Maulnier) and the "Mediterranean sensualist wary of ideology" (Brasillach). Thierry Maulnier wrote on "The Dramatic Art of Racine according to his Prefaces," while Bardèche pursued his interest in the history of art: "The Urban Landscape in Fifteenth-Century Flemish Painting." Meanwhile, at the Sorbonne, future literary (and political) collaborator Paul Gadenne wrote on Proust while Maurice Blanchot wrote on skepticism.[64]

Student teaching as well as written work reveals insights into the personalities of our *normaliens*. Brasillach and Thierry Maulnier did their student teaching at the same time as Gadenne, Bataille, and Georges Izard. Brasillach was a good teacher, and his teacher's appraisal also describes his remarkable qualities as a critic: "His speech is easy, the delivery fluent and good humored. He sets forth what he knows simply and without pedantry . . ." Evaluations of Audibert

Table 3. Subjects of the *Mémoires* for the *Diplôme d'Etudes Supérieures*

Student	Subject
Raymond Aron	"La notion d'intemporel dans la philosophie de Kant." Mention: Très Bien
Maurice Bardèche	"Le paysage urbain chez la peinture flamande du XV siècle"
Georges Bataille	"L'influence des sciences de la nature sur la poésie française, 1840–1900"
Maurice Blanchot	"La conception du dogmatisme chez les sceptiques"
Robert Brasillach	"Balzac et Paris, les rues, les maisons"
Pierre Brossolette	"Washington et les relations des Etats-Unis avec l'Europe." Mention: Honorable
Georges Canguilhem	"La théorie d'ordre et du progrès chez Comte"
Paul Gadenne	"Proust"
Claude Jamet	"L'amour dans l'oeuvre de Victor Hugo." Mention: Honorable
J. Hyppolite	"Mathématique et Méthode chez Descartes."
Georges Izard	"Géraud de Cordemoy" (seventeenth-century philosopher and historian). His adviser was Etienne Gilson
Daniel Lagache	"Croyance et Délire." Mention: Très Bien
M. Merleau-Ponty	"Multiple intelligence chez Platon." Mention: Honorable
Jacques Monod	"L'évolution réligieuse de Maurice de Guérin." Mention: Honorable
Thierry Maulnier	"L'art dramatique de Racine d'après ses préfaces"
Paul Nizan	"Fonctions de meaning: mots, images, schèmes"
Henri Quéffelec	"L'idéalisme de Villiers de l'Isle Adam"
J.-P. Sartre	"Les images de la vie psychologique (et la role de la nature)." Mention: Très Bien
J. Soustelle	"Les phénomènes d'extase chez les non-civilisés." Mention: Honorable
Pierre Vilar	"La vie industrielle dans la région de Barcelone." Mention: Honorable
Simone Weil	"Science et perfection chez Descartes"

Names set in bold represent cohorts at the Sorbonne.
Source: 61 AJ 188, 250–256

and Bardèche are also in character. Bardèche was complimented on his "very solid and varied qualities." Audibert has a "biting sensibility —a brisk style."[65]

Rightist *normaliens* were equally "typical" in other variables, such as foreign travel. John Talbott has documented the shift from classical studies to modern humanities.[66] Students exchanged countries as well as languages. It is interesting to note the interrelation between foreign travel and foreign language. English was the most commonly used modern language for the *concours d'entrée*. German was the next frequent, although it was marginally more common among rightist-identified students. *Normaliens* of both right and left identification benefited from the Fonds Lavisse for Easter and summer vacations. Audibert visited Spain (during the same time as Pierre Vilar); Bardèche visited Belgium; Pelorson, England; Thierry Maulnier, Switzerland (Davos); Jamet, North Africa; Quéffelec, North Africa and Hungary; and Etiemble, Italy. As Talbott noted, many students were lastingly affected by these sojourns. Of the destinations of students who availed themselves of either the Bourses Lavisse or Kahn, Davos, Switzerland, was the single most frequently visited place, followed by Algeria/Tunisia/Morocco.[67] Brasillach links these "ski vacations" to the political phenomenon of Briandism.[68]

An examination of the disciplinary files of the ENS reveals names of both rightist- and leftist-identified students signing a petition against the compulsory military service: Thierry Maulnier, René Chateau, Etiemble, Jamet, and Simone Weil.[69] Another "infamous" petition which appeared in *Humanité* included students of mostly leftist orientation: Weil, Nizan, Bruhat, Pierre Vilar, Albert Lautman (another of Brunschvicq's students). Bruhat and Vilar were censured for an incident with French officers ("Casa Velasquez").[70] Indeed, it appears that leftists were less docile students than rightist *normaliens*. If our rightist *normaliens* did have problems with authority, they were not manifested in student protest.

Our analysis of rightist *normalien scolarité* has revealed a "typical" career at Ulm. Moreover, analysis of the *Annuaire des Amis et Anciens Élèves de l'ENS* reveals that extramural contact between them and the French academies were strong, active networks. Most rightist *normaliens* received prominent literary prizes in the thirties and forties. Robert Brasillach received the Prix de l'Académie Française in 1936 as did his friend Thierry Maulnier in 1938 (he was also *membre titulaire*), as did Maurice Bardèche in 1941, Pierre Gaxotte in 1947, Jean Giraudoux in 1940, René Gillouin in 1931, Jérôme Carcopino in 1929, Henri Guillemin in 1927, Pierre Henri Simon in 1942 and 1943. Other laureates include Pierre Gaxotte (Prix Gobert 1947) and Jérôme Carcopino (Prix Louis Barthou). Carcopino was also elected to the Académie des Inscriptions. This is, indeed, an illustrious elite. The typical *normalien* extramural network was composed of the Académie Française and the Académie des Inscriptions, among others, as well as the Ecole de Rome. Carcopino and Maurice Bardèche were associated with this prestigious institution.[71]

It is only when we look for leftist names in the roster of literary prizes and academic honors that we see a pattern emerge which differentiates rightist and leftist students. Whereas a rightist student in a promotion of the twenties will receive some academic recognition in the thirties, his leftist cohort will usually appear in the mid-forties at the earliest. One searches in vain for a mention of Sartre, Merleau-Ponty, Vilar. Nizan wins a prize in 1939 for his *Conspiration*. This difference will increase in importance when we also consider that the rightist *normalien*'s political participation consisted largely of writing, whereas the leftist *normalien* had a more typical career pattern.[72]

Moreover, the receipt of literary prizes is a measure of integration in the *normalien* network. Péguy's experience is a strong negative example of the extramural influence of the ENS. Péguy wrote *Jeanne d'Arc* during two years' leave of absence from Ulm. (He also wrote *Pierre*, on Ulm scratch paper!)[73] Barrès nominated him for the prize of the Académie Française, and the decision was between Péguy and Robert de Louis. However, Lavisse intervened and "had the temerity to use the *normalien* fraternity to obstruct his [Péguy's] career." Lavisse exercised a right to nominate a third candidate—*normalien* Romain Rolland—and "drew in his wake the group of former students of the Ecole Normale, the *archicubes united from the right and left*" (italics mine). Péguy still had the lead, but in the absence of a majority he was awarded another prize.[74]

This typical career pattern changes abruptly when we turn to the *concours d'agrégation* and look at "débouchés." For rightist students turn disproportionately to careers in journalism and government. This is true for both *normaliens* and their rightist cohorts at other institutions: Drieu, Giraudoux, Gillouin, Pelorson, Morand, Jouvenel, Gaxotte, Brasillach, Thierry Maulnier, Guillemin, Etiemble, Déat.[75] It is difficult to assess whether the choice of a profession other than teaching is a direct result of failure on the *concours d'agrégation* or whether this failure is a result of a prior decision and commitment to journalist endeavors. Brasillach's many extra curricular pursuits, his literary collaboration on *Action Française*, may have left little time for concerted study or may be unrelated to his failure. In either case, success on the *agrégation* does not appear related to either *scolarité* or success on the *concours d'entrée*. One need only cite the profound surprise at Sartre's failure on the philosophy *concours d'agrégation*. In the words of Lavisse: "Experience proves that there are very mediocre students who are destined for careers in teaching, and very brilliant students who are not."[76]

One can further distinguish between leftist and rightist authors in that leftists first have a career in teaching and later go on to careers in letters.[77] Bardèche was among the *boursiers d'études supérieures*, Jamet and Beaufret joined the majority of their classmates in careers as lycée teachers. Among those *"sortis de l'université"* figure Brasillach and Thierry Maulnier (who failed to pass the *agrégation*) and Georges Pelorson, who was expelled.[78]

Our empirical sociology of rightist *normaliens* has generated the following conclusions: we have seen that they are an illustrative, non-aberrant elite that can look with pride to several generations of rightist *normaliens*. They do have their own history within the Ecole. There are small variations: More rightists have provincial origins. They have less representation in the liberal professions. Both right and left are equally likely to be fatherless. Extramural contacts between the ENS and the right are strong which is especially important when we consider the critical difference between the two elites. A change in career pattern occurs at the time of the *concours d'agrégation*. Rightist intellectuals more often go into careers in letters or government (perhaps owing to failure at the *agrégation*). Leftists first have a career in teaching, then go on to a second career in letters.

It should be noted that failure at the *agrégation* is not as determinative as it may seem. We will see, rather, following an analysis by Bourdieu, that the *concours d'agrégation* is not as significant as that ritual of initiation, the *concours d'entrée*. Indeed, the profitability of the title *ancien élève de* l'Ecole Normale Supérieure" remains high throughout the *normalien's* career. One is even tempted to say for his entire lifetime, in the sense that it is a mortal (or, in the case of Brasillach, a fatal) condition. The extramural contacts of the ENS—the literary establishment, its prizes and academies—continue to keep even the *"nonagrégé" normalien* within an elite network. Indeed, as Owen Lattimore has remarked about the Great Wall of China, it serves as much to keep them locked in as to keep strangers out. There is simply too great an institutional pressure not to *"démissioner."* The same act of passage—the *concours d'entrée*—that licits the passage *into* an elite discourages the obverse transgression: desertion. Our next section will, thus, deal not with the passage into Normale, or with the successive stages of a career: *licence, scolarité,* military service, student teaching, *agrégation, "détachement,"* but rather with the line itself, the frontier, or "arbitrary limit which the rite of institution . . . consecrates and legitimates."[79]

Instituting Rites

Robusson was drunk, tottering with joy. And he slept . . . and in
the great silence of the dormitory he dreamed. Normalien!
Finally! He was a normalien!
—Abel Hermant

Any theory of the mythic function of the ENS must explain a preoccupation with the *concours d'entrée* and the *canular*. The many different discursive levels—biological, genetic, zoological, mythological, occult, exotic (all couched in hyperbole)—continually raise the question of origins. The myth of ENS is all-encompassing, totalizing. It includes Kipling's *Jungle Book* ("Through novels, memoirs, and works of all sorts, the *normalien* flora and fauna of every period remains dispersed. We must gather them to constitute the *normalien jungle book* . . .")[80], a family romance, the retelling of Genesis, and a lover's discourse.[81] Moreover, even on a nonfigurative level, one witnesses a decentering of concerns such as *scolarité* to the early moments and gestures of initiation. But perhaps this decentering is but a displacement, pointing our attention to the act of passage and the line that is crossed in any such passage.

In an article on "instituting rites," Bourdieu asks a deceptively simple question: "What does the rite of passage separate? A before and an after—circumcision for example, or those that the rite concerns and those it does not—men and women?" Should emphasis be placed on mere temporal passage—the child becoming adult, the young *lycéen*, an eager *normalien*—or does such an emphasis mask the essential effect of this rite: to institute a lasting difference between those who are and those who can never be affected by the rite? The separation would thus be a constitutive part of a rite whose main purpose is to consecrate a preexistent difference. While the line draws attention to the act of passage, what is critically important is the line itself.[82]

The rite consecrates not only the difference between elected and excluded but between all that is associated with the excluded. Laloy, writing in the *Gaulois*, speaks of his philosophy initiation: "that's why we cannot remember these years almost separated from the world without a secret tenderness. We were delivered from all material worry . . . a sacred respite . . ."[83] Camille Jullian writes in *Le Temps*: "What creates this élite is that the *normalien*, relieved of material worries, lives from morning to night in an ideal atmosphere . . . the least literary incident reverberates without being diminished by any exterior vulgarity."[84] The *normalien* universe excludes the material, the real (nonideal). Its extreme interiority is juxtaposed with vulgar exteriority.

This separation is also central for Erving Goffman's analysis of "total institutions." For the "encompassing character of a total institution" is, above all, symbolized by those physical barriers to unrestricted social intercourse. The specificity of the total institution lies in its dual nature: part residential community, part formal organization. Total institutions depend upon a necessary separation of the young recruit from a home world as well as on the creation of a set of solidarities formed within the new boundaries. We have already noted the function of the *turnes* (dormitory study quarters) which united students of the left and right, creating friendships across ideological rifts. Goffman writes: "Sometimes special solidarities extend throughout a physically closed region . . . whose inhabitants perceive they are being administered as a single unit and have a lively sense of common fate."[85]

The separation, however, is projected onto the view of the school as an island, but this is no mere geographical unit. It is an island protected by patron saints:

> It was an island . . . an obsolete and unknown island with its bust of Pasteur . . . the island of Sancho, or moreover the island that everyone dreams about, the island of three years of vacation, miraculously accorded to a few.[86]

> The ceremony . . . takes place in places of retreat placed as is customary under the protection of our kings: St. Louis, Henri IV, Louis le Grand. The guardians of the holy grail . . . recognize their young equals and call to them.[87]

This "siren call" of the jury opens the gates to the island of the Ecole Normale. The notion of entry is nowhere more prevalent than in the memoirs of Romain Rolland, in which we find the recurrent metaphor of the door. We have mentioned Romain Rolland's "obligation . . . to force an entry into the Ecole." At length he describes the "omnipresent idea of the narrow door which had only been half-opened . . . on a world where we would be able to make a secure living without offending our sensibilities."[88] Again, we have juxtaposition of the world within Ulm and a vulgar, offensive outside. In other words, the Ecole is otherworldly. It is also denoted by a series of self-contained images: seminary, cloister, Jesuit convent, sanctuary, cathedral.[89]

The "excluded" is underlined in the numerous physical demarcations that constitute the *canular*.[90] The *canular* can be seen on one level as a ritual reconciliation of inside and outside; this passage is continually reinforced by movements up and down, on and off campus, and transgressions into "indecent places" in the Latin Quarter. The juxtaposition of transgression and consecration that inheres in the *canular* (hand-in-hand with the delineation of *normalien* physical space) draws continual attention to the line itself. One wonders, indeed, if there is any elusive content to the *canular* or rather the continual opposed motion that points to transition.

Yet the juxtaposition of transgression and consecration also shares an affinity with the logic of Goffman's total institutions. Physical separation may indeed contribute to strong, abiding friendship, but it is the separation of a recruit from his home world that is of the utmost necessity. In other words, a clear break must be instituted not just with the immediate environs, but also and more important, with the lived past of the recruit. This is most efficiently achieved by a series of abasements: "he begins a series of abasements, degradations, humiliations and a profanation of the self. His self is systematically mortified." The process of entrance is thus one of "loss and mortification." The transgression of entering indecent places in the Latin Quarter circumscribes "permissible" zones of *normalien* excursions as it also involves a "defiling" of the *normalien*. Yet this "defilement" plays a constitutive role in the socialization process, as it involves a necessary "breakdown of usual environmental arrangements for insulating oneself from one's own source of contamination."[91]

This mortification of the self will take many forms in the *canular*. The use of the term *"gnouf"* (see below) reinscribes hierarchical values of the institution as well as detailing the "plight" of the new arrival. Demeaning postures are also required such as kneeling and bending. Moreover, "Just as the individual can be required to hold his body in a humiliating pose, so he may have to provide humiliating verbal responses."[92] In sum, the *canular* acts as a "welcome" consonant with Goffman's criteria for total institutions. Thus gestural and verbal profanations correspond to the indignity of speech and action required of the new recruit. This loss of self-determination will be acted out. Subjects may be required to sing abusive songs or perform "ludicrously useless" tasks. We will see both at work in the *normalien* initiation rite. The function of these performances is to turn deference into a visual display.[93] Although Goffman's descriptions are to the point, his analysis differs from that of Bourdieu or Foucault in that he is concerned with the experience of these rites from the point of view of the recruit subjected to them. The French sociologists not only reject the possibility of this form of subject consciousness but also see the "deviant" case as being the purist example of the true norm.[94] Moreover, they are more concerned with institutional socialization than with the effect of total institutions on inmates.

With these theories in mind, we will now look at the *canular* in greater detail. *Gnoufs* (the word designates noninitiates, who will later become *"conscrits,"* i.e., first-year students) meet at a neighborhood café (outside) and walk to Ulm (inside). They ascend the staircase to meet "upper" classmen whom they meet with ferocious howls (aggression) and are then made to kneel and "prostrate" themselves (submission). They are tucked *into* bed and then *tossed out* along with their mattresses.[95]

The second day consists of a single-file lineup (order) and a forced visit to "indecent places" (disorder). They are then forced to kneel before the Méga—a skeleton left to the school by Cuvier (it signifies prehistory)—and to respectfully kiss the end of its tail (signifying extension). This vision of a *normalien* perpetuity is terrifying: "Tremble, conscripts, the Méga is lying in wait for you." After a few days of such heady dialectics—obscene "homework assignments," "ethics exams," and roll calls—the temple does not fall. Rather *gnoufs* stand on stovetops and listen, without moving, surrounded by upperclassmen in disguise (hiddenness), to demeaning poetry (the revealed word). Teachers and alumni are also present, testifying to that unbroken faith that links the generations, and the school ritual ends appropriately (i.e., by denial) with the solemn words attesting to that never-ending history: "there never were *gnoufs*, there never was a *canular*, there are only *cubes, carrés,* and conscripts."[96]

This is a most "selective" amnesia; it represses the act of institution that created the *normalien,* the *canular,* and its analogue, the *gnouf,* while affirming its product—the *conscrit, cube,* and *carré.* It is this particular "amnesia of genesis" that Bourdieu so aptly captures in *La Reproduction.* It gives a naive impression of "always thus" (*"toujours ainsi"*) which is a necessary part of a "collective unconscious." It serves to naturalize what is a historical product.[97] Yet, what is the purpose of such an appropriation?

This negation of any history prior to the moment one becomes a *conscrit* is indeed a constitutive act. As much as the *canular separates* the *normalien*—circumscribing him from the nonelect, from the outside world, situating him both within Ulm and within the Latin Quarter —it *unites* him to his fellow *normaliens.* It is thus a principle of generalization that proceeds through the very denial of historical change. The denial of a *normalien* prehistory leads to the "family romance."

As with Freud, "real," "historical" parents are replaced with those of a higher stature (i.e., Pasteur, Poincaré, other famous authors).[98] Concerns with origins are similarly displaced onto concerns with the birth of ideas, with the library as delivery room ("between the world and us, there was a library") and Herr as midwife: "He knew all the works in progress. He aided their birth."[99] If the before/after, *gnouf/conscrit* transition cannot be a historical product, it is thus a difference *in essence*. Any *normalien* is separated by a difference, not in time (before/after) but in essence, from even the "best" non-*normaliens*.

The act of initiation which consecrates difference is thus also an act of *investiture*:[100] "The future *normalien* is, from this moment, promoted as a family member of the great moralists, the great aesthetes, and the great authors. He could remain small and mediocre, but he is of their race. He often speaks and writes their language poorly, but he employs only their language . . ." This investiture can be juridico-political —as is the *investiture de chevalier*. One recalls Pompidou's pronouncement: "One is born a *normalien* as one is born a chevalier (knight). The *concours* is the only dubbing."[101] Investiture, however, consists of making this inner essence known and recognized: "the diploma belongs as much to magic as do amulets: in the power that belongs to them, to act on the real, through acting on the representation of the real." This recognition combined with the *normalien*'s unique relation to cultural capital, i.e., language ("he employs only their language") allows the *normalien* to become the "*porte-parole*," the one who speaks for the collectivity. The role of *porte-parole* constitutes the *normalien*'s "competence" in both a legal (Bourdieu) and a linguistic (Chomsky) sense.[102]

The act of institution is thus a communicative process. The *normalien* is recognized by others, certainly by those in his "family": "the guardians of the holy grail . . . recognize their young equals and call to them."[103] This encourages him to realize this essence: "Become what you are. Such is the slogan that underlines the performative magic of all acts of institution." But this slogan "become what you are" conceals a fatality. Bourdieu notes that "all social destinies are mortal," because once the line is crossed, it is virtually impossible to go back.[104]

Yet this barrier to "resignation" is more easily understood when one looks at the *concours d'entrée* as a door that is locked on both sides. The barrier that keeps one locked out can also keep one locked inside. Just as the *canular* proceeds through an "amnesia of genesis," the *concours d'entrée* creates a "second" nature through a specific form of education that Bourdieu denotes elsewhere as *habitus*. *Habitus* is the internalization of the "cultural arbitrary." It is self-perpetuating and thus continually revalorizes this interiorized "arbitrary." (It is the analogue of "genetic capital.")[105] This can proceed, as Durkheim has noted, through hardship and suffering. The *concours d'entrée* is often described as a "burden" (e.g., Rolland), as a physically demanding ordeal (*épreuve*), an apprenticeship designed to produce exceptional students. The *normalien* way of life is Spartan and ascetic, recalling those metaphors of "cloister, seminary, convent" enumerated previously. This is another reason for the *canular:* the "fête" is but the obverse of the sacrifice necessitated by the *concours d'entrée*. If the drunken revelry of the *canular* is Dionysian, the austere and rarefied *normalien* mode is Apollonian.[106]

The notion of sacrifice was expressed in Rolland's feeling of "obligation" to pass the *concours d'entrée*. Among the numerous obligations are the learning of dead languages (both Latin and Greek) and forced lycée study for as much as three years. Pierre Henri Simon's proclamation that what is really crucial is to be *khâgneux* ("this ascetic trial of one, two, three years in order to acquire . . . a general culture . . .") reveals a profound understanding of *habitus*.[107] Indeed, Bourdieu's discussion of *habitus* bears uncanny similarity to Simon's discussion. For one of the examples continually cited by Bourdieu is a professorial aristocratic asceticism which functions as a distinctive sign (analogous to petit bourgeois pretension): "When one speaks of the aristocratic asceticism of teachers or the pretension of the petite bourgeoisie, one is not only describing these groups by one, or even the most important, of their properties, but also endeavoring to name the principle which generates all their properties and all their judgments of their, or other people's, properties."[108] This is not a gratuitous example, for it occupies a strategic place in Bourdieu's discussion of the "theoretic space" of *habitus*. "Aristocratic asceticism" becomes a generative principle of the professor.

Bourdieu's depiction of professorial asceticism underlines the importance of denegation of aristocratic essentialism as part of the generative matrix of *habitus*.[109] This aristocratic asceticism delineates a separation from the petit bourgeois. Indeed, Bourdieu notes the great attempts at euphemization in teachers' appraisals of students precisely to avoid using the adjective *petit bourgeois*.[110] *Habitus* connotes a generative principle which is also a life – style (or an "art of living") as well as a secondary signifier of all the attributes and practices of its corresponding social condition and position.[111] A "cultivated naturalness" is produced, and this cultivated disposition ("an ideology of natural taste") presents itself in the guise of an innate disposition.[112] This is a form of "knowledge without concepts," a reflexive mastery of social codes. As such, *habitus* is a "practice-unifying and practice-generating principle" corresponding to an internalized form of class situation and the conditioning this entails.[113] It is not just a mechanical reflection either of demographic variables (education, occupation, geography) or of a relation to productive forces, but part of a whole set of super-impositions. *Habitus* partakes of an Althusserian overdetermination and structual causality; that is, its generative principle is nonlinear, but overdetermined and superimposed—indeed, polysemic.[114]

The unconscious aspect of *habitus* should also be noted: it is an unconscious strategy which partakes of a whole set of tacit principles of selection and exclusion. These can be read at a glance in the most minute and trivial techniques of the body (posture, gestures) that Bourdieu describes as a bodily *hexis*. Thus the "general culture" learned and attained by aristocratic asceticism is an appeal to the body of an entire person. The various *concours* (*d'entrée* and *d'agrégation*) as well as the memoirs and necrologies of alumni attest to the importance of the physical persona as a sign of *normalien* moral attributes.[115] Simon is uncannily apposite to Bourdieu in his underlining of the importance of *khâgne,* as it is here where naturalness and facility are first inculcated.

This *habitus,* however, is reinforced by a series of signs and passwords. Peyrefitte's *Rue d'Ulm* offers a *lexique* of *normalien* slang, a startling percentage of which refer to the *canular* (*gnouf, cirage, bizouth, conscrit, méga*), or the *concours d'entrée* (*cacique* [first place], *culal* [last place], *intégerer* [to be accepted in the *concours*], *mégaliser* [to be accepted by the school]). This self-consciousness is reinforced by other slang used to designate separateness from the outside, e.g., *exo* (all that which is not *normalien*) "designates the pitiful part of humanity that has not passed through the rue d'Ulm" (*sorbonicole* is an especially contemptible part of *exo*). Separations within Ulm attest to a structured hierarchy: upperclassmen inhabit the *palais;* illegal residents ("*goimmards*") have a name as do practicing Catholics ("*talas*"). Relationships are established: *sevrienne* (the women's coestablishment): *normalien:* Benedictine: benediction."[116]

Goffman concurs on the importance of a specialized language to denote superiors and outsiders: "Along with a lingo, inmates acquire knowledge of the various ranks and officials, an accumulation of lore about the establishment and some comparative information about life in other similar institutions."[117] Bourdieu's conception goes beyond the *content* signified by the slang to its structural role. For Bourdieu, affinities of style are constitutive of social practices (and classes) and are linked to a concept of *habitus* as *writing.* Bourdieu gives the analogy of *habitus* as a "unique way of tracing characters which invariably produces the same writing."[118] Yet this shouldn't be taken too literally. Bourdieu cautions that this same writing has a familiar resemblance whether written in large or small letters, on white or colored paper, or on a blackboard, whether with pen, pencil, or chalk. Despite these "apparent" differences, a family resemblance is created with a unique signature like that of a painter, a writer, or a distinctive stride. We will see how the *normalien* institutional socialization (of which the slang is a part) plays a key role in neutralizing both political and demographic differences, creating a signature or handwriting which can be read at a glance.

There are certainly many external signs which reveal the *normalien*, but what signifies the *normalien* is, above all, "incorporeal signs." Both Thierry Maulnier and Georges Pompidou see the Ecole as an occult or secret society. "For the true, without doubt . . . there are no exterior signs." The school belongs to the world of the unspoken: "The Ecole: proper noun with a definite article: cannot be defined."[119] Those who are *normaliens* don't talk about it. The moment one says "when I prepared Normale" he has revealed himself as an impostor or, more accurately, as a "pretender" to this royal family. Indeed, the lack of words signifies that only a glance is needed: *normaliens* recognize each other at first glance and they say in unison: "it's a *normalien*."[120]

This stress on incorporeal signs underlines the point that *habitus* is a generating principle which is never explicitly formulated. We have previously noted that *habitus* partakes of an unconscious strategy. Imbedded in what we call values[121] are networks of secondary signification connoted by body language (body *hexis*). Bourdieu is concerned with a series of symbolic aggressions which are explicitly codified as well as with the idea of "the pure gaze as a social break." This mutual recognition denoted by Suzanne Langer as "the self legitimating imagination of the happy few"[122] is admirably captured in Peyrefitte's *normalien* hagiography. This is not a rational calculus but a metaphoric perception based on an affinity of style.[123]

Thierry Maulnier writes of the occult imperceptible ties that bind *normaliens*. This difficulty of grasping *normalien* essence is understandable in terms both of *habitus* (unconscious internalization of pedagogical principles) produced by the *concours d'entrée*, and of the "amnesia of genesis" that is the end product of the *canular*. "For the Ecole Normale Supérieure is really a secret society with its coded language, its signs of recognition, its solidarity among its members which appears to be stronger than political or religious divisions. Everyone knows that the Ecole Normale, which prepares one for nothing . . . leads one to everything." [124]

The act of institution is so powerful that it restricts many apparent contradictions. Even if the *normalien* does not ever do anything noteworthy (or even if he does indeed commit infamy), his lack of achievement is seen as an expression of his will. It is an example of the autonomy of ascription vis-à-vis achievement, or Kant's "institutional charisma." [125] It is no more easy for a *normalien* to disown the school as it would be for a child to renounce his parents. Indeed, the parental condescension toward a "problem child" is also revealed in this discussion of "*normalien* detractors": "certain *normaliens* have become detractors of the *normalien* spirit, but they have contempt for its virtues as Seneca had contempt for riches, while possessing them." [126]

During Bouglé's tenure as head of the ENS he noted that the school had come to replace many of the functions of the family.[127] Part of the success of the act of institution must be seen in this transference. While Sibony has stated that a "group is ordered around a sexually symbolic pattern, in this case an appeal to the father," [128] and Bourdieu has remarked, "whoever teaches becomes a father or a priest," it is at least evident that the *normalien* is no mere civil servant. Durkheim was right in situating a homology between professorial and priestly functions.[129] The Ecole has been often described as a seminary.[130] But it is a curious combination of the sacred and the uncanny. The fusion of the priestly and the occult resides in the incantatory power of the *parole lettrée*, the delivery of which is likened to the white jacket of the chef and gestures of the surgeon.[131] The *normalien's* verbal pyrotechnics (demonstrated beginning with the *concours d'entrée* and revealed in the clever parodies and speeches of the *canular*) transmit not only a specific content but, most important, an affirmation of the value of that content.[132]

If the function of the *normalien* is that of the *porte-parole* or spokesman, the act of investiture is, indeed, crucial. Symbolic efficacy is dependent on the "*destinateur*"; words in themselves don't constitute speech acts. Illocutionary strength is restricted to authorized spokesmen.[133] This necessitates collective belief guaranteed by the institution and materialized in titles and symbols, which are testimonials of respect and confer authority. It is not by accident that the postwar purge trial indictment of Robert Brasillach begins with the words "*Ancien élève de l'*Ecole Normale Supérieure." [134]

This elite identity created by the *actes d'institution* of the *canular* and the *concours d'entrée* also explains the seeming paradox of the French intellectual whose role as an effective ideologue increases with his separation from a mass base. For this very separation inaugurated by the rites of initiation "invests" the *normalien* with his "competence" as *porte-parole*. The *actes d'institution* not only insure a *normalien's* authority, they also offer a lifetime (money back) unconditional guarantee.

4

THE RETURN OF THE REPRESSED

THE ECOLE NORMALE SUPÉRIEURE

AND THE RIGHT

Normal: *1) Réglé 2) Naturel*
Normalisation: *Rationalisation*
Normaliser: *Régler*
Norme: *Règle*
—Hachette, Dictionnaire des Synonymes

It is in the play between the two synonyms for *normal*
—*réglé* (ruled, regulated, ordered) and *naturel* (of nature, natural)—
that the peculiar status of the Ecole Normale Supérieure is grounded.
For the ENS as arbiter of elite culture rules, regulates, and hierarchizes
intellectual production in France. Yet, as we have seen in Chapter 3,
the mythic functioning of its institutional mechanisms (i.e., *concours
d'entrée* and *canular*) invests an "essence" and "authority" in its students as *porte-paroles*. To be a *normalien* connotes both a certain style
(*mode*) and a (higher) essence. It is, thus, both form and content. Moreover, like money in Marx's *Capital*, the label "*normalien*" is convert-
ible currency. It operates, in short, as both measure (*règle*) and value
(*nature*).

One can not underestimate the political effect of these dual functions. *Normalisation* (standardization, rationalization) is the process by
which real, historical differences are effaced (e.g., provincial/Parisian)
to create new allegiances and self-concepts. *Normalisation* regulates
the standards of elite discourse, its articulation, its reception, and as
we will see in the postwar purge trials, its judgment. In such a way,
the role of *normalisation* itself must be reexamined. For, following the
analysis of two *normaliens*, Foucault and Bourdieu,[1] *normalisation* is the
way a dominant ideology works to coerce without resort to direct repression. This will be extremely interesting in the case of a "liberal"
institution with linkages to the right.

Yet it should be no surprise to the etymologists that this same "rule" that connotes measure and standard conceals the more obvious political association of power and domination. We will examine the role of the ENS as a standard in relation to the diverse ideologies of the right and their reception.

Rhetorics of Establishment

> *It's the institution which speaks in a certain rhetoric of establishment and the formal procedures betray the objectively inscribed intentions in the constraints and necessities of a social position.*
> —Pierre Bourdieu

Normalien style, its "book culture," is an instrument of power. And it is an instrument peculiarly suited to the ideology of the right. Indeed, it would be difficult to find an important theme of the right that does not have its parallel in either *normalien* discourse or some structural mechanism of the Ecole Normale. Not only do the two mechanisms discussed in the previous chapter, *habitus* (interiorized compliance) and the *amnesia of genesis* (produced by the *concours d'entrée* and the *canular*), foreground the very issues of occultation and the naturalization of history that lie at the heart of fascist ideology, but also the codes of *normalien* discourse become the perfect mode of articulating the central issues of elite and mass, hierarchy and subordination. The antidemocratic, anti-egalitarian bias is nowhere more appropriately situated than in the loftiness (*hauteur*) of the "philosophical discourse of importance," cited by Bourdieu in theorists as diverse as Heidegger and Althusser or, in our case, as opposite as Hubert Bourgin and Paul Dupuy.[2] However, where the "discourse of importance" contravenes certain (i.e., egalitarian, committed) norms of the leftist/liberal ideology, it serves to reinforce rightist moral conceptions.

Let us return to the leftist caricature of Ulm. This portrait rested on the fact that *normaliens* were well represented in the parliament; moreover, one half of those who became deputies also became ministers. As Suleiman stated: "It was *normaliens* like Jaurès, Blum, Painlevé and Lebrun who directed attention to the intense political interest of the Ecole Normale Supérieure."[3] Hubert Bourgin's classic volume *De Jaurès à Léon Blum: L'Ecole Normale et la Politique* reinforces this predominant vision.

Bourgin's version becomes especially noteworthy when one considers Bourgin's political itinerary. Police dossiers at the Archives Nationales document Bourgin's many affiliations with rightist and fascist groups of the twenties and thirties such as Bucard's Francisme, Valois's Faisceau, and Colonel de la Roque's Croix de Feu. A brochure written to launch Valois's *Nouveau Siècle* boasts of Valois's illustrious academic career, beginning with the Ecole Normale: "ENS 1895–1898, *agregé lettres*—#1, 1898, *doc ès lettres* 1905, *doc en droit*, 1906."[4] Bourgin's presentation of the Ecole Normale as a leftist political institution may be politically motivated, or at the least suspect, but I will argue that both his exposition and his denegation are profoundly typical.

If we have seen (in Chapters 2 and 3) that the political history of the ENS denies its linkages to the right, we will now see how its historians have denied the thematic confluence between the ENS and the right. Bourgin's rewriting of the history of the ENS articulates two thematics shared by rightist intelligentsia and *normaliens*, albeit often in latent forms: anti-Semitism and the tension between political leaders and the elite in a vanguard party.

The tensions between leader and follower reveal themselves in Bourgin's diachronic exposition of the ENS in the guise of a meditation on intellectual *"maîtres."* Lucien Rebatet's distrust for the leader succinctly resumes a fundamental tension between vanguard party and its leader: "Where there is a leader, the elite no longer exists."[5] Similarly, intellectuals such as Drieu La Rochelle or Bertrand de Jouvenel[6] concur in their discussions of the Doriot question whether the emotions aroused by a leader or the qualities admired in a leader will weaken the aristocratic elite. For if the goal of the right is to "remake the aristocracy,"[7] the leader plays an ambigious role.

The role of an intellectual *maître* is more complex and is perhaps more clearly revealed in the denegation of those *normaliens* interviewed who when asked about *maîtres* announce flatly that they have no *maître* and in the next sentence reveal the opposite; "But there was Nietzsche, Barrès . . ."[8] There is, too, a poignancy about this denegation as it reveals the inherent tension between the leadership principle (and rivalries) and the much-valued intellectual independence, sought in the *concours d'entrée* and cultivated throughout a *normalien*'s career. One may read in Bourgin's documentation of Dupuy's, Herr's, and Andler's role as *maître* a tension between belonging to established social circles and the much-heralded "personal reflection." Moreover, it should be noted that *maîtres* are more easily followed by leftist students. A statement such as: "Alain led me to the left, once and for always . . ."[9] is simply not uttered by *normaliens* of the right. The influence of Bellessort, Massis, Gaxotte, Maurras, etc., is couched in more qualified and mediated terms.

The question of anti-Semitism is not disjoint to these concerns.

The Return of the Repressed

Bourgin's conception is of Jews as lawgivers who deform the school. If Herr is a linchpin in *normalien* and socialist social circles, Halévy and Eisenmann are the "sacred to Herr."[10] Bourgin's *De Jaurès à Léon Blum*, if read as a companion piece to the history of the ENS, reveals an anti-Semitism equal to that of *Libre Parole* and *Cocarde* following the Dreyfus Affair. His vision of Jews as Anglo lawgivers and as commercial geniuses will be examined in a later section, but a few examples should suffice to demonstrate the persistent stereotypes. An entry in the *Correspondant*, December 25, 1896, underlines the complementarity between Judaistic pursuits and business acumen: "The press, literature, teaching, saturated with Talmudism, completed the power of money."[11] Jewish writers are critical and assimilate ideas as easily as they do nations: "Small Jews who place themselves like insects in our finest fruits."[12] They work for enemy nations: "all those who are the agents of Germany and England."[13] *Libre Parole* affords us with perhaps the most interesting example of the Jew's purported cosmopolitanism: When asked where he comes from, a Jew responds: "I *live* in France where I *write* in English."[14] The "capitalist intello-Jew" also contributes heavily to *Humanité*.[15] *Libre Parole* of August 18, 1906, lists some influential *normalien* contributors to Jaurès (780,000 FF) in an editorial "Tout aux Juifs." Contributors include Lévy-Bruhl, Herr, and Léon Blum.

Let us consider the leftist caricature as a point of departure, for it produces a fundamental accuracy albeit through a distortion of size, or in this case, a mirror vision. Just as a written history of the right is lacking because their political activism consisted of writing, so too the leftist depiction of the ENS which assumes parliamentary praxis as a primary criterion will be singularly inappropriate for an elite whose ideology was profoundly antiparliamentarian! Intellectuals such as Brasillach and Bardèche were extremely wary of political leaders and political parties and turned away when the ideologue eclipsed the poet or moralist (as in the case of Barrès and Maurras).[16] Montherlant and Drieu concurred in this contempt for narrow political processes which were seen to substitute electoral or economic criteria for moral or spiritual ones. Drieu's disillusion with political parties (joining them only when he was depressed),[17] his disillusion with Doriot and the PPF as well as with the *"parti unique"* during Vichy, have been documented by his numerous biographers and historians of the period.[18]

Drieu most succinctly poses the problem in two entries in *Sur les Ecrivains*, writing on Maurras and Barrès: "The writer who is a political leader, he's always a phony. Supreme example: Maurras." "Every year I reread some of Barrès' books and more and more, it's the author and not the thinker I admire."[19] Soucy states that if Drieu appeared to succumb to "an old sclerotic fascism which focused too much authority on a single leader" such as he inveighed against in 1937, his collaboration in 1940 with the Nazis was in spite of the *Führerprinzip*, not because of it.[20]

Paxton remarks that for French intellectuals the critique of parliament and the critique of decadence are allied.[21] Maurras will thus see party interests as replacing a more general public good, as will Barrès contrast political parties with France's national interests. In a journal entry Barrès writes of his meeting with Maurras: "We didn't speak of political parties, only of France."[22]

The movement toward redefinition of politics away from parliamentarianism conceals various themes both shared by rightist intellectuals and expressed in pamphlets of right-wing groups during the twenties and thirties. First, electoral success is seen as a betrayal of principles. Ethical interests are seen to be in contradiction with political interests. Second, there is the belief that quantity/mass is synonymous with degradation. The equation of democracy/number with impotence and mediocrity is a closely related subtheme. In short, political questions as traditionally defined by narrow political parties and parliamentary praxis are seen as "baser," less "spiritual," and more materialist than the ethical claims of the polis. A cursory glance at leaflets from rightist and fascist groups corroborates the prevalence of this thematic.

Semichon of the Étudiants Royalistes (a dissident organization of the Action Française) concurs in the equation of electoral politics with man's baser instincts: "Politicians ever ready to betray their program for lowly electoral interests."[23] Laudatory press coverage of Colonel de la Roque's trip to Oued Smar (Algeria) is quick to point out that the colonel is no ordinary parliamentarian: "A young leader, still vigorous, neither parliamentarian nor politician . . . the Croix de Feu were . . . simply men . . .[24] Even Bourgin expresses his sympathy for Valois (as he resigns from the Ligue des Patriotes): "There is sympathy for Valois in *anciens combattants*, in those who place questions of patriotism and nationalism above political questions."[25] Politics for the right is something clearly larger than a narrow parliamentary focus.

And it is not the number of politically identified *normaliens* or their parliamentary behavior that is at issue in our analysis: "It's the institution that speaks in a certain rhetoric of establishment" which belies any leftist appraisal. Our next section will examine the institutional mechanisms of the ENS as one form of institutional discourse. I argue that institutional discourse speaks louder than expressed content—in our case, the number of leftist-identified *normaliens*.

The Return of the Repressed

Concours d'Entrée

> *Today, writing a monographic history . . . would involve making*
> *the whole archive . . . emerge in the movement of its formation as*
> *a discourse in the process of constituting itself and interacting at*
> *the same time with the development of . . . its institutions,*
> *inflecting and informing them.* What one would thus try to
> reconstitute would be the enmeshing of a discourse in the
> historical process.
> —Michel Foucault, *Power/Knowledge*

The comparison of Ulm's caricature with its institutional discourse at once raises the question of inaccurate representations, or the uncanny accuracy of misrepresentation. What does a
"myth" seek to remedy or restore? We will first regard caricature as
a specific form of compensation. Borges notes that nations tend to
pick as national authors those that suit them the least: Victor Hugo
for France, Cervantes for Spain. Yet he argues that this is not unin-
tentional: "each country thinks that it must be represented by someone who differs from it . . . as a sort of remedy, an antidote against
defects."[26]

The leftist caricature of Ulm can now be more closely understood
as a form of compensation. But what does it compensate for? What is
the repressed content it seeks to exclude? A reading of the archives
of the ENS shows that the preoccupations of the right in the twenties
and thirties startlingly parallels the preoccupations of the ENS during the same period.[27] We will first examine institutional mechanisms
and their thematic analogs, starting (as does the ENS) with the *concours d'entrée*. The *concours d'entrée* will be analyzed on four different
levels: (1) as a mechanism of selection which seeks to cultivate difference and encourage idiosyncracy; (2) as an expression of the horror of
mediocrity; (3) as an act of investiture which turns history into nature;
(4) as a physical ordeal (*épreuve*).

SELECTION: DIFFERENCE/IDIOSYNCRACY

The *concours d'entrée* is the first step in the recognition
of that cultivated difference (or studied eccentricity) that is the true
mark of a *normalien*. Idiosyncracy is evinced in mundane sartorial con-
ceits. Jaurès returns to his provincial hometown during one spring
break garbed in the latest Paris fashions.[28] Similarly, the political itinerary of Brasillach can be metonymically traced through his muffler's
journey from Ulm to Fresnes prison. Paul Dupuy's green cape is as

fondly remembered by his students as he is; it epitomizes the fact that "a fanciful taste as also a great disdain for fashion are among the *normalien* traditions."[29] Cultivated eccentricity, the mode of the "*démodé*," is also recounted in the celebrated meeting of Montherlant and Massis. Montherlant arrives wearing an American officer's uniform.[30]

Maurice Merleau-Ponty gives an early recollection of Nizan: "One day while we were preparing for the Ecole Normale, we saw entering our classroom with the aura of one of the chosen few a former student . . . He was admirably dressed in dark blue and wore the tricolor cockade of Valois. They told me it was Nizan. Nothing in his dress or carriage advertised the labors of the *khâgne* or the Ecole Normale."[31] Indeed Merleau-Ponty situates Sartre's inability to understand Nizan (until twenty years after his death in the preface to *Aden, Arabie*) in Sartre's misreading of Nizan's dandyism: "Sartre did not understand Nizan because Nizan transformed his suffering into dandyism. His books, the sequel of his life . . . were necessary before Nizan was finally understood."[32] Déat, on the other hand, was a more able fashion critic. Déat immediately recognized a link between style and political itinerary in the case of his friend Pierre Pucheu. Déat presents Pucheu's new beige suit and yellow shoes as a signifier for his opportunism.[33] Pucheu's trajectory away from the rue d'Ulm to the technocratic circles of alumn A. François Poncet is presented as an allegory of his wardrobe.

Nonconformist dress and affectations are shared by *normaliens* of the right and left. However, rightist critical style is seen as more idiosyncratic and more consonant with their sartorial style. Leftist critical style appears more traditional and scholastic. Pascal Ory's recent biography describes Nizan as a pedantic critic in spite of his flamboyant (or extremist) affectations. Nizan as a scholastic Marxist correcting student copy[34] is contrasted with the frivolity and ease of the "*moi, je*" school. "Assuredly Nizan isn't a Thibaudet, a Thérive, a Brasillach . . . ready to speculate on the unsaid, the elusive, and the trivial."[35] Yet it is precisely those qualities that Nizan lacks that are sought first on the *concours d'entrée*, and later in the speeches of the *canular*, the *stage pédagogique*, and the *agrégation*.

Idiosyncrasy/eccentricity are not just themes in a narrow discussion of *normalien* style (i.e., the much-lauded categories of "originality" and "personal reflection").[36] Rather they are linked to a larger political critique that will be examined in our next section. For one of the salient features of fascism was its critique of mediocrity and the "*moyenne*." Indeed, this feature played no small part in the moral attractiveness of fascism for an already selected elite.

The Return of the Repressed

Table 4. Declining Basis of Recruitment

Year	Number of Candidates
1880	169
1890	240
1900	212
1904*	195
1905	200
1910	170
1912–14	197–212
1920	140

Source: Archives Nationale (AN) 61 AJ
166, 192
*The decree of November 10, 1903, that
united the Ecole Normale with the Bourse
de Licence didn't greatly affect the number presenting themselves.

HORROR OF MEDIOCRITY

The emphasis on originality and individual creativity is heightened in the archival documents which reveal a horror of mediocrity similar to Montherlant's savage *"morale de midinette."* [37] The concern with the declining birthrate after the war finds its echo in those who lament the numerical weakness of the post–World War I *concours:* fewer candidates presenting themselves means less adequate ones are chosen. Admission no longer represents a meaningful selection. [38] An editorial in *Le Temps* (January 16, 1927) discussing recruitment to the ENS speaks of the effects of the 1903 reforms which led to both a decrease in the number of candidates presenting themselves and a concomitant decrease in quality. Table 4 and Figures 1 and 2 show this decline.

The relation between nonconformity, mediocrity, and the creation of an elite is ambivalent for Montherlant. In this essay "La Qualité" he puts forth the view that eccentricity is a type of social service. Questions of style are thus also political questions. "The simple example of nonconformity . . . is in itself a social service. Precisely because tyranny makes such a crime of eccentricity . . ." Moreover, the amount of eccentricity in a society is a measure of the amount of genius. The problem for Montherlant is the very notion of elite, as it contains within itself the concept of a minority of exceptional people. Just as the "leader" posed a problem for an intellectual dedicated to recreating an aristocracy, so too does an elite undermine the very notion of quality. It should be noted that Montherlant shares a dismal view of *maîtres,*

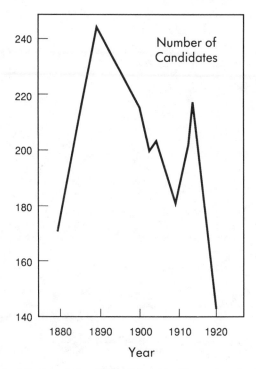

Figure 1. Declining Number of Candidates Presenting Themselves for Admission.
Source: Archives Nationale (AN) 61 AJ 166, 192

albeit phrased in a backhanded way: "A protégé who succeeds! My God! One dies all over again!"[39]

The horror of mediocrity leads to the critique of democracy and that of representation in the works of the rightist *normalien* René Gillouin, as well as informing the critical essays of Pierre Henri Simon on "heroism." Glory, grandeur, and honor, all "essentially heroic virtues," must be cultivated in the same manner as a student in *"hypokhâgne"* prepares for the arduous *concours:* it is impossible to achieve without the "surpassing of the self" produced by ascetism. This *"surpassement"* echoes the writings of a fellow *normalien*, who articulates this same notion as *"démesuré"*—an exaggerated excess, the opposite of "moderate," "ordinary," or, more apt in our analysis of the *concours*, "average." Indeed, *l'homme démesuré* is beyond all standards.[40] "Heroism" would appear alien to democratic values or in Gillouin's words, "Democracy rests on a false premise . . . that politics is within the reach of anyone, and that it is the only trade along with unskilled labor, which does not require any special knowledge."[41] He will thus argue for the

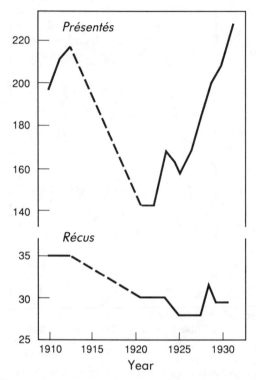

Figure 2. Number of Students *Présentés* and *Récus* as a Function of the Year. Source: Archives Nationale (AN) 61 AJ 166, 192

duty of the elite to combat the obstacle of democracy and the mediocrity of the representatives that are elected officials, and urge the formation of *"aristarchie"*—a government of the *"meilleurs"* (best). The theme of mediocrity will prove central to the critique of parliamentary representation. This *surpassement* further reinscribes ascetic codes of distinction just as the notion of *aristarchie* highlights the aristocracy of taste detailed by Bourdieu.

INVESTITURE: DENIAL OF NATURE

> *All* normaliens *look alike. Like Negroes.*
> —G. Tery

It was noted in the previous chapter that the *concours d'entrée* marks the first step in the process of investiture. One does not historically "become" a *normalien;* in Pompidou's celebrated phrase,

"One is born a *normalien*." Historically acquired culture (lycée training for the *concours*) becomes transmuted into a second nature, creating, in Giraudoux's words, "*une race*," a race apart. The goal of institution-alization and "normalization" is to deny real, historical difference and substitute created "cultural" difference. Nature is denied; culture is affirmed in the celebratory excesses of the *canular*. The combined goal of the initiatory rites and the *concours d'entrée* is to turn meritorious success on a state examination into a mythic identity. *Normaliens* are no longer merely the top twenty *boursiers d'études supérieures*.[42] Initiation marks an end, as well as a beginning; in as much as it signals entrance into the ENS, it serves as an end. Once "named" or designated, they have arrived and "are."[43] The discussion of *normalien* nature turns into a question of race. *Normaliens* are not better merely in degree. The process of investiture assures their superiority in essence. When we look at French anti-Semitism what is noteworthy is that it, too, is a reaction to a second, "created" nature, i.e., cultural, and not a more literal (biological) nature.

Normaliens as a race apart leads to a rhetoric of exclusion. It is interesting to note the similarity of discourse and image in two characterizations of the ENS from ex-fascist sympathizer Thierry Maulnier and ex-communist Alain Tourraine.[44] A persistent image of the door haunts the recollections of these two *normaliens* considering their selection into Ulm. "This small universe singularly closed, behind its large open doors" (Thierry Maulnier).[45] "I found that my milieu remained extraordinarily closed despite the opened doors" (Alain Tourraine).[46] The rhetoric of exclusion yields to the theme of anti-Semitism in the guise of an analysis of the Jews at ENS. Bourgin presents us with the image of a Jewish "cabal" at Ulm comprising Durkheim, Lévy-Bruhl, Henri Berr, and Elie Halévy who meet fortuitously in the corridors of Ulm. This portrayal is characterized by a sardonic tone (consistent with similar discussions of the Jewish question). "Meditate on a most fortuitous meeting between Elie Halévy and Louis Eisenmann around Lucien Herr . . ."[47] Jewish *normaliens* play a role in the disfigurement ("*déformation*") of the ENS. Moreover, this presentation of Jewish *normaliens* is not exempt from stereotypes, often contradictory. Jews are endowed with special moral and spiritual qualities; Halévy and Eisenmann are thus the "sacred" for Herr. Analogous to this high station is their role as lawgiver: "Halévy is the depository of the law, the interpreter of the law." The law that they hand down is, alas, an English law: "He came with his English erudition, to announce and to impose this law on the French."[48] Nomads, countryless, Jews do give a law, but it is an English law that must be imposed upon the

The Return of the Repressed

French. Bourgin neatly presents two important fascist elements: anti-Semitism and anglophobia. Nor was anti-Semitism at the Ecole solely a twentieth-century phenomenon. The anti-Semitism against Suarès affected Romain Rolland's feelings for his *turne*. It will be remembered that the *turne* usually was responsible for the integrative function, even uniting students of right and left, such as Brasillach and Claude Jamet, one of Alain's students, as well as *talas* and *antitalas*. In June of 1887, the president of the anticlerical league asked Rolland for "names of students on whom the league could count." Rolland observed that for his promotion the religious had a different character. Until then, the salient difference was between the *talas* and *antitalas* (practicing and nonpracticing Catholics). Now, with two Jews, the question itself was transformed: "It was no longer a question of religious belief in the broad sense of the word, but of Catholicism confronted by Jews, Protestants, and Atheists."[49]

Fortunat Strowski, a teacher at the ENS and *Membre de l'Institut*, as well as a contributor to *Gringoire*, reviews the Tharaud brothers' (promotion 1884) book on the Jews and offers the following anecdote about a visit to his father's hometown in Poland. There were many Jews in his town that went to a Jesuit school. His sarcasm is readily apparent as he describes Radek, the best student in this Jesuit school: "A Polish-born Jew, brilliantly raised by Jesuits, nourished with Latin and one of the martyrs at Lenin's side. Is this the announcement of a new world? But one sparrow does not a spring make."[50] Here, the Jews are linked to Bolshevism. The humor serves only to highlight the saliency of anti-Semitism as a critical issue. It is also important to note that whereas Strowski presents the Bolshevik, idealist Jew (also well versed in Latin), Bourgin's Anglo-Jew is more capitalist. In a discussion of the Alcan bookstore, Bourgin muses, "The Jewish race appears to have commercial genius if this genius is audacious."[51] If Bourgin has seen Jews to be spiritually and morally superior, he has not neglected their materialist capacities.

ORDEAL/*ÉPREUVE*

> *There is nothing more to say about my examination. It is over.*
> *My corporal punishment is finished. If I have a bit of advice to*
> *give to talented boys it is never to take such an examination. First*
> *of all, it requires a physical strength . . .*
> —Romain Rolland

As Célestin Bouglé noted, the *concours*, originally intended as an *épreuve de technique* was becoming an *épreuve de morale*.

Romain Rolland's description of his grueling ordeals with both the *concours d'entrée* and the *concours d'agrégation* underlines Pierre Henri Simon's testimonial address: "this ascetic trial of one, two, three years . . . Let us remember, Monsieur, the pain and the charm of those long days when uncomfortably housed and crudely nourished, over-whelmed by work and often frustrated for pleasures . . ."[52] Preparation for the arduous examination is likened to that for any competitive sport, with older *normaliens* as trainers. Indeed, the archives of the ENS reveal a preoccupation with sports and the body. Physical culture was seen as an important contributing factor to moral culture, and if Descartes could separate the mind and the body, his readers at the Ecole Normale could once again reconcile them.

This notion of "ordeal/*épreuve*" can also be traced to Durkheim's discussions of the role of discipline in education and his attendant focus on regimentation and normalization. Durkheim's notion of discipline is a bifurcated one and appears to be sex segregated: "Discipline is society seen as the father, as commanding us, as prompting us to do our duty. Attachment to the group implies society as mother, the image of the good attracting us."[53] Yet it is the application of the rule which allows for both the experience of *épreuve* (trial) and regimentation. Rolland is accurate in his description of the *concours d'entrée* as a physical ordeal akin to corporal punishment. For, as the *concours* establishes the norm, it is experienced as a "forcing": "The rule is outside the person. It is felt as an order, which implies a source outside ourselves."[54] What Romain Rolland experiences on the individual level is true for any "body in authority":

> When a body in authority, any body in authority is fired by a love of regimentation, when it has a tendency to make anything conform to a single unique norm, it experiences an instinctive horror for anything which is the result of whim and imagination. Anything which might disturb the established order takes on the appearance of a scandal to be avoided; and since elective affinities are necessarily incompatible with programmes which have been decreed . . . every effort is made to suppress them by restricting freedom. Hence the tendency to impose a style of life which is uniform . . .[55]

Thus Durkheim situates the boarding school as the mechanism necessary to curb excesses (and that which also parallels, on a pedagogical plane, the French emphasis on centralization.) Indeed, Durkheim's examples of regimentation within the boarding school are relevant for our purposes as well, focusing on the body via various mediations: sports, fasting, and abstinence.[56]

The Return of the Repressed

Life at the Ecole Normale has been seen as Spartan. Archival documents of directors of the ENS reveal a persistent worry that intellectual overwork (*"surménage"*) will cause the body to deteriorate. Bouglé's radio address notes aptly resume the basic symbiosis of mind and body: "We risk under the pretext of developing the mind, to damage the body of our youth. And once the body is injured, the mind quickly suffers."[57] Bouglé will thus argue for a modern form of Sparta. Bouglé's concerns are not a recent phenomenon. A student summation of life at the Ecole dated 1859 states with philosophic understatement that there is not enough recreation: "One must be in some communication with the outdoors."[58] These preoccupations with physical hygiene will reach an intensity during the Vichy years, and one witnesses similar concerns to that of leftist Bouglé (removed from his post as *secrétaire* of the ENS during Vichy) in the correspondence between Abel Bonnard and Jérôme Carcopino (Bouglé's successor). The propaganda aimed at French youth exhorted: "Healthy bodies, attentive hygiene, methodical training of the vigorous, the reeducation of the puny."[59] The much-heralded benefits of fresh air afforded a nice contrast to the dust-covered sofas of an Ulm *turne* eulogized in Brasillach's *Notre Avant Guerre* and Claude Jamet's memoirs: "the little dusty gray sofa still speaks to us of our youth."[60]

The notion of sports and the attendant focus on the body will have important conceptual consequences in the formulation of an *esprit d'équipe* which is in more than one sense an *esprit de corps*. Indeed, Suleiman writes: "There is no other country where the term 'esprit de corps' has such a literal meaning."[61] This will be crucial in any reconceptualization of the literary and journalistic circles of the thirties. Moreover, the priority of sports will lead to two interesting equations for a fascist discourse: sport as art, the body as text (or machine). A critic of Montherlant demonstrates that Costals, protagonist of *Les Jeunes Filles*, worries about his fitness (*forme*) as others worry about their works of art (*oeuvre*).[62] Sports furnishes as rich a metaphor as school, war, or bullfighting for a proving ground. Henri Pourrat, winner of the 1942 Goncourt prize will echo these sentiments, writing in *Comoedia*: "Sports is an art. A moral recipe whose excuse is physical."[63]

The reintroduction of the corporeal into intellectual, political, and aesthetic discussions is not absent from the discourse of the ENS. Indeed, at Ulm, language can not be disassociated from the body producing it. Lucien Herr's invectives are remembered for their "robust" nature: "this greenness of language, this robust invective was one of the principal traits of Lucien Herr . . . a superb athlete."[64] The friends of Herr are stimulated by this exemplary presence to live in an atmosphere of "virile frenzy."[65] Herr's figuration evokes his athleticism just as Montherlant's athleticism evokes his estheticism; again a comparison with Montherlant is apposite. Just as the body becomes an ideological object in fascist discourse, either a tabernacle for Drieu[66] or a site of renewal for Marinetti's "new man,"[67] it will prove crucial for *normalien* instruction.

The power of seduction lies at the heart of identification with a fascist leader and a *normalien* mentor. Political seduction, as well as intellectual initiation, is above all an erotic induction. The description of *maîtres* parallels the description of political *chefs* (leaders). Charles Andler cites Herr's incredible magnetism, his "radiance," his gift "to magnitize souls."[68] Bourgin, in turn, describes Andler's magnetism in a chapter of his memoirs appropriately titled "Friends and men of liaison of Lucien Herr." Erudition and the uncanny play equal parts in the seminars of Andler, said to be characterized by "a sort of elegant and serious casualness, fanciful . . ." Ideas are "hurled" and rebound off his harsh Alsatian accent, which syncopates and stimulates attention. The power of Andler's instruction is not wholly rational, it is a charm, a spell, sacred, confidential, sui generis: "It was a spell, which was not released from the teachings of any other master."[69]

Intellectual "masters" are endowed in all senses, intellectual and physical. Initiation is both an intellectual and a physical response of attraction. Drieu's writings on Doriot and his fictionalized political leader, Lehalleur in "Double Agent," echo the idea that gifted leaders possess "intellectual-political vision as well as a prepossessing body and magnetic personality."[70] Drieu's admiration for Doriot was quite literally body worship; the son of a blacksmith, a former metallurgical worker, Doriot is a metallurgical person, who communicates by the "bristling of this thick head of hair, in the vast perspiration of his forehead." Or, as Nizan cuttingly argues, "Doriot is a messiah because he is male, because he sweats a lot, and because he can speak a long time."[71]

It should not be surprising that the language describing intellectual *maîtres* should be so rich in metaphors both erotic and seductive. Bourgin describes the captive crowd to Jaurès' hypnotic figure; Paul Dupuy's discovery of Virgil is linked with visceral memories of his professor, M. Bernase. Dupuy recounts his first time: "His memory remains for me united to my first encounter with Virgil who was for a long time one of my *delights*."[72] The themes of homoerotic identification and the correlative initiation, both physical and intellectual, will prove important in understanding group formation and a fascist aesthetic with misogynist tendencies. It should also be remembered,

The Return of the Repressed

following Roland Barthes's analysis in *Fragments of a Lover's Discourse*, that a lover's discourse is an extreme discourse: "A lover's discourse isn't a balanced state, but of such disequilibrium that it is part of this black economy that stands out for me in its aberration, or in other words its intolerable luxury."[73] The inadequacy of language, the lack of congruence between language and feeling, or between words and action is an essential theme of fascists and one that finds its counterpart in the excessive elegies to the Ecole.

Jaurès' letter to his school friend Salomon reveals his depth of feeling: "This memory of our good years at the Ecole and of good friendship and the inability to renew it and to grasp it again in living together is becoming to me almost a suffering."[74] Jaurès' nostalgia, with its all too palpable wistfulness, can be understood in light of a lover's discourse. Is it any wonder that he aches for his school years? The extremities of discourse and of feeling that characterize a fascist discourse are similarly revealed in the inability of *normaliens* to find a name worthy of the love object, "*école*." Why do all the titles thrust upon the school fail to satisfy those living in it?[75] "Because to all great loves, there is no better definition than the name of the beloved. Perhaps that's why it will always be sufficient for *normaliens* to say: 'The School [*l'Ecole*].'" The "unnameability" of the ENS provides it with a cultic cachet, and it is not an accident that its illustrious alumn Michel Foucault refers to it as the "holy of holies."[76]

In conclusion, the *concours d'entrée*, with its emphasis on physical *épreuve*, reveals latent parallels between sports and art, with the body as the site of an initiation which is both philosophic and erotic. Fascist discourse and *normalien* memoirs share two thematics: the split between the mind and the body that lies at the core of the decadent critique, and the inadequacy of language to express profound realities, either affective or political. The group psychology of hypnosis and seduction is a related subtheme.

This cursory overview of an institutional mechanism of the ENS is intended to reveal the presence of an institutional discourse which parallels and supports central issues in fascist thematics. This institutional discourse, consonant with many preoccupations of the right, is revealed even among leftist *anciens élèves*. The focus should shift from that of the usual literature which purports to explain the presence of a "few" rightist *normaliens* to an explanation of why there are not more of them! For there would appear to be a fundamental compatability of notions of cult, athleticism, physical ordeals, eccentricity, dandyism, self-conscious elitism, and distrust for the *moyenne*, evidenced in the *normalien's* self-perception of its rite of institution (the *concours d'entrée*) with those themes of fascist ideology. The similarity of concerns as well as a shared metalanguage underlines the position of an institutional discourse in the power-knowledge nexus. For as an illustrious *normalien* writes: "In the end we are judged, condemned, classified, determined to a certain mode of living or dying, as a function of the true discourses which are the bearers of the special effects of power."[77] The role of the institutional discourse of the ENS in the classification and determination of its rightist students is profound and reinforcing.

Canular

Je vous parle comme instituteur et comme père.
—Petain

The future normalien *is . . . promoted as family of the great moralists, esthetes, writers. It's the* cour d'honneur *of the school that offers the* spectacle of family . . . *(emphasis mine)*
—Giraudoux

The children are peculiarly fond of their school.
—Peyrefitte

We have seen in Chapter 3 how the *canular* signals initiation into the royal family. But if rightist ideology has been stereotypically seen as unambiguously natalist, one wonders if it could more accurately be described as profoundly familial. The ENS will play a crucial role in the reconceptualization of a familial ideology. We have seen initiation into the ENS as a process of investiture creating a new breed, the *normalien,* which is likened to a blood prince, "chevalier" (Pompidou), or the offspring of celebrated authors (Giraudoux). The initiation also engendered a family romance, as it denied any history prior to entry into the Ecole Normale. Real historical parents were replaced with those of a higher status (e.g., Poincaré, Pasteur, Racine, and other famous authors.) We will see how the frantic search for the father, typical of the "family romance," will characterize a *normalien* discourse as well as foregrounding a split crucial in understanding rightist ideology: the distinction between *nation* and *patrie.* (It should be noted that while Bouglé did adumbrate a detailed article on the word *nation,* most of his cohorts focused on *patrie.*)[78]

Patrie derives from the Latin, meaning literally "father's place." This is especially noteworthy as we witness the demographic effect of the

The Return of the Repressed

Table 5. Pater Semper Incertus Est: Incidence of
Fatherlessness among *Normaliens*

Normaliens with fathers	*Normaliens* without fathers
Raymond Aron	Robert Brasillach*
Raoul Audibert	J. Chauvet*
Maurice Bardèche	René Etiemble
J. Beaufret	J. Guéhenno
Marc Bloch	J. Hyppolite
Pierre Brossolette	Daniel Lagache
J. Bruhat	M. Merleau-Ponty
Georges Canguilhem	Jacques Monod**
René Gillouin	Henri Quéffelec*
J. Giraudoux	J.-P. Sartre
Henri Guillemin	Jacques Soustelle
Claude Jamet	Thierry Maulnier
V. Jankélévitch	
Paul Nizan	
Georges Pelorson	
P. H. Simon	
Pierre Vilar	
J. Wahl	
Simone Weil	

$n = 31$
% fatherless = 38.7
Pupille de la nation
**orphan
Source: Archives Nationales 61 AJ 14, 17–22, 251, 256, 166

First World War on our sample; this father's place is literally *absent* (Table 5). The remarkably high incidence of fatherlessness among these students lends a certain poignance to that slogan of Freud's (writing about the family romance): *pater semper incertus est*.[79] Certain knowledge of the mother and vague conceptualizations of the father will mark two extremes of rightist ideology in France: nation as embodied myth, linked to nature; culture as created artifact, which will be linked to science. For this generation, fathers—or, more specifically, "hero substitutes"—will be known from books. Malraux's grandmother as well as Drieu's will give them biographies of generals and other famous men to read for excitement.[80] However, this reading will take place in a highly protective maternal environment, and there is a tension between the exhortation to action and adventure in the texts and the maternal constraints. This will result in a curiously ambivalent pattern: "authority"/the father's word will come from books/the written word, at the same time that the passive activity of reading will be deprecated.

These notions are supported by the etymologies of *nation* and *patrie*. *Nation* is linked to concepts of birth and origin implicit in its root: *natio, nascor, naître*. Emile Littré's *Dictionnaire de la Langue Française* situates *nation*: "*Nation* marks a relation of birth, of origin, and of togetherness. Thus in everyday use *nation* is considered above all as a representation of the body of inhabitants of the same country and people: a body in political relationships."[81] Paul Robert in his *Dictionnaire Alphabétique et Analogique de la Langue Française* concurs: *nation* is defined as a "group of men to whom one imagines a common origin, a race, a people."[82] Moreover, Robert distinguishes nation from state (*état*). State is seen as an artificial creation. Nations are separable from both states and governments. *Nation*, both dictionaries underline, is linked to a notion of race. Bainville writes: "It's better than a race, it's a *nation*." Renan sees in *nation* a spiritual principle: "A *nation* is a soul, a spiritual principle. Two things that, truthfully, are but one . . ." Valéry finds the notion of *nation* difficult to summarize easily: "Sometimes a race, sometimes a language, sometimes a territory, sometimes memories, sometimes interests institute diversely national unity from an organized human agglomerate."[83]

Patrie derives from the root for father and shares its etymon with both patriotism and patrimony. *Patrie* (fatherland) in distinction to *nation* signifies a *political* community to which one either belongs or feels as if he belongs. "A place where one finds oneself at home, by metaphor or extension, an environment where one feels at ease, with which one is in harmony. The Republic, this moral *patrie*."[84] Similar to *nation*, *patrie* is not strictly defined by territorial considerations. Chateaubriant writes: "when liberty disappears, a country remains, but there is no longer a fatherland." Two of the attributes of *patrie* will concern our discussion, namely, its tie to science and its tie to internationalism. "The proletariat has a fatherland."[85] In addition, we note that patriotism distinguishes itself from both *good citizenship* (it is less concerned with the respect of the common good and more with the defense of *patrie* from an external aggressor) and *nationalism* (as it does not presuppose an exclusive cult of the nation). Chauvinism is seen as a *caricature* of patriotism.

The split between *patrie* and *nation* parallels that between *Vaterland* and *volkisch*. *Volk/volkisch* parallels *nation* in both its old usage ("ein Volk, ein Nation betreffend") and in its more contemporary usage in Nazi race ideology ("Rassenideologie—begrundeten, entscheiden antisemitischen Nationalismus"). *Vaterland* is similarly that place where one feels at home: "Land, in dem man geboren oder aufgewachsen ist, Heimat (land)." *Vaterlandisch* corresponds to *patriotic* as well as signifying conservative and rightist groups under Dollfuss (1933): "Zusammenschluss aller konservativen und rechten Krafte in Österreich unter Dollfuss."[86]

With these etymologies in mind, we will examine variants of the *normalien* familial discourse. There are two variants. Entrance into the ENS carries admission into both a "royal family" (which has the ideological consequences outlined above) and a "holy family." The ENS is continually compared to a seminary; the *sacerdotal* function of the institution, examined in a previous chapter, is cited by Durkheim, Kant, and Bouglé.[87] The parallels between Jesuit book culture and the *"culture livresque"* of the ENS are striking. Between the Book and the book, between the interpretation of written, sacred texts and Lanson's *explication*, between the meditation on the written word and its oral instruction[88] lies the ENS dual insistence on the written word ("something of permanence and death") and its spoken substitute: *Scripta manent verba volant*. These two requisites are reconciled in the *normalien* pedagogy which strives to "speak like a book."[89]

We will now turn from priestly fathers to their more secular and conceptual counterparts. The familial discourse of the ENS is eloquently revealed in a moment of disruption—death of a member of the *normalien* family. The *Bulletin of the Assocation of Anciens Elèves* contains a necrology that precedes the enumeration of academic and literary honors, a listing of its extant members and commemorative addresses. "After the necrology, some prizes: *mortuous plango, vivos appello*."[90] These addresses are rich sources for ideological analysis. Here, the school is repeatedly linked to the *patrie* and to science. The favoring of *patrie* over *nation* in Emile Boutroux's words on the importance of literary prizes during wartimes is typical and ends with the following *éloge*: "The School, such as it is, very simply, but with all its strength and with all its heart, serves, in every way, with the same devotion, and without separating one from the other, according to the motto of the *normalien* Pasteur, 'Science and the Fatherland.' "[91] This extract is also typical in its elite form, exemplifying that "pompous repetition" that sets it off from ordinary language and pointing to itself as a "discourse of importance," in Bourdieu's words. *Patrie* is opposed to *nation*; it is linked to science, and an impressive patrimony ensues, usually Barrès, Poincaré, Pasteur. *Patrie* is clearly an abstract, conceptual term. Its political correlative may well be internationalism: "Science has no fatherland."[92] Indeed, it would be interesting to compare the conceptual language in which the debates around internationalism were carried out among fascists with the more embodied metaphors of the nationalist right: blood and soil. If science is linked to *patrie*, *nation* is a mother myth. If we recall Freud's family romance in this context—i.e., "you always know who your mother is"—the concrete vision of nation as mother is understandable.

Let us compare the various discourses of the right and fascist groups such as the Croix de Feu, the Faisceau, and the Jeunesses Patriotes with these conceptions. Valois, writing for the Faisceau's *Nouveau Siècle*, is typical of one approach: He distinguishes between *état* and *nation* in a manner that links blood and nation and uses a metaphor of illness. The nation as a sick body for which fascism is a cure is a view expressed by Maurice Bardèche in an interview.[93] As Valois's pronouncements are typical, I will quote at length: "There is a great sick state that is attempting to give its sickness to the nation to show its own end. The state malady is financial and monetary anemia. The state is losing its blood through inflation. The state is attempting to detour the nation's blood."[94] The Jeunesses Patriotes reiterate a polarity of embodied characteristics of the nation with the conceptual categories of the *patrie:* "The state must be the emanation of the national collectivity. The very representation of the country (*pays*)."[95] *Pays*, sharing its root with *patrie*, is spoken of as a second-order metaconcept, either "representation" or abstraction. "Nation" is, on the contrary, an essentialist concept, hence "emanation" is possible.

The Croix de Feu play on this conceptual distinction with a reversal of mother love and father abstraction: "The idea of the nation (which is your nation), the love of country (which is your country)."[96] Or, in other words, Love Thy Father, Honor Thy Mother. A poster dated July 23, 1935, continues the separation of *patrie* from *nation:* "I work neither for capitalism nor for Marxism, but for the family, for patrimony, and for the nation."[97] Réaction, a Christian royalist group, publishes its manifesto in 1930 and uses similar language: "Political reaction against democratic decadence: It's upon the certain base of the fatherland, setting out from the national element of the nation, that we wish to erect the spiritual cooperation where the entire world will have its share."[98] The nation's base is natural (*"l'élément naturel"*), whereas the metaphor for *patrie* is architectonic (*"la base . . . édifier"*), i.e., it must be constructed.

These figurative associations are most effectively made in a book review of Montherlant's *Service Inutile*, appearing in *Comoedia* during the Occupation: "Still, it has love of fatherland; *Patria*—of father and us: France, our mother . . . Always one sees us as children of our fatherland."[99] We will now turn to the enunciations of the *patrimoine* in the discourses of the necrology. It should be remembered that *patrie* will be the operational category here, as we are concerned at Ulm with created, cultural (second-order) difference. The commemoration of Paul Appell projects the following vision of Barrès and is typical: "We must quote M. Barrès (in first place among men): 'science and all the highest life of the mind.'"[100] As Barrès himself said: "to belong to the team of science is somewhat equivalent to a priest or a soldier in orders or in the army." It is the scientist who is the true patriot. We have already mentioned Pasteur's motto "Science and Fatherland" quoted ad nauseam in these commemorative addresses.

The linkage of science and *patrie* plays two roles in fascist and some variants of rightist ideology. First, it expresses a thematic that finds its echo in discussions of fascist intellectuals concerning internationalism and technology. This will be fused into a focus on the war machine (e.g., Drieu's fascist parable *Gilles*, which complements his writings on the machine in *Les Derniers Jours*) as well as displaced into discussions of the role of technology in the possible "reproduction" of works of art in the forms of photography and film.[101] The role of technology in the creation of both leisure and the new forms of mass culture which inhabit this space of leisure is a related elite concern which will be addressed in our later chapters on the literary politics of the thirties and forties.

There is, however, a second dimension in these discussions of science and *patrimoine* more germane to our immediate analytical purposes. These celebrations of an illustrious *patrimoine* ground elite conceptual self-representation in both explicit (i.e., the overt thematic: heirs of Poincaré etc.) and implicit ways. The separation of scientific, abstract concerns from concrete, ordinary nature reproduces the separation of elite from mass at the heart of French fascist intellectuals' dogma and (I will argue) at the heart of its appeal. The thematic link between *patrimoine* and science (with *normaliens* as heirs apparent to both realms) reinforces an elite image of *hauteur*.

There are formal consequences as well. The two commemorative addresses cited above reveal a language of *hauteur* that cuts itself off even further from mass concerns. Not only are the masses excluded from a specific thematic register (science), they are excluded from that very form of language which clothes the elaboration of the theme. We have seen how Boutroux's address reinforced elite perceptions through the device of pompous repetition, which is outside of ordinary language. Barrès' invocation to join the team of science reveals another type of device ("equivalence"). These formal devices will be elaborated in our next section. For the moment, we will consider the separation of "scientific" philosophic discourse from ordinary language as a reinforcing mechanism for an elite who formally and thematically exclude the nonelite. Our next section will consider how "elite" language sets itself off from ordinary language. What does this separation allow one to articulate?

5

LANGUAGE AND AUTHORITY

Nevertheless, I cannot see him somehow as a real traitor;
he had too much culture . . .
—Claude Jamet

Indeed, one of the basic questions which led to this study
was: how could such a sensitive, intelligent, cultivated
intellectual . . . become a fascist?
—Robert Soucy

One must immediately add that our author comported
himself in such a way as to escape polemics and
tendentiousness and find a place on the level of political
philosophy where opinions may be true or false but none
deserve to be condemned . . . he showed that he had a sense
of historical responsibility, and he understood that a writer
in an even partially occupied country, especially *if he had*
been interested in fascism, could no longer put his name to
a political chronicle. This *is what gives him the complete*
right to publish his reflections today and gives us the
complete liberty to discuss them . . .
—Maurice Merleau-Ponty

A specter is haunting scholarship on fascism; the specter of liberal humanism. Moral indignation provides a unifying theme of a decidedly heterogeneous body of writing. Indeed, judgers and judged, as well as revisionist historians, concur in the purported separation of support for fascism and heightened awareness. In Jamet's petulant disbelief that Brasillach is sentenced to die for treason[1] as in Merleau-Ponty's recuperation of Thierry Maulnier by those same criteria that executed Brasillach,[2] as well as Soucy's revisionist psychobiography of Drieu La Rochelle,[3] the question of how or why someone becomes a fascist assumes center stage. Nor are these isolated concerns. Soucy situates Sartre's preoccupation with this question in his "Childhood of a Leader" and asserts that the theme of "What is a collaborator?" plays a major role in existential psychology from Sartre's *Anti-Semite and Jew* to Fanon's *outre-mer* version, *Black Skin, White Masks*. Nor have psychoanalysts been backward in their attempts. The choice of fascist ideology is clearly something to be explained, either by the sexologist (desire to dominate/be dominated) or the analyst seeking an Achilles' heel in the form of a personality flaw (e.g., Drieu's narcissism) or a situational variable (absent father/domineering father/errant father). Thus it should not be surprising that this highly motivational literature is itself highly motivated. Soucy writes: "to prevent the occurrence of fascism moral indignation is not enough; it has too often hindered a serious understanding of the causes of fascism."[4]

It should be noted that these motivations can involve either positive or negative appreciations. For Julien Benda, Drieu is inspired by "moral passion." Similarly, the indictments of two *normaliens* sentenced in the postwar purge trials demonstrate that good faith can be as culpable as bad faith; there was no doubt as to either Jamet's or Brasillach's sincerity (yet each received the maximum of their respective penalty.) What Frederic Grover wrote about Drieu—"In a generation haunted by the obsession of sincerity, he has outdone Gide"[5]—could be equally argued for Brasillach, Thierry Maulnier, Jamet, or Béraud. Indeed, those cases without opportunism provoke the most indignation. Sartre writes: "What is it that leads such men to collaborate? The lure of gain? But some of them are already rich and also the Germans pay badly?"[6] The stance of indignation goes hand-in-hand with a language of errance. But "one of the fundamental tenets of democracy is that intellectual error is innocent."[7] This formulation makes one wonder, when can intellectual error be separated from political error? We witness a separation of strategic-political concerns from intellectual commitment; the first is performative, the later "merely" cognitive. If the right to err is a privilege of democracy, the separation of political from literary judgment is vital to guard against the "historialization of letters" (what Thierry Maulnier calls the suicide of literature).[8] One of our concerns will be the possibility of "nonhistorical" literature.

Soucy focuses on why Drieu erred, rather than if he had the right to err. Yet errancy is still the operative term. This is not meant as a critique of what is an illuminating piece of scholarship on a fascinating author. Soucy does answer the questions that he chooses to answer. His example is illustrative of the symptomatic denegation that influences much research on fascism. Although he ably demonstrates that fascism is a highly developed intellectual doctrine that draws on much of Western intellectual history and has attracted many intellectuals of the callibre of Yeats, Pound, and Heidegger, as well as university students (such as the Jeunesses Patriotes), these explanations are simply insufficient. Something remains to be explained: "What is troubling is that he is an artist . . . ."[9]

Language and Authority

The language of errancy conceals a double standard. Maurice Merleau-Ponty begins an insightful essay, "On abstaining," with the following anecdote that will be useful for our purposes. "Gide, it is said, did not vote under the pretext that his concierge's vote counted as much as his own . . . If Gide wanted plural voting for cultured men, the claim would be exorbitant on his part."[10] Gide wondered why voter-intellectuals should be granted "all at once in a vote what we would not accord them in a conversation."[11] It is important for our purposes to note that Gide distinguishes between two different verbal formulations—the conversation and the vote. Studies of elite intellectuals suffer from a double standard, at the same time as they traditionally neglect the *mise en forme* (verbal formulations) of elite discourse. Whereas the question of the appeal of fascism to the masses would be left to studies of mobilization or "by a questionable interpretation of electoral sociology," to quote Raymond Aron's felicitous expression,[12] the case of the fascist intellectual requires the ministrations of the technical expert, i.e., the psychoanalyst.

We will not concern ourselves with the question of either why intellectuals err or how they err, but rather focus on the formulation of the problem around the notion of errancy as a point of departure. The assumed (or projected) separation between aesthetic sensibility and fascist support (i.e., "What is troubling is that he is an artist . . .") and the stance of moral indignation that either implicitly or explicitly accompanies it will be seen as a peculiar form of denegation that represses the common ground between the two in the form of a "cult of the self," "politics of disengagement" (as opposed to a leftist politics of engagement) as well as a high degree of aestheticism and elitism.

From Barrès onward, generational revolts against decadence garbed themselves in the "cult of the self." Both Drieu and Jamet are seen as "lyrical souls": "Look at Drieu La Rochelle; he is a lyrical soul, he never stops talking about himself, he fills the pages of the *Nouvelle Revue Française* with his petty angers, his emotional crises . . ."[13] A critic of *Au Pilori* reviewing Jamet's *Carnet de Déroute* makes a similar indictment: Jamet never stops talking about himself! Even Jamet finds this critique to be just: "The truth, which he saw . . . was that I didn't have a sense of *camaraderie*." Jamet does provide situational variables to explain his woeful lack of camaraderie: "An only son, *externe* at the *lycée*, *externe* at Ulm." Jamet expresses a similar thought consonant with these Barrèsian preoccupations when he admits that if he talks about himself, it is only because "my person is only a sample, a type of a universal form."[14]

As for the high degree of aestheticism and elitism, these were not disjoint concerns for an ideology that above all (as Girardet tells us) was a spirit (*esprit*).[15] For Drieu, fascism represented ethics; for Brasillach it was aesthetic. Or, as Maurice Bardèche would write after the war, it was a "dream" ("*rêve*").[16] Girardet cites Brasillach's own words: "Fascism wasn't a political doctrine for us nor was it an economic doctrine . . . fascism was just a spirit . . ." Above all, it was a certain form of lyricism, "the exaltation of certain sentimental and moral values."[17]

The *"politique dégagée"* can be tied to difficulties and paradoxes involved in the notion of engagement for the fascist enthusiast of action. *Normalien(ne)s* Simone Weil and Paul Nizan concur in the antagonism implicit in the stance of a "writer of engagement." There is an unresolved conflict between being and action and writing and living. For Simone Weil, "philosophy is exclusively an affair of action and practice. That is why it is so difficult to write about it. Difficult in the same way as a treatise on tennis or running, only much more so."[18] The *"politique engagé"* presents the following paradox for Nizan: "One can write about politics only if one lives it, and they say that if one lives it there is no longer time to write about it."[19] He proposes as a solution a rhythm, alternating between action (engagement) and *récit*. Malraux's *Espoir* is a close approximation of this ideal. Or, conversely, whereas Raymond Aron sees Drieu's objectivity to be part of his "problem"— "a sort of superior indifference to events, a pure spectator . . ."[20]—it is precisely this disengagement that gives priority to writing. (It is interesting to note that Aron's recent memoirs provide a liberal solution to this dichotomy in the form of a *spectateur engagé*.)[21]

There would appear to be some common ground between aesthetic sensibility and fascist support. However, our concern is with the assumed separation of the two, perhaps all the more interesting as it is unwarranted. If a pattern of denegation has repressed the common ground between the two, recent literary studies have focused on this disjuncture as a point of departure. Fredric Jameson's volume on the relationship between reactionary politics and revolutionary aesthetics, i.e., modernism, in the works of Wyndham Lewis, is a case in point.[22] Let us then displace the question "how can such an intellectual be a fascist?" and focus instead upon the way repression works, agreeing with Pierre Bourdieu that the verbal formulations (*mise en forme*) are the *Aufhebung* of repression.[23]

Bourdieu's recent work on *mise en forme* is especially apt as it was formulated in part to solve an analogous problem—the debasement of Martin Heidegger from the philosophic heights of *Sein und Zeit* to the Hitler celebrant of the *Rektoratsrede*. For when it comes to university logocentrism, the verbal fetishism of the Heideggerian corpus is unparalleled. In a scholastic universe the pen is indeed mightier than the sword; it is no longer might that makes right, but "write" that makes right: "good form that makes for good sense." [24] Habermas asks a rhetorical question: "How could a thinker of his stature abase himself to such an obviously elementary way of thinking which reveals itself (to any lucid eye) as the unstylized pathos of this call to the auto-affirmation of the German university." [25] This "unstylized pathos" is an embarrassment to those who laud the "stylized pathos" of *Being and Time*. Yet Bourdieu shows that it is not at all surprising that the author of *Being and Time* is also a Hitler enthusiast for he demonstrates that Heidegger's seemingly "innocent" epistemological categories of authenticity (*Eigentlichkeit*) and inauthenticity (*Uneigentlichkeit*) merely reproduce the same distinction between elite and mass in a higher form—that is, in pure philosophy.

This is especially important for our analysis of the Ecole Normale Supérieure and its relation to both rightist ideologies and their fascist variants. For just as certain "rites of institution" (*canular, concours d'entrée*) act as a "routinization of charisma," transforming, or more accurately, transubstantiating an elite, so too the *mise en forme* acts on a linguistic level to transform and transubstantiate elite discourse. It is this process that will separate the elite intellectual or aesthete from the hack journalist, and it is constant reference to this form that will dictate reception and judgment.

What is crucial to our concerns is that formal devices which Bourdieu denotes as "stylistic loftiness" recall the hierarchy of a discourse in relation to ordinary discourse and dictate reception for its utterer with all the respect due to his rank. Indeed, as Bourdieu notes, one simply does not treat the phrase "the true housing crisis resides in that which mortals are always searching for in the being of habitation, that which it is necessary to teach them to inhabit" as one would treat the ordinary language version, "the housing crisis worsens," or even its scientifico-technical formulation: "In Berlin, on the Hausvogteiplatz, in the business district, the value of a square meter has risen from 344 marks in 1880 to 990 marks in 1895." [26] *Discours en forme* imposes its own norms of perception. It can be argued that without understanding the ENS as the norm for all elite discourse in France, one cannot begin to understand a rightist ideology of a literary elite. For, on the linguistic level, it performs those crucial roles of transformation and transubstantiation and will prove as suitable a subject for interpretation as that of the "dream work" for Freud. Let us examine the content of a rightist ideology as the signifying form through which it is realized: "the substance signified *is* the signifying form through which it is realized." [27]

Language and Legitimation

> *The head of a clinic in one of the large hospitals in Paris,*
> *interviewed by a newsman on the final fast of Gandhi, answers,*
> *"Here we stick a tube in the esophagus of a guy like that and feed*
> *him by force . . . period!" The* doctor who dares to express
> himself in the language of a medical student, *the paper that*
> *dares to quote him, the public which swallows these words*
> *without wincing—what emulation of baseness.*
> —René Gillouin

René Gillouin's rather polemical example of desacralization underlines the relation between language and legitimacy.[28] It is the form of the utterance that dictates its reception; neither its explicit content (degree of sympathy for hunger strikes) nor the elite position of the speaker (head of a clinic in a large Paris hospital) is at issue as much as the fact that a doctor speaks in the language of a medical student. The use of inferior codes is what constitutes transgression. René Gillouin's example posits a normative model of expression, as well as reception (or in this case, ingestion), relating language and legitimacy at its negative moment, its zero degree of legitimacy. It is interesting to note that nonlegitimate discourse can be pronounced even by authorized speakers. A title (doctor, *normalien*) isn't a sufficient condition. A title is a promise, but one which can be broken. Bourdieu notes that even the *porte-parole* is subject to what he calls a "structural censor." For Bourdieu situates the language of the specialized corps as a compromise between their own expressed class interest (*"intérêt expressif"*) and the censorship constituted by the very field (*"champ"*) in which this language both is produced and circulates. Moreover, this censorship is especially pronounced in the case of "authorized" speech: "This censorship . . . imposes itself on all producers of symbolic goods, without exception of the authorized spokesman (*porte-parole*), whose authorized word is more than any other submitted to the norms of official propriety; it condemns the occupants of dominated positions, the alternative of silence, or scandalous speaking of one's mind."[29] In addition, political action, Arendt tells us, is transacted in words, but most importantly, in finding the right words at the right moment. There is always a performative dimension in creating authorized speech.

Durkheim saw language as a form of collective representation that contributed to social integration, as well as complicity. Gillouin's quote, which admonishes those newspapers that print this transgression as well as those consumers who, unlike hunger strikers, "swallow without wincing," underlines the complicity of those receivers of authoritative discourse. Both doctor and newspaper readers have broken with a normal expectation of civilized discourse. Indeed, Durkheim's notion of collective representation is regulated by a form of consensus, or, in other words, a linguistic contract. We witness the displacement of the word *code* from law to linguistics: "The code regulates written language, which is identified as proper language, in opposition to conversational (spoken) language, implicitly seen as inferior." Moreover, for Bourdieu, codes acquire the force of law "in and through the educational system."[30]

The educational system, along with the family, provides the basis for what both Bourdieu and Basil Bernstein refer to as the *elaborated code*.[31] This elaborated code is defined in relation to the absence or deprivation of linguistic capital. Formation of an elaborated code leads to the canonization of the discourse of the dominant classes in society. Legitimate "competence" necessary to speak legitimate discourse comes to depend on a "social patrimony." Social differences become retranslated into verbal *distinction*. In short, the heirs to Pasteur, Poincaré, and Barrès inherit not only a thematic register—"Science and the higher life"—but also and more important the linguistic capital which is an essential part of the "social patrimony" along with the title *normalien*, which gives them the right to speak this elaborate code: "Acts of authority are first and always enunciations proffered by those who have the right to state them."[32] Style becomes an element of the "apparatus" (in the Pascalien sense) which contributes to credibility regardless of the content of the enunciation. "There is no symbolic power without a symbolics of power." Just as robes and ermine "create" the doctor and the judge, so too the legitimate elaborated code "creates" an elite intellectual: "One must be authorized by the institution and not just anyone is so authorized."[33]

Authoritative language requires authoritative speakers and adherence to an elaborated code. But context is also important; recognition of legitimate language is qualified: it must take place before legitimate receivers and be pronounced by legitimate persons in what Bourdieu calls "liturgical conditions." Priests, poets, professors speak in situations where there is "an ensemble of prescriptions that direct the form of a public manifestation of authority, ceremonial etiquette, gestural codes . . ."[34] Public nomination is a special case of this "quasi-magical" power of words in that objectivication and officialization are achieved *in front of* everyone. Legitimacy no longer merely represents power; it is now power gone theatrical, turned into a scenic display.

If we have focused until now on authoritative spokesmen, on the guarantee, let us turn to consider what we are protecting. Language has been described by the metaphor of treasure. Auguste Comte likens language to a universal treasure. The notion of treasury similarly haunts Saussure's model of social and economic conditions for linguistic appropriation.[35] Language is a storehouse, a repository of value, and as *normalien* public addresses proclaim, the Ecole Normale Supérieure is a repository of language, furnishing thirty-one academicians to guard the treasury. The elite self-perception of *normaliens* as guardians of language will be evident in our next example.

We will now examine a paradigmatic instance of a *normalien* public address concerning the contribution of the ENS to the illustrious corps of "immortals"—that is, to the French Academy. As Boutroux's remarks are noteworthy for both their language and their content I will quote at length.

> The Ecole Normale Supérieure, dedicated to the service of science and letters, product of over a century of arduous work, strong in all the young intellects that it knew how to choose and form in the highest disciplines, conscious of having collaborated in the general progress of human knowledge and of having defended the spiritual heritage of France, in communicating it to minds capable of transmitting it to generations to come, does not count it as a mediocre honor having donated to the French Academy thirty-one *normaliens*.
>
> Therefore, when all eyes turn to this renowned company, which justly prides itself on its royal birth, its august mission as guardian of the language and style, the brilliant minds that it has called to her and this immortality that its choice confers, the Ecole Normale Supérieure associates itself with all its heart with the festival which will celebrate the third century of a body so old and so illustrious.[36]

Boutroux implicitly equates the French Academy's mission as guardians of the language and its choice of immortals with selection into Ulm: "that it knew how to choose . . . conscious of having collaborated in the general progress . . . of having defended the spiritual heritage." The Ecole quite definitely "associates" itself with this venerable institution "so old and so illustrious."

The view of *normaliens* as guardians of the language is seconded by the student of myth Claude Lévi-Strauss, as evinced in his peroration on the occasion of Alain Peyrefitte's reception into the Académie Française. What qualifications does this minister have for the Académie's mission? *"Rue d'Ulm*, a collection of texts" written by *"nos confrères"* who were students at Ulm. "You have contributed three brilliant pastiches and two essays, in addition to a learned glossary of *normalien* language that augurs well for your collaboration on the work of our dictionary." In addition, Lévi-Strauss cites a *canular* directed at a famous academician by Peyrefitte as an auspicious beginning for his career at the Academy. Peyrefitte has traveled that royal road of language that leads so directly to the French Academy. Peyrefitte's "ontogenesis" is recounted in his semi - autobiographical *Roseaux Froisés* and is different from that of most men: "Even when most lives design their own course progressively as they fulfill themselves, my curve that I trace already will precede my life and will assure my victory." Peyrefitte's accomplishments are assured from the beginning ("my curve will precede my life"); they are not "historical" ("design their own course progressively as they fulfill themselves"). This natural evolution recalls the "phylogenesis" of social institutions described by Vico: "first there were forests, then huts, next villages, afterward cities, and finally academies."[37]

Professorial Language and Authoritative Discourse

> By this chain it appears that there is no other master but the signifier. All powerful master: We built a house of cards on this fact of discourse.
> —Lacan

Roland Barthes, commenting on the relation between the sentence and hierarchical discourse, notes: "The professor is someone who finishes his sentences." The professor, in other words, is an "agent" of the sentence. Similarly, the writer is no longer someone who expresses his thoughts, but according to Paul Valéry, "someone who thinks sentences." If the word (*parole*) in Saussurian linguistics conceals a priority of the signifier over that which it signifies, authoritative discourse conveys a hierarchy of the sentence over the fragment. For what concerns us is how the completed utterance itself signifies an elite content in the form of "mastery" of an elaborated code. "The power of completion defines sentence mastery and marks, as with a supreme, dearly won 'savoir-faire,' the agents of the sentence."[38] Professor-intellectuals as *porte-paroles* (spokesmen) have a determinate relation to authoritative discourse, not only due to their social position, or the titles conferred upon them, but to the formal structures of their discourse.

If it is not merely the person pronouncing the words, that is, an authorized speaker, that is sufficient to situate elite language, what then constitutes the peculiar distinction of elite discourse? Moreover, can one argue, with Pierre Bourdieu, that this elaborated code is the perfect mode of articulation of hierarchy, exclusion, domination; these themes in turn becoming retranslated into formal questions, more readily interpreted by a linguist than a political analyst? The first requisite of an elite code is a completed utterance, i.e., the sentence. Yet what really delineates elite speech is its separation (*écart*) from "ordinary" language. We will now examine linguistic features which denote this separation. Among those cited by Bourdieu are strategies of "preemptive verbalism," "pompous repetition," neologisms, as well as poetic devices: alliteration, assonance, repetition, equivalence. Extensive use of quotation marks as well as italicization of words that are in common usage, but are employed in a different sense, also implies a separation from ordinary language. Neologisms are also useful in decoding elite speech as they serve an analogous function to that of "euphemization" for Freud, i.e., in compromise formation or as a type of censorship.[39] Analysis of archival documents, memoirs, speeches given at anniversaries of the Ecole or its alumni association meetings, addresses surrounding the candidacy of a member of the French Academy, and critical essays of *normaliens* reveal preemptive verbalism to be the most frequently employed device and repetition (and equivalence) to be the most common poetic device.

For Pierre Bourdieu, preemptive verbalism marks the limit form of all authoritative discourse. Preemptive verbalism is also related to a violent or offensive style, including nastiness and innuendo in some cases. Brasillach's essay on Paul Morand is typical of this type of figure: "No one is more trendy than M. Paul Morand. It is never he whom one calls a has-been. Were he to live two hundred years, he would still be talking about what they're wearing this year. Except, of course, for purely literary questions, which would be bad taste for a man of his society."[40] Preemptive verbalism can take a defensive tone as well as an offensive tone, as in the case of Claude Jamet's reaction to his removal from teaching after the war due to his literary collaboration under Vichy. In a journal entry headed "Ne jugez pas" ("Don't judge"), his defensiveness turns oddly lyrical: "The extremes move me . . . all together, Pascal and Voltaire, the duc de St. Simon, Michelet and Kropotkin, Sade and Claudel, Alain-Fournier and Jean-Paul Sartre. There is no one thought, no one system, one form behind which I cannot rediscover man . . ."[41]

Much of this preemptive verbalism concerns the ENS or its related themes: camaraderie. Borel muses: "I will not have the optimism to pretend that this *normalien* camaraderie could suffice to resolve all political and social problems that trouble us. Nevertheless, if it could contribute to a resolution, by creating more fraternity, this would be one of the greatest services that our school could give to the country." [42] One might contrast Pierre Gaxotte on the *esprit* of ENS with a newspaper clipping of the twenties: "One may say that there is a *normalien* spirit. It's possible." [43] "Even if the *normalien* spirit is but the university spirit, one could already admire it." [44]

Both the believer in and the detractor of the *normalien* school spirit employ a similar figure that curtails discussion: "it's possible," "even if." The status of ENS as "higher" than its sister institution, the Polytechnique, is articulated preemptively as well at the hundredth anniversary of Pasteur's death: "It's very simple, monsieur, if you want to do science, come to the Ecole Normale, if you would like to place pebbles on the road, go to the Ecole Polytechnique." [45] The contrast between engaging in science and placing pebbles in the road is reenforced by the form of the enunciation: "It's very simple, monsieur . . . go . . ." The use of "possible" as a preemptive dismissal of all possible critiques should be noted: "That there is the exercise of pure thought, a bit of playfulness. That philosophy itself is subject to fashion, like women's hats. *It's possible.*" [46]

Preemptive strategies also include "false humility"; in a commemorative address, the Conseil Supérieur de la Récherche Scientifique is condescendingly referred to: "Scientific research is at least as important to the nation as teaching." [47]

Excessive *éloge* is yet another preemptive strategy. We have already noted how Boutroux's *éloge* used the device of pompous repetition. "The Ecole, such as it is, very simply, but with all its strength and with all its heart, serves, in every way, with the same devotion, and without separating one from the other, according to the motto of the *normalien* Pasteur, 'Science and *Patria.*'" [48] Léon Blum's preface to a work of memoirs by Abel Hermant is an extremely precious example of the *éloge*, using repetition and hyperbole:

> It's a truism to affirm that the author . . . has his place at the head of contemporary literature. But it is true that M. Abel Hermant is one of the rare, one of the very rare writers whose originality and mastery have never suffered from their fecundity. He has touched, little by little, on almost all the branches of literary activity . . . M. Abel Hermant belongs to the literary family of Retz or St. Simon. But while classical authors of *Memoirs* work only for posterity, M. Abel Hermant has preferred not

to wait. He has given to his contemporaries his work all fresh
. . . Imagine a Retz or St. Simon alive today . . .[49]

Blum goes on to enumerate Hermant's superior qualities; he possesses
almost "all" distinguished literary virtues. Moreover, Hermant has
created with his *Mémoires* a new genre which is "rare." Indeed, "nothing is more rare." A language of superlatives characterizes much of
the discussions of the School; one notes the overuse of words or expressions such as "nowhere," "a similar X," "so," "always," "all," "the
most," "the least." Paul Dupuy reminisces about that asylum presided
over by Pasteur: "Perhaps there isn't anywhere in the world another
house where the persons of the young elite meet each other with a
similar intensity, and a similar variety of curiosities, where the shock
of ideas is *so* sincere, *so* cordial."[50] *Normalien* passion, an alumn recounts, is *"sans doute"* a fervent desire for mastery: "nowhere in France
is the contact between the student and the book more continuous
than at the Ecole . . . the least incident reverberates there . . ."[51] *Normaliens* can be defined by superlatives: authors of the greatest number
of books with the least diffusion.

The effect of superlatives as with preemptive verbalism is to pre-
clude serious examination or criticism and provide a unified total
explanation. Even differences of outlook or formation are dismissed
via these devices: "It engages all of the man for his entire life. In
power or in prison, on the good or sometimes on the bad road, the
normalien is never alone. Near him, one almost always finds the *camarade* with whom he experienced the exalted dawdling of his first
years . . . Thanks to this fraternity where Catholicism, existentialism,
communism are but first names . . ."[52]

Neologisms function in a manner which does not dismiss real, historical differences (e.g., Catholicism, existentialism) or mythologize
these differences in the celebration of *camaraderie* (where differences
function merely as "first names") but are rather, in Freud's formulations, elements of "compromise formations." They are attempts to
conceal differences by "changing value without modifying the under-
lying substance."[53] Difference is repressed; value is expressed. Nowhere is this more evident than in the neologisms of *normalien* argot
(reproduced in Peyrefitte's *Rue d'Ulm*). Here differences are encoded
not only to manifest exclusion/inclusion but also to provide positive
appraisals of that inclusion. This will take either of two forms, both
consonant with the definition of neologism: "use of a newly created
word, formed either by deformation, derivation composition, or loan
or use of a word in a new sense." The *normalien* "lexicon" contains

both newly created words and words borrowed from ordinary or conventional usage employed with a different connotation. Verbal malformations for Freud exhibit condensations. The two conditions that qualify Freud's examples in *The Interpretation of Dreams* concern us as well: (1) Malformations must bear or represent a compound meaning; (2) this meaning must be solidly related to an intention.[54]

Let us examine the various forms of "syllabic chemistry" evinced in *normalien* slang. Most of the argot is in relation to the presence or absence of status in or outside of the Ecole. Those *"exos"* who are not part of Ulm are designated by pejorative adjectives: contemptible, base, without value. This is apparent in the term used to denote *normaliens* of the Ecole Normale de St. Cloud who are referred to as *"cloutiers."* *Cloutier* is a compound word containing the stem *clou* recalling the phrase *"ne vaut un clou,"* an expression connoting valuelessness. *Clou* also has the figurative connotation of a worthless car, a "jalopy." It clearly signifies that which is lacking in value defined in relation to the *exo.* "*Sorbonicole*" is an analogous neologism, substituting for the more proper "Sorbonnard" which is the conventional term employed to denote those *exos* who attend the Sorbonne. *Sorbonicole* conceals a multiplicity of pejorative figural associations. *Bonnasse* signifies weakness; *boniche* is a pejorative term for a young maid; *boniment* is a discourse of charlatans; and there is a homonymic association with *barnacle*, that which is a hanger-on. States prior to full initiation to Ulm are similarly designated by deprecating phrases. For example, the term *bizuth*, used to denote a first-year preparatory student at *khâgne*, has the etymon of a young recruit of Spanish descent (*d'origine espagnole*): Spanish connotes vulgarity and a lower state of being, e.g., she dances like *"une vache espagnole"* (a Spanish cow).

The term that connotes the last *normalien* to be received in a promotion, that precarious position so near the nonelect, is rife with the pejorative and excessively vulgar associations from its stem, *cul—culal. Culasse* is that worthless part of a precious stone; *cul* also denotes imbecility, cretinism, and idiocy. Those *normaliens* who desire to associate with the nonelect (by virtue of their gender) at the Ecole Normale Supérieure des Jeunes Filles-Sèvres are given the penultimate linguistic insult: the term *Sevrien* is formed from creating a masculine noun from a feminine form. In like fashion, those outsiders that are "stowaways" at Ulm (i.e., making use of the facilities, sharing *turne* space, receiving table scraps from meals at the refectory, etc.) are referred to as *goimmards* or in the case of female "stowaways," *goimmardes. Gomme*, like *clou*, is a noun which connotes little worth. *Gomme* is without value, *sans valeur. Goimmard(e)* also shares the stem *goim* from the

Yiddish *goy*, denoting those outside the faith. The compound association and inference is that those outside the faith (or institution) are
without value. The *goim*, like the *goimmard*, are *gomme—sans valeur*. A
student being tutored by a *normalien*, a *tapir* is metaphorically linked
to the sedentary beast of the same name.[55]

Those terms employed to denote entry into Ulm or inclusion in Ulm
partake of higher or more complimentary adjectival forms or com-
parisons. *Reconciliation* denotes the traditional "punch" offered by the
new initiates to the alumni. Its connotations derive from the liturgical
sense of the term: a Catholic ceremony through which one is reinte-
grated into the church, as well as the more common associations of the
overcoming of hostilities, interpersonally or between enemy nations.
Tables 6 and 7 demonstrate the differences between connotations and
denotations as well as positive or negative normative values ascribed
to these connotations or, in certain cases where there exists no explicit relationship to these values, their relation to the institutional
norms of the ENS itself. Denotations refer to the conventional usage/
meanings in *normalien* slang; connotations refer to all possible associations, etymological, conventional, figurative revealed in the *Petit
Robert*. Connotations—as well as, in some rare instances, denotations
—can have negative or positive values (or normative associations).

It should also be noted that many definitions of *normalien* argot
figure among those definitions given by the *Petit Robert*. Moreover,
normaliens and elite intellectuals alike continually employ this slang
in memoirs and essays, as well as interviews. Indeed, Brasillach realized how (linguistically) capital intensive was the vocabulary of the
Ecole, and he was bemused by the way in which this language was
used *en famille*: "We see that the vocabulary of the school is abun-
dant. I have always found it somewhat comic that alumni practice it
with perseverance and sometimes teach it to their wives and to their
children."[56]

Neologisms are not only to be found in the "lexicon" of *normalien*
slang, but figure among critical works of alumni as well as memoirs.
Gustav Téry creates an interesting neologism from both positive attributes as well as "elegant" personality defects of *normaliens: normalig-
nity*. "Make a synthesis of these discrete qualities and these elegant
defects: you will obtain *normalignité*."[57] *Normalignité* provides an en-
lightening example of a compromise formation as it is a compound:
normal + malignité. *Malignité* connotes cleverness with dissimulation.
Its negative associations (baseness, hatred, malice, malevolence, per-
fidy, perversity, as well as pettiness) in no way abrogate the positive
ones (intelligence, cleverness, skillfullness, cunning). *Normale* con-

Language and Authority

Table 6. Neologisms: Verbal Malformations/Compound Words

Word	Denotation	Connotation/Institutional Norm*
bizuth	first year at *khâgne*	green, *origine espagnole;* pejorative value (−)
cloutier	student at ENS-St. Cloud	worthless (*ne vaut un clou*), worthless car (jalopy); pejorative value (−)
culal	last student in a promotion	derrière, asshole, cretin, imbecile, idiot (*culasse:* inferior part of precious stone); pejorative value (−)
culage	initiation rite, consisting of touching posterior to ground while chanting a song	same as *Culal*
gnouf	a *conscrit* before initiation	"*gnothe seauton,*" Socrates' dictum: "know thyself." *Gnose:* knowledge ("tout savoir qui se donne comme le savoir par excellence")
goimmard(e)	clandestine lodger at ENS	*gomme* (without value), *goim,* from *goy* (outsider); pejorative value (−)
p.q.	all-purpose writing paper, anything that could be written, but is given as an oral address. Pecufiage, pecufier: to give a long address	Institutional norm "*parler comme un livre*" Value (+)
sorbonicole	"a particularly contemptible & widespread form of exo," a student at the Sorbonne	*bonnasse* (weakness), *boniche* (pejorative form of "young maid"), *boniment* (discourse of charlatans), *barnacle* (hanger-on); pejorative value (−)
sevrien	a normalien who frequents ENS-Sevres	Pejorative value (−) creates unmasculine associations

notes that which serves as a rule, as well as denoting a student of the ENS. Indeed, the positive value of the denotation *normal* is only fully achieved in conjuncture/combination with *malignité;* for *normal* connotes that which is by definition not exceptional, i.e., the rule. *Normale* connotes the ordinary, the most frequent and conformist, but also that which is correct and legitimate.

René Gillouin's neologism "*aristarchie*" is another euphemism which ably expresses the thematic content of this reformulation of democracy as well as conceptions of legitimate representation. *Aristarchie, ou Récherche d'un Gouvernement* begins with a declaration to the reader ("the unintelligent reader without good faith," because for the intelligent

Table 7. Neologisms: Loans (*Empruntes*) from Ordinary Language

Word	Denotation	Connotation
ecole	with indefinite article common noun value (−)	with definite article, proper noun capital Ecole: undefinable Value (+)
exo	outside	"that pitiable part of humanity that has not passed through rue d'Ulm" Value (−)
cacique	first on concours	Indian chief, a person with importance in a political or administrative position Value (+)
cirer/cirage	an initiation rite consisting of rubbing the subject against a table to tune of a song	*cire* (wax), a person who is influenceable (*frotter de cire:* flatter) Value (−)
reconciliation	traditional punch offered by new recruits to alumni	liturgical: reintegration into the church, reestablishment of friendship, cessation of hostilities Value (+)
sevrienne	student at ENS-Sevres	Pejorative value (−): use as epithet as in "*sevrienne: normaliene:* Benedictine: benediction"
tapir	student who is being tutored by a *normalien*	herbivorous, sedentary animal, *approvoisable, comestible* Value (−)
turne	room, student quarters	a dirty room without comfort, workplace Value (−)

reader with good faith, Gillouin states, such a warning is unnecessary) which includes an explanation of the neologism *aristarchie:* "I do not call it aristocracy which is the government of a class, but ARISTARCHIE, which is the government of the best." The separation from ordinary language implicit in the adoption of neologisms is insufficient for Gillouin; he must set his conception off even further typographically, through the use of all capital letters. Gillouin's deconstruction of the question of representation will turn on this question of the "best," which is the primary connotation of *aristarchie.* For the "best" are the "most true."[58] Analogous neologisms that appear in other philosophical essays of Gillouin highlight a religious concern; Gillouin employs the term *mysticite* to convey the civilizing power of a doctrine such as Christianity in distinction to the "rationalizing" tendencies in mass culture: "Modern culture, having undertaken to rationalize the totality of life and with this end in view, having declared war on religion in general as on the Bastille of the irrational . . ." Modern culture (value −) is defined in relation to *mysticite.* This is not a disjoint concern from that of his first neologism (*aristarchie*) for, as Gillouin states, "there is no way of having a sane society nor a durable civilization

Language and Authority

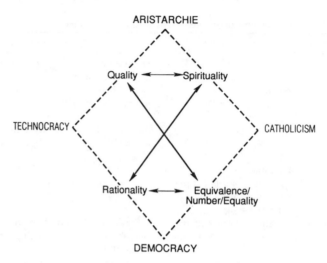

Figure 3. Neologisms and Ideological Closure: The Case of René Gillouin

without a strong spiritual power, itself leaning on an undisputed temporal *aristarchie*."[59] Neologisms here function to highlight conceptual uniqueness and innovation. But as with the *normalien* lexicon, in connoting "difference" they are ascribing value. *Mysticite* is clearly superior to "modern culture." *Aristarchie* is more highly valorized than mass or, indeed, all types of *class* society, including aristocracy.

We will now examine the way in which neologisms article ideology. What are the social contradictions implied by Gillouin's two neologisms: *mysticite* and *aristarchie*? We might find Greimas' semiotic rectangle an interesting heuristic model for the universe of ideological closure. Gillouin's conception of the possible social universe (or, choices) is revealed in the *aporia* between that which his two neologisms designate. *Aristarchie* points to the question of *quality* (*les meilleurs*) (the best), whereas *mysticite* underlines the salience of *spirituality* as a political concern inextricably tied to the problem of quality. Quality-spirituality represents a fundamental tension, a "dilemma" (to use Jameson's formulation)[60] rather than a logical contradiction. The semantic rectangle schematically represents this "dilemma." The tension between the two terms are designed by S and $-S$; in our case, between quality and spirituality. The other two components or terms of the rectangle are generated by the opposites of the original pair; we will take rationality to be the opposite of spirituality and equivalence/ number (or quantity) to be the opposite of quality. The synthesis of the four terms will provide the four concepts that represent the field of ideological closure.

Neologisms are only one form of distinctive circumscription from ordinary language. It should be remembered that it is this separation (*écart*) from ordinary language or conventional usage that distinguishes elite discourse. We will now examine other types of devices. Typographical marks, quotation marks as well as italics, set off parts of discourse from other parts (i.e., the main body). What Denis Hollier notes for the printed text of a play is also apposite: "The printed text of a play generally utilizes three different sorts of typographic elements: roman capitals, roman text and italic type faces." Names of characters (or in our case, concepts) are in capitals, the words they exchange, i.e., the content, are in roman type, and italics mark the stage directions. I would like to argue that italics function in much the same way as stage directions to the reader known more conventionally as the "*mode d'emploi*"—"directions for use." Gillouin's preface to the reader in the beginning of *Aristarchie* is printed all in italics, as is Léon Blum's preface to Abel Hermant, with an analogous function —to "direct" the reader. Hollier argues that in a play, the italic type functions as a "desperately silent insistence": the mark is only "perceptible to the reader's eye." [61] It is precisely this "silent insistence" that characterizes elite forms.

Gillouin uses italics to set off words that are used conventionally —that is, there has been no active *mise en forme* to transform or deform these words as in the case of neologisms. Examples of italicized prose are strewn liberally throughout his writings. Italics function as a physical sign of the concept he is adumbrating: "He who *creates* an idea has the impression of grasping reality itself by means of it, directly . . . But he who *receives* that idea finds it between himself and things . . . Thus, *inheriting* generations lose." Italics function to underline the notion of quality and the separation from mass concerns. His use of quotation marks is yet another device to achieve the same ends: "as 'crude' materialism, born in laboratories, diffuses and 'popularizes' itself in the garb of 'democracy,' very serious *consequences* on the practical plane can not fail to ensue." Often, quotation marks highlight pejorative assessments: "Christian spirituality, less delicate, limited itself to forbidding cruelty toward our 'inferior brothers.' " [62] Both quotation marks and italics emphasize an already hyperbolic and extreme discourse. To distinguish between two types of democracy he has presented, Gillouin reiterates: "if there is one more true than the other, it's the second one, and it also will follow that being the *most true*, it is *the best . . ."* [63] It is important to note that the use of italics is not subject to a typographical rule; it is strictly the author's choice. Hollier cites the example of Claudel's use of italics in *L'Annonce Faite à Marie*. Here they function—as with Gillouin's use of *creates, receives,* and *inheriting* —as words the utterer *does not mean*. They may not be a foreign language, but they function as a foreign discourse. "The italics . . . clearly stress that . . . [she] does not mean the words she is pronouncing . . . it is not her language . . . the words he or she pronounces are printed in italics in order to make clear that they are not his or her own." [64] Whenever Gillouin employs the term democracy, it is clearly a foreign notion as is *clerc* and "technical imperative." [65]

Poetic devices such as alliteration, assonance, repetition, and equivalence are forms which signify that the speaker partakes of an extremely restricted number of people who possess the mastery of the language to the extent that they can manipulate poetic forms. Indeed, use of poetic devices may mark a limit form of separation from ordinary, "prosaic" (in all senses) language. Analysis of *normalien* language reveals repetition to be the most commonly employed poetic device.

Repetition and the Articulation of Power

> *Now, encratic language (the language produced and spread under the protection of power) is statutorily a language of repetition; all official institutions of language are repeating machines: schools, sports, advertising, popular songs, news, all continually repeat the same structure, the same meaning, often the same words: the stereotype is a political fact, the major figure of ideology.*
> —Roland Barthes

Roland Barthes notes that the language of power— "encratic language"—is primarily a language of repetition. [66] And *normaliens* have not been exactly backward in their attempts to employ this device in the service of elite preoccupations. Poncet's address is only one example: "The cloister, the garden, the library, the convent . . . You rediscover them here, you find science and sometimes piety here, in any event the piety of science." [67] Repetition serves to underline all the aforementioned stereotypes concerning Ulm—"cloister, garden, library, convent"—both the extra - institutional appeal to the seminary and the secular-rational, institutional features, i.e., the library and garden.

Claude Jamet enlists the device of repetition to bolster his argument that ideological collaboration is only "words." It should be noted that repetition is often most effective when it is combined with another figure. Jamet's use of repetition is used alongside a strategy of denegation:

> It will be these sentences that will kill him, indefensible sentences, certainly, I am convinced that under his too light pen, it was only sentences, rhetoric, literature . . . Nevertheless, I can not see him somehow as a real traitor, he had too much culture, too many human nuances . . . He was born, certainly, to speak to us of books, to write them himself, books of souvenirs, of nostalgia. There was a little music in him, sensitive, sad, and gracious . . . that one finds all over, in his poems, in his essays, to his most rapid papers, a sort of Proustian haste of time past, of youth, of pleasure and of days gone by.[68]

Repetition forms a counterpoint, a baseline to the poetic rhythms of this remarkable *éloge*. Preemptive verbalism is used ("certainly," "that one finds all over").

Alliteration is a poetic device that relies on repetition, that of initial consonant. Thierry Maulnier's entry in *Rue d'Ulm* provides an example: "sociétés secrètes, avec son langage codé, ses signes de reconnaissance, cette solidarité entre les membres qui semble plus que les divisions . . ." (secret societies with their coded language, their signs of recognition, their solidarity between members, which seems stronger than their divisions . . .)[69] Maulnier's example also uses an internal rhyme, "membres qui semble." Alliteration is not a trope merely of the right; Bouglé's papers reveal his fondness for this figure: "tout ce milieu materiel et moral . . ." (all this material and moral milieu . . .).[70] As quotation marks and italics are to the eye, alliteration, assonance, rhyme, and cadence are to the ear.

The Binary Opposition and the Articulation of Difference

Our analysis of the *normalien* lexicon has shown that in connoting difference one is also ascribing value. Social differences become retranslated into verbal distinction. *Normaliens*, as heirs apparent, inherit not only a specific thematic register—science and the lofty life—but also and most important, the linguistic capital/competence that is part of their "social patrimony." Neologisms as well as distinctive use of ordinary language through italics, quotation marks, or transforming an ordinary usage into a new specific connotation, as well as discursive strategies such as preemptive verbalism and hyperbole, serve to separate elite from nonelite discourse. But one can argue that binary oppositions are an especially privileged mode of articulating difference.

We will begin with Fredric Jameson's historic reexamination of the binary opposition, "a form which confers signification on the various types of content it organizes." It should also be noted that the binary opposition as adumbrated by Saussure is itself a vehicle that not only describes two features of the linguistic sign, but also ascribes value to one of its units: i.e., in structuralism, the division of the linguistic sign into the signifier and the signified is but one mechanism to insure the priority of the signifier over the signified. This reexamination of the notion of the binary opposition is characteristic of poststructuralism as well, associated with the works of *normalien* Jacques Derrida. For Derrida is concerned with the "unmasking of binary oppositions such as speech and writing, presence and absence, norm and deviation, center and periphery . . ." All these axes serve to ratify the centrality of the dominant term by means of marginalization of the inessential term. Derrida calls this process of exclusion/dominance "metaphysical," but Jameson's reformulation around the Nietzschean problematic is more to the point. The dominant/excluded opposition is only masquerading as "presence and absence"; the opposition is really about ethics —good and evil. Following Nietzsche, Jameson convincingly argues that "it is ethics itself which is the ideological vehicle and the legitimation of concrete structures of power and domination." Good and evil coincide with the categories of otherness. Evil for Nietzsche is that which is radically different from me. "The other is not feared because he is evil; rather he is evil because he is Other: alien, different, strange and unfamiliar."[71]

Pierre Bourdieu demonstrates how many binary oppositions—between "distinguished" and "vulgar," between "high" and "low/base" —appear in Heidegger's writings and how these binary adjectives function to reinforce his discussion of exclusion. Prephilosophic states are not merely temporal (before/after); they are "lower," "cruder," more vulgar. Moreover, for Bourdieu, to "think in pairs" is motivated by censorship and repression, and the "relation of opposition between social groups." In this sense a *mise en forme* (verbal formulation) is always a *mise en garde* (challenge).[72]

The binary oppositions in the *normalien* discourse reveal a striking parallel to those found in the "university aristocratism" of Heidegger. If, for Bourdieu, Heidegger's opposition of *Eigentlichkeit* (authenticity) and *Uneigentlichkeit* (inauthenticity) is only one particularly "subtle" articulation of the opposition between elite and mass, the binaries which will most closely dovetail with the *normalien* corpus are those distinctions between "frivolity/facility" and "trial/responsibility" seen in the couplet "leisure/school," and "originality/secret/occult" as opposed to massifying culture. Mass culture is synonymous with frivolity and facility, "with television and Plato in paperback." Heidegger wanted to show how mass society is engendered by scientifico-technological society leading to the "flight of the gods and the primacy of the mediocre." Yet in the case of the Ecole Normale this same binary—"leisure/school"—functions as a double articulation or, in Derrida's phrase, a "double séance," a double meeting, wherein the lower term is recuperated.[73] Leisure may be lowly for the masses, and the elite observer may regard such past times with disdain, but disdain quickly is transformed into *"éloge"* when "facility/leisure/ease" is evinced by one of the elect. This use of the binary opposition in which the "lower" or unvalorized term becomes revalorized even further circumscribes elite usage from common usage, functioning as quotation marks or italics. Let us now examine the particular *mise en forme* wherein facility becomes a positive attribute.

Bourgin recalls Andler's mixture of "decisive ease and sometimes exhausted lassitude."[74] Giraudoux notes that what is characteristic of the *normalien* is that he is always *at ease*, and Giraudoux further describes the high degree of euphoria and facility at Ulm. Sartre recounts that his discussions with his professors at the ENS took place in an atmosphere of "aristocratic leisure." Indeed, Gaxotte links facility to the *normalien's* "learned pranks."[75] Moreover, teachers' appreciations of their best students often cite the student's facility: Quéffelec had a facile elocution; Brasillach's teacher writes, "he speaks with ease, good humor, a facile discharge . . . taking account of his facility . . . so clear . . ."[76] We have already witnessed Jamet's *éloge*, which continually referred to Brasillach's "too light pen" and his "facile sentences" which were to kill him in the postwar trials. Pierre Henri Simon's study of comparative heroism in three authors—Montherland, Drieu, and the *normalien* and ex-student of Alain, Jean Prévost—links the writer's vocation of "surpassing of the self" to eventual facility which characterizes all great works. What was remarkable about Jean Prévost was his patience; he waited for years and covered innumerable notebooks with worthless scribble in order to become "absolute master of his thought and of his pen, to acquire this *ease* which makes masterpieces possible . . ."[77]

The facility on one literal level is the obverse to the trial that afforded entry to the ENS, and on that level should not be confused with that superficiality characteristic of the masses or the superficial facility of trendy authors, as in Brasillach's dismissal of Paul Morand. For Brasillach (who was seen as well to be "too fashionable, not serious") Morand's ease and comfort are one further sign of his vacuity: "He has installed himself comfortably in our epoch . . . he isn't stupid: He has a Baudelaire in his suitcase, sometimes." Morand's thinking is simply ready-to-wear or *"prêt-à-penser."* His books may reveal an ease, but it is merely his ability to follow trends that makes such facility possible. Ease here connotes superficiality; indeed, Morand is characterized by his "will to be superficial."[78] Brasillach's facility in contradistinction, like that of his cohorts at Ulm, is achieved, acquired, or, at least, the sign of a status achieved or acquired. It is facility of a *second order*, created and willed. And it is this second-order specific connotation that extends even further the *écart* already inscribed within the binary opposition ease/ordeal (*"aisance/épreuve"*). Other terms which convey the sense of facility and ease include *"désinvolture"*: offhanded, airy, ease, freedom. As with the case of *loisir*, when applied to Ulm, the word *désinvolture* is often coupled with an adjective that provides the transubstantiation into an elite rather than pejorative epithet. Pierre Henri Simon writes of Jean Prévost's "aristocratic casualness."[79] One witnesses a similarity of image in Bourgin's description of a master at the ENS, Charles Andler. Andler's magnetism is due only in part to his erudition. Behind this erudition and professed dogmatism lie "a kind of elegant and sober offhandedness, fancifulness, and oddness."[80] Offhandedness (*désinvolture*) in this example must be modified—or, more accurately, "normalized"—with sober (*sérieuse*) and elegant which negate possible associations with "off-handed, ease."

Yet Bourgin's insistence on the *"étrangeté"*—the uncanny, odd, or in Freud's words, the *Unheimlich*—is to the point. For if *normalien* facility is posited in distinction to superficiality, one of the salient oppositions is between surface and depth: the secret, occult, original, mysterious. Jean Guéhenno, an *ancien élève*, compares the role of a writer with that of a professor. The professor, for Guéhenno, is a type of sorcerer, who with the aid of texts must recover the secret life "beyond words and sentences" as an initiation to a mystery, "a certain overshooting that certain men, artists, exemplify."[81] We have already discussed in a previous section the occult, elusive, imperceptible ties that bind the *normalien*. The *normalien* fraternity closely approximates the model of a "secret society." The polarity surface/depth is only a displaced form of the opposition between inside and outside, high and low, which articulate the concepts of hierarchy and exclusion. What is deep is also "higher." The *normalien* response to superficiality runs in two directions: *below*, the mysterious, uncanny, occult, and secret, where originality and the artistic impulse reside; and *above*, in the form of self-transcendence coded as "surpassing oneself," "overshooting" (*dépassement*), "superiority."

For these authors surpassing oneself is a continual theme, a counterpoint to amusement (*divertissement*).[82] Jean Prévost's heroism is one of culture, in distinction to the heroism of Montherlant ("heroism of play") or of Drieu ("heroism of anguish"). This type of heroism is a vocation of "transcendence," of "personal elevation." Indeed, for Pierre Henri Simon, glory, honor, and grandeur, the three "essentially heroic values," are cultivated only with a "deep and constant will to control and surpass oneself." Drieu's writings reveal a "superiority complex."[83] It is only through "innate aristocratism" that Drieu finds fascism (according to Simon). An allocution pronounced on the occasion of the reception of Alain Peyrefitte into the Académie Française states: "In the hearts of men, you distinguish a fundamental element, the instinct of surpassing of the self. You have written superbly: surpass yourself, surpass routine behaviour, surpass others. It was one friend, Thierry Maulnier, who made me aware of the unforgettable word of St. Augustine: 'He has bread who is hungry and water who has thirst.' Is there a more beautiful explication, for a Christian, of the instinct of surpassing."[84]

The rhetoric of *surpassement/dépassement* points to yet another set of binaries which articulate the difference between the elite and the nonelite: "sacred/profane" and "high/low." The preoccupation in elite discourse with status, with *hauteur* reveals a profound concern to distance oneself from the everyday, the routine (or *quotidien*), and the mediocrity of life in a "mass society." As in the case of Heidegger (described by Bourdieu), the articulation of difference from the masses will take place via adjectival constructions comprising "high/low/base" and through the separation of pronouns which refer to the elect *nous* in distinction to those forms that level individual differences —"*on*".[85]

"Philosophic loftiness" is not an accessory attribute of an elite discourse. The preoccupation with loftiness, along with the positive appraisal of anything that is "high," is one response of an elite to a mass society which is leveling (*niveleur*). The continual references to *hauteur* should thus not be so surprising. Jamet writes of his defense attorney's speech on his behalf: "He situates the problem at the appropriate level."[86] The problem of recruitment and selection into Ulm is one of achieving the same *level* as in the past.[87] Henri Massis, Georges Izard tells us, had the opportunity to be born in the "loftiness" of Paris' highest geographical point: Montmartre! This demographic quirk or accident affords an intellectual distinction: "To be born on the heights . . . permits one to grasp things a bit higher: it broadens the gaze, it obliges one to rise up . . ."[88] Massis is thus able to rise above the picturesque and seize the essential. We have already seen how this notion of *hauteur* is contained in the notion of *surpassement* and *dépassement* as higher states of being. It should be remembered that height and loftiness are linked to descent, and with descent comes diminution. "There seem to be times when man . . . climbs too high, sinks and gives up, 'aspires to descend,' and like Flaubert's St. Anthony, experiences a certain nostalgia/desire to be matter."[89]

Diminution of quality is tied to the idea of number and the majority. For a *normalien* journalist to be in the majority "leads to a diminution of his talent." The minority status of the elect is heightened by a use of the *nous* form. If *on* functions to efface difference and to "massify," *nous* is linked to *noblesse*. *On* acts as a leveler, and it also linguistically functions to free the individual speaker from direct responsibility, contributing to notions of facility, frivolity, *désinvolture*, offhandedness, and freedom. *On* relates to the theme of the *moyenne*, mediocrity, all that threatens precious, original attributes of an individual's *Dasein*.[90] Oscillations between the twin poles of *on* and *nous* articulate horror at all egalitarian ideologies that threaten exertions of effort and expressions of free will. Mass culture threatens these moral exertions: sports and war. War comes to be seen as a moral and physical contest, similar to boxing. Number/quantity implied by *on* is clearly opposite to the higher associations of *nous*. Gillouin argues: "Who wants to belong to this new type of human society? It would have small beginnings, no doubt, but that is always the way great things begin; and the issue here is not *quantity* but *quality*."[91]

Nous forms continually stress the linkage with the higher life: *noblesse intellectuelle*. "Our school . . . a democratic institution in the most noble sense of the term . . . Thanks to it, each year youth from the modest social classes acquire a precious title of intellectual nobility . . ." The rhetoric of this one-hundred-year anniversary of the Association of Friends and Alumni of the ENS echoes those sentiments of Paul Appell's commemorative address: "We witness together . . . the large place that our school holds among all the intellectual manifestations of national and international life . . ."[92] The self-referential discourse of *normaliens* continually refers to "our school," "our community life." Indeed, "our school . . . renders its service to the country" in the form of *camaraderie*. Memoirs both of *normaliens* who consider themselves on the right and of those on the left share the use of the *nous* form which figures prominently in their titles: Brasillach's *Notre Avant Guerre* and Claude Jamet's *Notre Front Populaire* have little commonality but for their use of *nous* and the relative importance of the school for their political beliefs.

It should also be added in conclusion that the choice of *nous* and the choice of what one links to this use of *nous* not only reflect a present ordering and hierarchy, but can dictate a future as well. Jean Guéhenno writes of the importance of a speech by Jean Jaurès in determining his intellectual itinerary away from manual labor. As Jaurès spoke, his voice rose as in a call (*appel*): " 'Citizens, citizens': he addressed himself only to our pride. He painted us a world that we carried with us . . . only then, at the end of his discourse, he called us that most tender of names—'*camarades*'—and for the first time, I had a presentiment of our true destiny." [93] This presentiment of his future evoked by the apposition *nous-camarade* closes chapter 1 of his memoirs, and chapter 2, entitled "Intellectuel," begins with his enchantment at rue d'Ulm.

Jaurès' elocution displays an analogous opposition that can be described as follows. The relevant terms are *"il citoyen"* (third person) and *"nous camarades"* (first person plural). The separation between these two realms of the citizen and the *camarade*, between the *he* and the *we*, is at least as great as the difference between the Socrates of the *Apology* (the elite philosopher/gadfly) and the Socrates of the *Crito* (one of the ordinary men who must "always obey the laws" of society). A world separates them or rather an *aporia* or gap which constitutes them even (and especially) as it separates them. And it is not only their essence or ontology that is inscribed in the *nous* or *il* form but a *telos* (or future) as well.

Conclusion

Our analysis of *normalien* discourse as a prototype of elite discourse has revealed the presence of certain rhetorical tropes and strategies: preemptive verbalism, neologisms, repetition, alliteration, rhythm. Both binary oppositions and neologisms function to denote membership in an elite group as well as ascribe value to this status. *Exos* are not just excluded outsiders; they are a lower form of being. The many binary oppositions that concern vulgar/distinguished, high/base are other mechanisms to articulate difference

Language and Authority

and with it, distinction. Poetic devices such as repetition, alliteration, rhyme, etc., further delineate this elite language as they convey an *écart* or separation from ordinary language, as do the use of quotation marks for a specialized use of a common word, and italics to similarly denote exceptional usage. The separation from ordinary language at once distinguishes and valorizes elite discourse at the same time as it articulates a distance from the ordinary or common (or mediocre) life in a mass society. *On* signifies not only nonelite speakers; it also serves as a critique of the leveling tendencies in mass society, of statistics, impersonality, and the average.

We have also seen that the *normalien* as *porte-parole* (spokesman) is a necessary but insufficient condition for authoritative discourse; he must also display a mastery of the elaborated code. Nor is mere use of this code sufficient to classify one as a member of the elite. For it must be stated that these devices are not wholly unique to this elite. Other groups do use the *nous* form; other people do alliterate and repeat. Anyone who has used the French postal system has probably encountered some example of preemptive verbalism! What concerns us is, however, the ways these forms are used to reinforce an already conferred elite status, and how in so doing they articulate notions of hierarchy, difference, and exclusion implicitly, in a manner similar to that of the right. How are elite forms used by an already powerful speaker? At the very least, these forms serve as a politically powerful reinforcing mechanism of the authoritative bearers of the word.

6

THE ECOLE NORMALE

SUPÉRIEURE AND THE

SCENE OF WRITING

The primal scene of politics is the prince with his scribes.
—R. Debray, *Le Scribe*

The social intervention of a text . . . is measured not by the popularity of its audience or by the fidelity of the socio-economic reflection it contains or projects to a few eager sociologists, but rather by the violence that enables it to exceed *the laws that a society, an ideology, a philosophy establish for themselves in a fine surge of historical intelligibility. This excess is called writing.*
—Roland Barthes, *Sade, Fourier, Loyola*

"There is a story that when the first German military governor came to Paris, he had a letter in his pocket telling him that two non-military objectives were to be taken as a matter of priority: the Hôtel de Ville and the *Nouvelle Revue Française*."[1] Nonmilitary, but no less strategic. For we will see that the crucial connections between writing and political power and writing and political position, as evinced in the writings of *normaliens* Debray and Derrida, afford an in(tro)duction into the journalistic-intellectual circles of the thirties, circles marked by a certain opacity and "social incompletion" that is, for Debray, the sign of the intellectual.[2] And in this Parisian *Umwelt*, whose appearance recalls "the bush, if not the jungle,"[3] it is difficult to tell which institution has greater authority: the *NRF*, that commanding "salon-chapel" with its impressive stable of authors, or the Hôtel de Ville, "that edifice in which municipal authority of a large city resides."[4] Nor are these disjoint figures if one recalls that a second connotation of *edifice* is itself discursive: "portes à la vertu, à la piété par l'example ou *par le discours*."[5]

Debray's example of the military governor is far from innocent: the blind opposition "Hôtel de Ville/*NRF*" recalls the disjuncture between culture and politics that Debray assails in his three recent books.[6] Debray attacks the Marxist designation of culture as just one type of signifying practice, and replaces the dichotomy with a "genetic brotherhood of culture and politics under the common parentage of the religious."[7] The theoretical resistance to such a notion, to the equation of culture and politics, is evinced in Le Roy Ladurie's critique of Debray's *Critique*: "Perhaps Debray would have a clearer vision of these matters if he stopped muddling culture and politics except where the two really do intersect."[8] Yet I will argue, echoing Debray, that the relation between "thought and authority, between ways thought is transmitted and communicated and the facts of government,"[9] do intersect—in the totem of the Hôtel de Ville and the taboo of the *NRF*.

Writing/Politics

Let us begin our presentation of the relation between political and literary authority with Debray's "primal scene of politics"—the prince with his scribes. Derrida situates the possibility for political power in *Of Grammatology* in the access to the written sign: "that all clergies, exercising political power or not, were constituted at the same time as writing and by the disposition of graphic power; that strategy, ballistics, diplomacy, agriculture, fiscality and penal law are linked in their history and in their structure to the constitution of writing."[10]

Moreover, the origin assigned to writing finds analogous formulations in different cultures (evinced in confluence of myths) and this assignation is communicated in a "complex, but regulated manner with the distribution of political power as with family structure."[11] Derrida notes: "The solidarity among ideological, religious, scientific-technical systems and the systems of writing which were therefore *more* and *other* than the means of communication or vehicles of the signified remains indestructible."[12] In short, writing appears only as an intermediary vehicle for symbolic power; it is really coorigenary with the requisites of politico-administrative power—monetary and premonetary signs.

Balzac's zoological discovery in the nineteenth century—the *gendelettre* (men of letters)—can look to a similar matrix. Debray writes: "Historically, the birth of 'literature' from the ashes of *belles lettres* coincided with the birth of *politics* from the juridico-ethical ashes of the *art of government*."[13] Between 1830 and 1880 France was mother to a multiple birth, that of the politician and the professional writer. The first parliamentary groupings appear in 1838 coincidental with the emergence of the Société des Gens de Lettres.[14]

The entire Dreyfus Affair might be read as another "Battle of the Books" were it not for the overturning of the rivalry between the Sorbonne and the Quai Conti, the "secular fault line" of the Parisian intellectual milieu. Debray is correct to remind us that if the Dreyfus Affair were the "triumph of the intellectuals," it was only at the cost of the writer's defeat.

> The Ligue des Droits d l'Homme versus the Ligue de la Patrie Française meant the provinces versus Paris, the schools versus the salons, the scholarship men against the inheritors . . . It meant the 'German' university against 'French literature,' the *Revue Historique* versus the *Revue des Deux Mondes* . . . the left versus the right bank; the university corporation with its learned journals, its seminars, and *L'Aurore*, the black sheep of the popular press . . . versus the entire Academy. Such was the underlying drama acted out by actors called Barrès, Bourget, Lemaître, and Coppée on the one side and Monod, Herr, Andler, and Péguy on the other.[15]

The meaning of the Dreyfus Affair is dialectical. The author's promotion is the teacher's demotion. Publication increases in importance as lecturing/teaching diminishes in prestige. "The twilight of the University is the return of the Academy: the Dreyfus Affair in reverse. Today's Dreyfuses . . . will stay on Devil's Island."[16] The Dreyfus Affair in this reading is a bridge to the modern world in two senses. It signals an alliance between high intelligentsia and the mass media, a triumvirate between the salon, popular press, and the elite.

The victory of the university over the Academy is not without political consequences. For neither institution—University nor Academy—is a neutral term. René Rémond and Thibaudet concur. "The right, as usual, is not involved in politics—nor is the Académie Française."[17] Meanwhile, back at the Cartel des Gauches, the left is not content to be merely *involved* in politics: "the Sorbonne has on occasion *gone into politics* by fully identifying itself with the state."[18] The Academy is situated on the right, along with the profession of writing. Moreover, Thibaudet suggests that the "writer's trade inevitably leads those who practice it to the right" and equates him with the economist or financier.[19] For Debray, the wall of letters, "like that of money, is still standing and the left breaks against both."[20]

Debray proposes the following schema: "Until well after the war, a left-wing intellectual was a professor who wrote books, and a right-wing intellectual a writer who played the professor."[21] This is especially interesting when we consider that our sample of *normaliens* displayed similar patterns of *scolarité* until the crucial moment of the *concours d'agrégation,* when a disproportionate number of rightist-identified students, most notably Brasillach and Thierry Maulnier, entered careers in journalism. In an earlier generation, academician Abel Hermant resigned after placing first in the *concours* in order to pursue a full-time writing career.[22]

Intellectual history of the nineteenth and twentieth centuries reveals a sequential development. A chronological progression of filters ensues—first university, then publishing, recently media. The power of the political party is displaced from licencees of teachers to those of authors. The shift is thus from teaching to writing, from left to right, from the Cartel des Gauches to the Action Française.[23]

Writing/Position

We will now explore the Ecole Normale Supérieure as a *pépinière* to literary circles. A *pépinière* is an "establishment or land that furnishes a large number of people to a specific profession of state."[24] To examine the ENS as a *pépinière* requires an empirical analysis to underline the range, breadth, and interconnection of literary-journalistic circles with the rue d'Ulm. The picture becomes somewhat clearer if we remember the botanical root of the word *pépinière:* "the ensemble of plants that spring up in a similar ground." *Pépin* is a pit or seed, difficult to swallow, even harder to digest. Secondary associations of the word are also apt for our purposes if we recall the everyday usage; these seeds (*pépins*) are highly soft, *molle,* impressionable. *Pépins* can signal whimsical difficulties (*caprice, amourette, béguin*) or more material complications.[25] If Balzac's schema for classification of the species *gendelettre* resembled Linnaeus, our foray into *normalien* literary-publishing circles will look toward Cuvier.

We have seen that journalism provided an alternative route of *débouchement* for *normaliens,* more notably those of the right. But journalism is an especially privileged path in two senses consonant with the *normalien* experience. The pedagogical mission of the ENS in Bourdieu's words was to prepare the student "to speak like a book" (*parler comme un livre*), a standard encumbering in the classroom, but perfectly suited to publishing.[26] The literary style cultivated throughout a *normalien*'s career, beginning with the verbal display of the *canular* and the *concours d'entrée* which ratifies the newly elected's writing style in the form of selection into Ulm, prepares the *normalien* as much for the career of author as for that of teacher. Again, etymology proves illuminating. *Author* derives not from the common root for audience but shares its origin with authority, *auctor,* one who adds or founds.[27] The author is one who adds something; one who may do so in writing, itself a "supplement."

Pierre Andreu recounts in his autobiographical memoir of the period, *Le Rouge et le Blanc* (1928–1944), the necessary credentials for pursuing a career in journalism: "Good writing is *the* criterion demanded of a future journalist" (italics mine).[28] Hamon and Rotman in a scandalous book concur that a stay at the rue d'Ulm is an undeniable asset for any "intellocrat."[29] Residence at the ENS provides an "open sesame" to the portals of publishing.[30]

But the institutional mechanisms prepare the future author in yet more subtle ways. The initiation into the closed, familial world of the Ecole—brotherhood, secret society, corporation, family business —prepares the *normalien* for another closed shop, that of the small but influential publishing houses. The transition from the *"sigle"* ENS to that of Gaston Gallimard's *NRF* is easily made. Debray describes the world of Gallimard in such terms, calling it a "salon-chapel"; entry is comparable to "adoption into a family or even incorporation into an order."[31] One "regime" of symbolic production does indeed displace another: from Ulm to Grasset, a different place, the same "Imaginary." "The *NRF* imprimatur meant adoption into a family . . . That is why Proust finally went over to it, as did Martin du Gard, who went to see Gide when Grasset turned down his *Jean Barois:* 'The ranks of the *NRF* offered me . . . a welcoming spiritual family whose aspirations and quest were similar to my own and in which I could settle without losing any of my independence of mind.' "[32] J.-P. Sartre speaks in apposite terms of independence and spiritual asylum in his preface to *Aden Arabie.*[33] The transition from drawing one's stipend from the ENS (in the form of a *boursier d'état en études supérieures*) to drawing it from the house of Gallimard is made effortlessly. Robert Brasillach will speak in analogous fashion of the independence afforded by the ENS in his *Notre Avant Guerre,* and his love of independence will lead him to the ranks of Bernard Grasset, whose strength was seen to reside in his cult of talent and a "café-eclecticism."[34]

Indeed, there are many similarities between these publishing houses and Ulm. Gallimard's style was one of elegant indolence, facility, and dandyism. The *NRF* was a journal originally formed from Gallimard's Lycée Condorcet friends. But the *NRF* *"griffe"* most clearly

The Ecole Normale Supérieure and the Scene of Writing

resembles the ENS as an intangible mark of distinction. It should not be surprising that authors would greet acceptance within Gallimard with the same jubilation that they attend passing scores on the *concours d'entree*. "I'm in!" Marcel Arland exclaimed exultantly. Even the idea for the prestigious Pléiade series resumes the spirit of the "team" (*équipe*): *pleiada* in Russian means a group of friends. If Gallimard represents the *équipe* and aristocratic facility, Grasset represents the *normalien's* instinctive distaste for the mediocre and his disdain for anything other than his own opinion. Grasset had no editorial board, and his publishing house was a haven for iconoclasts and benevolent anarchism. Assouline paints a seductive picture of Grasset: a man of mischief, perversity, and daring with a quick, energetic, and impulsive intelligence. This was all terribly appealing to Brasillach.[35]

The career of writing shares an affinity with the pedagogical mission of the ENS, as well as with its institutional values stressing the "spiritual family" and independence. The initiation into a closed order is parallel. And the act of writing is indelibly linked to the career pattern of the rightist student. We saw in an earlier chapter that there was a disproportionate number of rightist students who went into careers in publishing/journalism directly from Ulm, short-circuiting the typical trajectory of Ulm: provincial lycée post—Paris—publishing. The rightist students on the whole had earlier literary careers and attained literary prizes a full decade earlier than their cohorts who had first embarked on a teaching career.[36]

Rightist students made good use of the very strong extramural contacts of the ENS that we saw prevail (Chapter 3). To cite just a few examples, we can look to the role of the older generation who admit the new generation in a manner comparable to Charles Kadushin's formulations for American intellectual circles.[37] Jean Prévost asked Robert Brasillach, a promising student, to spend a one month's internship at his paper *L'Intransigeant*.[38] Pierre Gaxotte provided the link to the Fayard *journals* and was the linchpin to student activism around the *Action Française*, which saw its culmination in the journal *Je Suis Partout*.[39] Older *normaliens* such as Guéhenno and Rolland furnished inspiration for the new right Catholic journals of *Ordre Nouveau* and *Réaction*. Thierry Maulnier served as a bridge from the older journalistic traditions of the *Europe* group (Rolland, Jean Wahl, Poncet, Guéhenno) that will have import for the journals such as *Sept* and *Esprit*.[40] In the first case, *Ordre Nouveau* is the filter; in the second, it is *Réaction*. Jean Prévost is a pivot for Déat's turn from the radical socialism of *L'Intransigeant* to *L'Oeuvre* and then to the far right *Gerbe*.

On the one hand, the strong extramural links of the ENS reinforce the symbolic-mythic clout of the title *normalien*. On the other hand, by affording entry into highly prized literary circles these contacts create strategic positions and alignments. Paris has long been seen by students of intellectuals as an extremely concentrated place for wielding symbolic power. All journals, the repository of the French language in the form of the French Academy, all the important national museums, as well as all major publishing houses and the star universities—Normale Supérieure, Polytechnique, Fondation de Science Politique—have their seat in Paris. Kadushin underlines this point when he contrasts the image of a decentralized American sphere of intellectual production with the concentrated European centers.[41] The rightist intellectual who foregoes a provincial professorial post is close to both his important contacts and to the locus of intellectual power. The combination is incontrovertible.[42]

ENS: Paradoxical *Pépinière*

The analysis of ENS journalistic circles reveals one startling discovery: although *normaliens* are represented in nearly every journal of the period, what is surprising is their disproportionately high degree of participation in the extreme periodicals, most notably *Je Suis Partout*. For our sample what is marginal is central, and *Je Suis Partout* is not only the most-contributed-to journal, it also functions as a way station. Table 8 and Figure 4 show the place of *Je Suis Partout* in the *normalien* journalistic universe. The journal with the next greatest number of *normalien* contributors is *Europe*, which shares second place with *Ordre Nouveau*, *L'Oeuvre*, and *Lutte des Jeunes*. Each of these journals (with disparate ideological tendencies to be discussed in a later section of this chapter) have four "well-connected" *normalien* collaborators. *Je Suis Partout* has a decisive margin of seven contributors. The term "well-connected" *normalien* has greater resonance when one looks at Figure 4. A well-connected *normalien* is one who occupies a strategic position in journalistic networks (Pierre Gaxotte is a case in point; although participating on "only" three journals, he plays the role of essential relay to the clearing house that is *Je Suis Partout*). A key position can also be due to overlap of journal membership in a way that reinforces one's strength. Both Robert Brasillach and Thierry Maulnier are examples of this phenomenon. Gaxotte also is an example of a third type of connection—that of the symbolic, assuming that role for a generation of young intellectuals like Brasillach or Bardèche. Thus, an intellectual may be important because he occupies a

The Ecole Normale Supérieure and the Scene of Writing

Table 8. Journals Represented by Well-Connected*
Normaliens in Order of Number of *Normalien* Collaborators

Journal	*Normalien* Collaborators
Je Suis Partout	7
Europe	4
Ordre Nouveau	4
L'Oeuvre	4
Lutte des Jeunes	4
Rive Gauche	3
Gerbe	3
Gringoire	3
Cahiers	3
Revue Française	3
Civilisation	3
Esprit	3
Etudiants Français	3
Revue Marxist	2
L'Assaut	2
Candide	2
Pamphlet	2
Revue du Vingtième Siècle	2
Reaction	2
Demain la France**	2
Cahiers des Revendications**	2
La République	2
Notre Temps	2
Combat	2
Rempart	1
L'Insurgé	1
Sept	1
Rajeunissement Politique	1
1933	1
Comoedia	1

*"Well connected" is a designation which refers to those *normaliens* who occupy a strategic location in the journalistic networks, due to either overlap of journals, position in a direct path between key pegs in journalistic social circles, or symbolic importance for a generation.
**Demain la France* and *Cahiers des Revendications* are included, although they are not regularly appearing journals, but are rather, a book written by a journalistic "*équipe*" (*Demain*) and a special number of an existing hebdomadaire (*Cahiers* is an issue of the *NRF*).

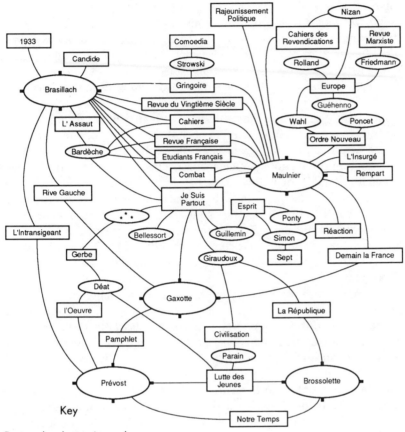

Key

Rectangles denote journals.

Ellipses denote *normaliens*.

A line connecting an ellipse and a rectangle denotes that the *normalien* wrote for that journal.

The ellipse with three stars represents three cohorts.

Figure 4. *Normalien* Publishing Networks

position in a direct path, because he is of symbolic intergenerational importance, or because he contributes to several reinforcing journals.

The centrality of an extreme journal such as *Je Suis Partout* for this elite when centrist journals such as *Candide* or *Comoedia* can look to only one *normalien* contributor is surprising at first sight. We will examine the institutional dynamics and ethos of *JSP* to see if it does capture

The Ecole Normale Supérieure and the Scene of Writing

salient features of the *normalien* experience, if not its more literal ideology. Yet, apart from the peculiarities of JSP, it appears from Table 8 that extreme or marginal journals do well with *normaliens*: *Gringoire* fares better than *Notre Temps*; *Gerbe* has more *normalien* collaborators than either of the two *NRF* special issues, *Demain la France* or *Cahiers des Revendications*. But it is the seven-to-one ratio of *Je Suis Partout* to *Comoedia* that is most striking.

How can one explain the centrality of the marginal journals for our sample, in terms of either number of contributors or position in a path? There would appear to be two plausible explanations. Beginning with the most tenuous and abstract, theoreticians on the status of the *logos* proclaim that it is the nature of the beast called writing to be excessive. Barthes in *Sade, Fourier, Loyola* links these three authors on the basis of their contribution to *logothesis* (as founders of languages);[43] what these three writers share is a certain excessive quality, despite dissimilar thematics. Debray also is concerned with the tendency toward the extreme that intellectual production for the media creates. Excess, thy name is writing.

Lottman notes how easily literary circles are able to contain or even assimilate violent extremism.[44] Despite his anti-Semitism, Marcel Jouhandeau, author of a pamphlet entitled *Le Péril Juif* and contributor to *Je Suis Partout* and *Action Française*, can remain a lifetime close friend of the Jewish editor of the *NRF*, Jean Paulhan. Paulhan in fact will break with the Comité National d'Ecrivains after the Liberation for their inclusion of Jouhandeau on a blacklist. One could equally cite the Drieu-Malraux lifetime friendship, as well as Robert Brasillach's close Jewish childhood friend and fellow cinéaste, Fred Semach. Do literary circles indeed easily assimilate political difference? Is the interpretation for this phenomenon more easily to be found in René Girard's *La Violence et le Sacré* (in his discussion of enemy brothers),[45] or does it reside in the institutionalized patterns of intellectual interaction imprinted at the ENS, where differences are not as salient as mere inclusion within the elite. Once one was a member of the elect, differences only served as "first names": "où le communisme, l'existentialisme . . . n'étaient que des prénoms . . ."[46]

If extremism is the content of this group, its distinguishing feature, what then is the overall structure and organization of these circles of *normalien* journalists? Our analysis of these circles will dovetail with that of Charles Kadushin. I will situate five *normaliens* as "pegs," who will function like their metaphorical mentor, Pegasus, as relays between the various journals. As most metro lines converge at Châtelet, one must pass through Pierre Gaxotte to arrive at other destinations, either pro-German fascist (Brasillach: *Candide, Rive Gauche, L'Assaut,* 1933) or Catholic right (Thierry Maulnier, Dandieu: *Ordre Nouveau, Réaction*) or radical socialist (Jean Prévost, Pierre Brossolette: *Notre Temps, L'Oeuvre, Pamphlet, L'Intransigeant*). *Je Suis Partout* also functions as a clearing house for the shared intellectual baggage of two *turne*-mates, Thierry Maulnier and Robert Brasillach, in the form of a common series of journals: *Gringoire, Cahiers, Revue Française, Etudiants Français* (mostly journals of youth surrounding the Action Française). This figure should also help in demarcating lines of cleavage between such apparently "similar" *normaliens* of the right, Brasillach and Maulnier, classmates and fellow travelers until the forties, whose final destinations (collaborationism/resistance, Fresnes/*Figaro*) are clearly prefigured in our diagram. The common baggage they share is not that of fascism, but a sympathy for Maurasian royalism. It is the Duc and not the Duce that binds them. Robert Brasillach's position is the more eccentric; his rightist pro-German alignment partakes of the common Maurasian ground with Maulnier, but Maulnier has the more centrist position. Maulnier is connected to a tradition that comprises a humanist center (*Europe, Civilisation*) as well as to the Catholic and Catholic right organs (*Esprit* and *Sept* via *Réaction* and *Ordre Nouveau*). Brasillach's only link to a journal such as *Esprit* is tenuous; it is made through *Je Suis Partout* via a marginal *normalien* collaborator to that journal: Henri Guillemin. It should be emphasized that Guillemin's "collaboration" was more of a flirtation. His primary affiliation was conservative and Catholic, after a brief period of participation in Marc Sangier's *Sillon* and the Young Republicans while a student at the ENS in the twenties. It was this participation that caused him to fail at his first attempt to pass the *agrégation*.[47] Similarly, an author of the caliber of Jean Giraudoux does not appear to have the institutional position befitting his literary stature. His position is augmented by his participation in *Je Suis Partout*. Giraudoux and Montherlant are among the most frequently interviewed authors in the *JSP* stable.[48] Giraudoux's other ties to journals are noteworthy. He participates in *Civilisation* with alumn Brice Parain who connects him to Brossolette and Jean Prévost via an influential journal of the period, *Lutte des Jeunes*. Other contributors to this journal include Bertrand de Jouvenel, Marcel Déat, Maurice Blanchot, Georges Gurvitch, Drieu, Georges Izard, Jean de Fabrègues, Robert Aron, and Pierre Dominique. *Civilisation* enjoyed the participation of the noted philosophers Gabriel Marcel and Karl Jaspers, as well as an influential teacher at the Sorbonne, Etienne Gilson. Table 9 shows some of the overlapping memberships between journals on the Brossolette-Prévost axis. These journals were bounded by a humanist center and radical socialist positions.

Before proceeding to analyze our five "pegs"—Brasillach, Thierry Maulnier, Pierre Gaxotte, Jean Prévost, and Pierre Brossolette—a few cautions are in order. The first distinguishing feature of these publishing circles is an aberration from the picture presented in our analysis of Ulm. Ulm was a closed, rigidly demarcated universe. For example, the *canular* via its ritual reconciliation of inside and outside circumscribed a tight universe. In contradistinction to this, literary circles appear to have a loose nature. There is a lack of easy closure between right and left within these circles. This looseness is also a crucial point in Kadushin's adumbration of social circles; the lack of easy definition is what separates the social circle from the more tightly defined network, which might be organized around a clearly defined interest.

Other similarities with Kadushin deserve consideration. The sponsorship by older intellectuals is in evidence in both France and the United States. The story depicted in Alfred Kazin's *Starting Out in the Thirties* and Norman Podhoretz's *Making It* has its parallels in the memoirs of Brasillach. One is tempted to compare Podhoretz's itinerary with that of *normaliens* such as Thierry Maulnier and Pierre Gaxotte, who started out in the political or aesthetic avant-garde to become, in the space of a generation, a voice of conservatism.[49] In addition to the role played by older intellectuals, the same phenomenon of sponsorship—small circulation journals feeding large cultural weeklies—is also the rule on both sides of the Atlantic. Book reviewing is a form of "salon critique" in Paris as in New York, whether it takes the form of Grasset's "café-salon" or Gallimard's "salon-chapel."

Pegs and Position

Our analysis of *normalien* networks will hinge on five pegs, functioning as pivots for ideology and paths to other institutions. These pegs denote not only topographical-political position but also time in the form of generational differences. These differences can be schematized as follows: we will distinguish between two early generations (Brossolette/Prévost/Guéhenno and Gaxotte) and two younger generations (polarized between Brasillach and Thierry Maulnier). We have *grosso modo* four determinations (although we must remember that the very concept of peg precludes neat conceptual demarcations).

Table 9. Brossolette-Prévost Journals

Lutte des Jeunes	Notre Temps	République	Pamphlet	L'Oeuvre
JEAN PREVOST	JEAN PREVOST	JEAN GIRAUDOUX	JEAN PREVOST	JEAN PREVOST
PIERRE BROSSOLETTE	PIERRE BROSSOLETTE	PIERRE BROSSOLETTE	PIERRE GAXOTTE	MARCEL DEAT
MARCEL DEAT	Bertrand de Jouvenel	Pierre Dominique	Pierre Dominique	RENE CHATEAU
BRICE PARAIN	Jean Luchaire	Georges Duhamel	A. Fabre Luce	ANDRE GUERIN
Bertrand de Jouvenel	Pierre Bost	André Maurois		JEAN PIOT
Jean Luchaire				
Maurice Blanchot				
Jean Fontennoy				
Drieu la Rochelle				
Robert Aron				
Pierre Dominique				
Jean de Fabrègues				
Georges Izard				
Georges Gurvitch				

Names of *normalien* contributors are in capital letters.

115

1. Brossolette, Prévost, Guéhenno: bridge between early radical socialism and internationalist humanism and concerns of the new Catholic right
2. Pierre Gaxotte: bridge between the Fayard journals and the marginal youth associated with the Action Française
3. Thierry Maulnier: second generation associated with both the far-right extremism of the *Combat* group and—through Maurice Blanchot and Jean de Fabrègues—linked to the Catholic and center-right journals
4. Robert Brasillach: link to the pro-German, fascist ultras of *Je Suis Partout*, as well as a bridge via *Rive Gauche* to the Plon publishing circle of Gabriel Marcel, Sylvia Beach, and Adrienne Monnier.

Each of these circles will be discussed in turn. Questions to be considered include possible lines of ideological cleavage (or consensus) as well as demographic or institutional quirks. Anti-Semitism will be seen to be a dividing line as will secular worldview. Can one construct a possible typology of intellectuals or in any way predict political commitment based on an examination of these literary circles?

The starting point for such an analysis is the literary review. Let us now review the review form. For Debray the review is isomorphic with the disparate fields of political action, academic research, and the aesthetic avant-garde.[50] The review has a determinant life span, that of a generation. Reviews discriminate not only between the ideas they traffic but in different manners and styles they cultivate. Place is very important; members of a review share the same locus; not the least important is address or *"siège."* Members of a review meet, for Debray, "in the same offices and in the same pages."[51] In distinction to more "modern" forms of media, "a review is ahead of its times, a magazine is after the fact . . ."[52] Kadushin echoes these sentiments when he states that to a very "large extent the small circulation journals germinate the ideas that are disseminated out to society."[53] After an article appears in the *Nation* or the *New Republic*, other journals pick up the story a year later.

The function of a review is thus prospective. In this context, Debray's facile slogan is best understood: "No review, no school." He describes the importance of the medium for the ideas it disseminates. Can one discuss "personalism" without discussing the centrality of the journal *Esprit*? But the importance of the review is not limited merely to the history of ideas; the whole history of political movements hinges on it. "Intellectual warfare is subject to the same organizational laws as social warfare. No political party, no paper; but if there is no review there is no school. Just as a party starts with a paper, a school starts with a review. The great epoch of isms was therefore that also of the periodicals."[54] To cite a few more pertinent examples: there would be no existentialism without *Les Temps Modernes*, no new-wave films without *Cahiers du Cinéma*, no historical school without *Annales*. Closer to home, one could ask if there could be democratic socialism in the academy without *Dissent*.

Undoing the Binary Opposition: The "Nonconformists" of the Thirties

The story of rightist literary circles of the thirties can be read as a struggle between three binary oppositions: young against old, political versus aesthetic (or literary), and the right-left antinomy. Nor are these disparate antagonisms; rather they hinge on and undo each other. The young-old polarity sought to redress a simplistic opposition between right and left via a blurring of literary and political criteria. Failure of a journal such as *Revue du Siècle* entailed both an increased politicization of debate (away from more literary concerns) as well as a reinscription of the right-left schema. For if there was one commonality to the diversity of new journals that presented themselves in the thirties, it was the seductive idea of a "solidarity of generation." Prolific publicist J. P. Maxence's major attribute was not his genius for forging *"équipes"* as much as his promise of offering the new generation a solution to "conservative immobilism and the imposture of Marxism."[55] And the young could certainly choose their journals: young radicals could look to *Notre Temps*, young revolutionists read their *Europe*, and young Catholics their *1929*.[56]

Yet even among these "youth" journals, one can not easily specify the appeal: Maritain's appeal, it must be argued, was not just religious but literary avant-gardiste and attracted a young following among not only Catholics but those youth rebelling against "intellectual corporalism."[57] Similarly, Massis's stamp on the *Revue Universelle* was not just religious but literary. It was in Maxence's Catholic-oriented *Cahiers des Revendications* that one witnessed support for foreign literature (one of the signs of modernism), and in a regular cinema column one could read a warm reception for Bunuel's *Chien Andalou*.[58] The Catholic journal *Cahiers* also experimented with typographic and format changes; to the traditional rectangle shape, it opposed a square. It can be argued (as does Derrida in *Dissemination*) that changes of spacing and form can herald changes more revolutionary than that of mere content.

But *Cahiers* is not just an example of literary modernism. It illus-

The Ecole Normale Supérieure and the Scene of Writing

trated the ambivalences of ideology, serving as the first example of a Péguyism of the right characteristic of the thirties.[59] This recuperation of the leftist *normalien* Péguy for the right is typical. We will see that Guéhenno's socialist humanist (and anachronistically Dreyfusard) *Europe* will also be championed by the young right who in Robert Francis' words "feel much closer to Romain Rolland or M. Guéhenno than to General de Castelnau or the editors of *La Croix*."[60]

NI DROITE, NI GAUCHE: THE EQUIVOCAL CENTER

Emmanuel Mounier, founder of a journal that can boast of even more *agrégés* than *normalien* Jean Jaurès' *Humanité*, suggested undoing the right-left opposition by combining their respective virtues. Although one might well wonder if this undoes the opposition as much as it might serve to reinforce these distinctions, we will turn to his schema. Honor, moderation ("measure"), and prudence are seen as rightist virtues, as audacity and peace are leftist attributes: "Charity is on the right with religion, the ministry of war, Spirit, M. Bourget, Latin, liberal economics, notaries, and families. Justice is on the left with Picasso, civil servants, M. Homan, social hygiene, feminism, liberty, and experimental psychology."[61] Whether or not one agrees with Mounier's checklist, it is clear that a putting into question of the traditional categories was on the journalistic agenda. In the periodicals to which *normaliens* contributed one does witness a blurring of the distinction between right and left. Nowhere is this more in evidence than in the case of *Europe*, started in 1923 by *normalien* Romain Rolland, who continued to preside over the journal from Switzerland like "a mother hen" during Guéhenno's tenure as editor. Indeed, Guéhenno helped to shape a journal that was "unabashedly internationalist, pacifist, anachronistically Dreyfusard." At first glance, *Europe* was superfluous. Lottman asks rhetorically: "Did the left bank really need two cultural journals?"[62] After all, the *NRF* appeared on the first of every month. Did Parisian intellectuals really need a double cultural dose every two weeks? (*Europe* appeared on the fifteenth of the month.) But to equate these as cultural weeklies is beside the point, for *Europe* placed social considerations over esthetic values. Guéhenno's humanism was the antithesis of the "art for art's sake" approach of the *NRF*.

In addition, Guéhenno exemplified that interface between publishing and the professoriat so admirably described by Debray; he continued to be a lycée professor at the same time as he served as editor, thus becoming the incarnation of the left for a whole generation of students. Moreover, like Guéhenno, the journal looked behind and beyond. While their Dreyfusism could be dubbed retrograde, their literary policy was decidedly avant-garde and international, as well as nonsectarian. During Guéhenno's tenure, Drieu and Giono appeared in the same pages as Faulkner, Silone, Gorky, Trotsky, Ehrenburg, and Victor Serge. This literary *détente* was continued even under Aragon's reign (which included active participation of *normalien* Georges Friedmann). The journal was far from the stereotypic communist *porteparole*, at home with Henry Miller, William Saroyan, Pasternak, Brecht, and Neruda. Closer to home, *Europe* accommodated authors as divergent as Montherlant and Supervielle, Nizan and Aragon.[63] That the journal was widely read among leftists such as Soustelle or Lefranc is of little surprise.[64]

But its curious appeal to rightists needs to be explained, and we need look no further than to the editor, Rieder, who in 1931–32 published a provocative volume, *Décadence de la Nation Française*. Guéhenno's pragmatic humanism had great appeal to youth tired of what they saw as a privileging of the abstract over the concrete which in their eyes led to France's decline and even to denatality (the preference for abstract over "real" men invariably leads to lower population!). Guéhenno's equanimity led to coparticipation with *Ordre Nouveau* groups, especially with Dandieu and Robert Aron. What these strange allies shared was a violent antirationalism which joined them to an illustrious register of *normaliens*: Lévy-Bruhl, Jean Wahl, Durkheim, Bergson, as well as Sorel, Maurras, and Heidegger. A preface to an antirationalist anthology reads, "All philosophic construction is in life's margins and problems in action."[65]

If *Europe* can be seen to appeal to both a center right (Robert Aron, Dandieu, Alexandre Marc) and a center left (Soustelle), another thirties journal, *Pamphlet*, also swung both ways, attracting radicals of all persuasions. Jean Prévost's participation served as a link to *conormalien* disciples of Alain, while the presence of radical authoritarian Pierre Dominique assured equal time for prefascist viewpoints. The ambivalences of the thirties journals are exceedingly difficult to categorize especially when we consider that even a pivot like Prévost can lead to alternating trajectories such as that of the resistant *normalien* Pierre Brossolette as well as that of Marcel Déat (founder of the rightist RNP) or to what Pascal Ory dubs the "left collaborationists"— *normaliens* René Chateau and Alain's disciple Claude Jamet.[66]

Pamphlet was co-edited by Fabre Luce, Pierre Dominique, and *normalien* Prévost. It also enjoyed the participation of *normalien* Pierre

Brossolette. It was closely linked to Luchaire's *Notre Temps*, sharing its advertising pages as well as its authors with them. Prévost and Brossolette also wrote for *Notre Temps*. *Notre Temps* advertised itself as "the great European weekly of the new generation." It extolled a European federation, Franco-German rapprochement, and state reform. And like so many thirties periodicals, the political agenda was fought out on the literary pages. Typical articles comprised Prévost's "Bourgeoisie et Capitalism," Dominique's "Une Atmosphère Préfascist," and Fabre Luce's "Eloge de Daladier." Fabre Luce's viewpoint expressed in a 1933 *Pamphlet* article could easily be read as an allegory of his own political position and that of the thirties journals: "I find it even impossible to vaguely situate the diverse movements which we consider rightist or leftist. Even their origin reflects two contradictory impulses."[67]

If the journals of the thirties eroded some of our more serviceable oppositions, let me now suggest another polarity in an attempt to situate rightist *normalien* literary praxis, that of personality. For in the absence of cultural or political signposts, the forceful personalities behind these journals served as a definition. Moreover, by distinguishing between journals headed by different figures, we can trace a difference between sets of authors who appear to be closely allied (Thierry Maulnier, Brasillach) yet whose paths diverge during the occupation.[68] For not all young rightist ideologues who contributed to a prefascism in France collaborate or willingly celebrate Nazism. And we have seen how difficult it is to situate differences among the heterogenous collection of names of contributors around philosophies that are even "ambivalent in their origins . . ."

Among the body of journals and authors that Loubet del Bayle refers to as the "nonconformists of the thirties," a salient opposition emerges between those journals headed by J. P. Maxence and those headed by Jean de Fabrègues.[69] While one should signal obvious differences in personal style—e.g., Maxence's absolute brilliance at organizing *équipes*—there are certain structural dissimilarities that point to political differences that might serve to map out this treacherous terrain. As with all mapping endeavors, however, one must remember an allegory of J. L. Borges and be careful not to prefer the map to the reality. Any map is solely for heuristic purposes—to situate the locations and tensions as symptoms of later political difference. With these caveats in mind, Tables 11 and 12 reveal the following generalizations. Although Thierry Maulnier contributes heavily to both sets of journals, Robert Brasillach has nothing to do with Fabrègues' journals. Moreover, it appears that Maxence's journals appeal to decidedly

Table 10. Ni Droite Ni Gauche

Cahiers	Europe	Civilisation	Ordre Nouveau
MAURICE BARDÈCHE	JEAN GUÉHENNO	ETIENNE GILSON	THIERRY MAULNIER
ROBERT BRASILLACH	GEORGE FRIEDMANN	JEAN GIRAUDOUX	A. PONCET
ETIENNE BORNE	PAUL NIZAN	BRICE PARAIN	JEAN WAHL
M. DE GANDILLAC	ROMAIN ROLLAND	*Jean de Fabrègues*	Denis de Rougemont
THIERRY MAULNIER	JEAN WAHL	*Gabriel Marcel*	*Robert Aron*
J. P. Maxence	*A. Dandieu*	C. Ramuz	Alexandre Marc
Jean de Fabrègues	*Robert Aron*	Karl Jaspers	*A. Dandieu*
René Vincent	Jean Cassou		
Robert Francis	J. R. Bloch		
Maurice Fombeure	Jules Supervielle		
Jacques Maritain	*Jacques Maritain*		
Georges Bernanos	Henri de Montherlant		
Henri Massis	Louis Aragon		
Max Jacob	Marcel Arland		
Henri Pourrat	Pierre Drieu La Rochelle		
Gabriel Marcel	RAYMOND ARON		
R. Vallery Radot	André Chamson		
Nicholas Berdiaff	Eugène Dabit		
Pierre Reverdy	Jean Blanzat		
Stanislas Fumet	Jacques Copeau		
J. Chauvy			

Names of *normalien* contributors are in capital letters.
Italicized names are those contributors to two of these journals.

Table 11. Maxence's Journals

Revue du Vingtième Siècle	Revue Française	1933	Rempart	Rajeunissement Politique
J. P. Maxence	J. P. Maxence	J. P. Maxence	J. P. Maxence	J. P. Maxence
ROBERT BRASILLACH	ROBERT BRASILLACH	ROBERT BRASILLACH	THIERRY MAULNIER	THIERRY MAULNIER
THIERRY MAULNIER	THIERRY MAULNIER	Henri Massis	Maurice Blanchot	Daniel Rops
R. Francis	MAURICE BARDECHE	Henri de Montherlant		
Maurice Blanchot	RAOUL AUDIBERT	Paul Morand		
Georges Blond	Henri Massis	Gabriel Marcel		
Pierre Andreu	José Lupin	René Clair		
Claude Roy		A. Thibaudet		

Capital letters signify *normalien* status.

Table 12. Fabrègues's Journals

Réaction	Combat	Revue du Siècle	L'Insurgé
Jean de Fabrègues	*Jean de Fabrègues*	*Jean de Fabrègues*	*Jean de Fabrègues*
THIERRY MAULNIER	THIERRY MAULNIER	Daniel Rops	THIERRY MAULNIER
Maurice Blanchot	*Maurice Blanchot*	Paul Morand	J. P. Maxence
J. P. Maxence	J. P. Maxence	Henri de Montherlant	*Maurice Blanchot*
Pierre Andreu	Pierre Andreu	R. Martin du Gard	*Georges Blond*
René Vincent	Robert Francis		
ALAIN	*Georges Blond*		
Georges Duhamel	Claude Roy		
Georges Bernanos	François Mitterand		
PIERRE HENRI SIMON			
P. Lucius			
R. Vallery Radot			
Emmanuel Berl			
A. Rousseaux			

Capital letters signify *normalien* status.
Italicized names contribute to two or more of these journals.

more *normaliens,* and this is understandable when we consider that his journals are largely composed of marginal youth associated with the Action Française. Indeed, one can look to the history of the *Revue Française* composed in forty-eight hours in Brasillach and Maulnier's Ulm *turne.*

Maxence meets Thierry Maulnier at the home of Henri Massis. Maulnier is described by Maxence as this young *normalien,* shy and ungainly.[70] It was in the spring of 1930 when students writing for the Action Française journal, *Etudiants Français,* abruptly quit the Action Française. The membership of *Etudiants Français* bears striking similarity to the roster of *Revue Française* which is of little surprise when we consider that both organs include what was fundamentally an Ulm *turne:* Robert Brasillach and Thierry Maulnier (who chooses his pen name at this moment) as well as Maurice Bardèche and their lycée friend who socialized at their *turne,* José Lupin. It is through this process that Thierry Maulnier is asked to collaborate on Massis's and Bellesort's *Revue Universelle* and then on the literary pages of *Action Française.*

If Maxence's journals can be seen as oriented toward both youth and a marginal Action Française milieu, Fabrègues's journals are more difficult to categorize. They are more heterogeneous, comprising rightists but also leftist and center positions: Emmanuel Berl, Drieu's "left" friend and coeditor of *Derniers Jours,* Georges Duhamel, Georges Bernanos, and the pacifist *normalien* Alain. Fabrègues' journals are more importantly marked by an *absence:* that of Robert Brasillach whose participation does appear restricted to Maurrasian oriented journals. He does not even contribute to *Réaction,* which is castigated by Guy Crouzet of *Notre Temps* as "It's Maurras without Maurras!"[71] Why should Fabrègues's journals, especially *Réaction,* not appeal to Brasillach? I believe this question is crucial in explaining later political and literary itineraries of Brasillach and Maulnier, especially as it has been argued that Maulnier's later position was in some ways a turnaround, either opportunistic or at least illogical from the point of view of his militant thirties positions.

Réaction shared common ground with Maurras, not the least in the figure of Fabrègues, who served as Maurras's secretary as well as being in charge of the press review rubric of *Action Française.* He shared some of Maurras's theoretical premises as well: his organizational empiricism, traditionalism, royalism, and naturalism. Yet the divergences from the Action Française prefigure the critical battle lines of the forties reviews. *Réaction* put literary questions second to religious and social problems. After all, it was not literature that was important to Fabrègues and no one expected a "poetic art from Maurras." And, most important, *Réaction* most differed from *Action Française* and *Revue Française* in its more explicit nationalism and lesser antipathy toward Jews and Freemasons. This presages Maulnier's positions as he was less Germanophilic or sympathetic to Italian fascism (than Robert Brasillach). Maulnier preferred that France find its own unique solutions, and he sided with his friend Maurice Blanchot of *Combat* against Brasillach's militant anti-Semitism.[72]

One might also see Maulnier's participation in *Rempart* and *L'Insurgé* as signaling his willingness to privilege social over aesthetic concerns. *Rempart*, founded by antiparliamentarian and anticapitalist Paul Lévy, echoed the sentiment expressed in the aftermath of the February 1934 days in the book *Demain La France* (co-authored by Maulnier, Maxence, and Maxence's brother, Robert Francis) that tomorrow's revolution must be fought on three fronts—spiritual, economic, and social—and of these three the social prevailed.[73]

The antiparliamentarian, anticapitalist themes grew more strident in the last issues of *Revue Française*. Indeed, a volume edited by Thierry Maulnier and Robert Francis, *Demain La France*, was both dedicated to those slain in the February 6, 1934, uprisings and written expressly to give a doctrine to these events. They argued for a strong state, a corporatist organization of the national economy. None of this was highly original, but Emmanuel Mounier noted the spirit of anticapitalism in his book review of *Demain La France* in *Esprit*.

Indeed, Brasillach's position is consistent and ties in with his support for monarchism. Was the support for monarchism among marginal youth associated with Maurras just juvenile rebellion, an "épater les bourgeois" stance akin to student movements anywhere? There may be grounds for such an appraisal; Maurice Bardèche suggests that the topic of monarchism was one of the great taboos, one of the *non-dits*, or unspeakable.[74] It would be easier to admit to homosexuality than to deep-seated belief in the monarchy. Yet I prefer to see more in the support for monarchy than the mere desire to be contrary. For the Maurrasians who surrounded the *Revue Française*, directed by Maxence, forged a review that showed little interest in politics. Brasillach chides a colleague that one of the great virtues of monarchism is precisely that it frees the citizen from political preoccupations.[75] Brasillach criticized his cohorts (around 1930) for being overly concerned with political questions. Brasillach will thus participate in the *Revue du Vingtième Siècle* of Maxence, given its support for the Count of Paris.[76]

Another major difference between the Fabrègues and Maxence journals concerns the question of style, and this also contributes to com-

The Ecole Normale Supérieure and the Scene of Writing

plicating matters. Although the Maxence journals might appear to be closer in their personnel and in their thematics (anti-Semitism, pro-German, etc.) to the extremist tendencies of the forties (*Je Suis Partout, Gringoire, Gerbe, Au Pilori*), the style of the Fabrègues journals provided the stylistic precursor. For all its antidemocratic and anticapitalistic sentiments, the *Revue Française*'s style was perfectly ordinary and doctrinal in tone. For real spleen, one had to peruse the pages of *Combat*, whose voluntary aggressive tone was first evinced in its provocative titles: "Terrorism: Method of Public Welfare" (Blanchot 7/1936), "Down with Bourgeois Culture" (Thierry Maulnier 10/1936), "Letter to the Cuckolded Right" (Brasillach 3/1936—he was to be removed from *Combat* in 1937 over the anti-Semitism issue).[77] If many of the participants did not become fascists, the shock of the titles reveals a rabid antidemocratic and anticapitalist sentiments that prefigure those of fascism. There were uncanny analogies between the reaction of *Combat* to the events of the day and those of the extreme right. Hostility toward the Popular Front, opposition to sanctions against Italy, support for *franquistes* in the Spanish Civil War, approval of Munich ("a victory of good sense") echo these positions of the far right. But the condemnation of Hitler's anti-Semitism will be a dividing line between *Combat* and *Je Suis Partout*. Indeed, Thierry Maulnier contributed to many of the journals whose invective was to set standards for fascist discourse of the forties (such as *L'Insurgé*, written under the dual patronage of Vallès and Drumont), while his political position itself remained moderate and in tune with the *normalien* motto of "personal reflection."[78]

PACIFICATION/NORMALISATION

Twenty years old in 1914 . . . To enter life through the door of war . . . After the hothouse of exhausting preparations for the concours, *to find oneself suddenly foot-deep in mud and blood, to hear sound one of the solemn hours that announces the collapse of a world.*
—Marcel Déat, *"Mémoires Politiques"*

If we have used personalities (Maxence, Fabrègues) to situate the opposition between two younger rightist *normaliens* (Brasillach, Thierry Maulnier), we will now turn to a journal that affected the older generation (promotions 1917–19), *L'Oeuvre*. And if the ambivalences and ambiguities of the centrist *entre deux guerres* journals were based on a conscious attempt to undo simplistic binaries, then this radical journal was ruled by an equally conscious insistence never to forget the polarity taught in the school of the First World War: that of war and peace. For Déat, the experience of the First World War was that of a civil war in Europe in which France sacrificed her elite, including three *normaliens* from Déat's promotion alone. All of Déat's education (as well as that of his cohorts at Ulm: Jean Prévost, Jean Piot, André Guérin, Pierre Pucheu) was marked by his insistent filtrage of peace over war, which culminated in a profoundly political engagement.[79]

L'Oeuvre was situated squarely within two traditions well represented by *normaliens*—pacifism and socialism—which were to converge in the Vichy journal of those who "would not wish to die for Danzig."[80] Pierre Andreu recalls the radical socialist tradition of the journal and presents his father as a typical reader of the mid-twenties (1924). "My father was more 'socialistic' than socialist and read *L'Oeuvre*—imbeciles don't read *L'Oeuvre*—and he voted for Paul Painlevé, a scholar."[81] Indeed, in more ways than one, the history of *L'Oeuvre* was one of old school ties. Yet the simple origin—disciples of Alain—leads to divergent destinations: Déat fleeing the scene of the Liberation toward Céline's "château" at Sigmaringen; Prévost shot by the Germans in the Vercors as he attempted to join the *maquis* in the Isère; Pucheu, dead in Algiers after a summary trial.[82] Moreover, a second generation of Alain students flanking Brasillach's promotion —René Chateau (1927) and Claude Jamet (1928)—pass through the journalistic circles of *L'Oeuvre* to form what Pascal Ory dubs the "collaborationist left," writing for *La France Socialiste* and *Germinal*. Chateau is emblematic of the bizarre itineraries and radical swings in position characteristic of this group. For if the journals to which Brasillach and Thierry Maulnier contributed could be seen as merely two sides of a Maurasian baseline, the *L'Oeuvre* participants had wild fluctuations.

Chateau was an ultrapacifist disciple of Alain, a member of the central committee of the *Ligue des Droits de l'Homme*, who passed through the independent left toward the "miniscule parti Camille Pelletan" to the left of Valois. What is even stranger is that he is elected as a Freemason in 1936 and enters *L'Oeuvre* in 1940. He will then serve as political director of a new worker's daily, *La France Socialiste* (115,000– 130,000 copies), with a heavy German subsidy under the same Hibbelen trust that will in March 1944 sponsor Jamet's *Germinal*. Jamet is chosen because he is a symbol of *normalien* literary quality, and he will accept largely for literary reasons, as we will see in our next chapter which explores his postwar trial.[83]

Ory suggests an interesting caveat for this group of authors; one must be extremely wary of exaggerating position-taking. Rather than logical internal coherence or some deep-seated belief system, it is the event or historical conjuncture that is the defining trait. It is toward Laval's return to power with Lagardelle in his entourage (as minister of work) that we should seek an explanation of literary behavior. Here politics provides for its own mediation or at least mediates literary praxis, rather than the reverse which we will see at work in *Je Suis Partout* and which we have seen to some extent in the personalistic journalistic circles around Maxence and Fabrègues. Indeed, one need only look at Alain's dictum "Peace for Peace's Sake" evidenced in his telegram (collectively written with Giono) to Daladier and Chamberlain: "Be assured that the overwhelming majority of the French people (desire) to keep the peace by whatever equitable arrangement." [84] Yet Déat will later speak of the irony of his teacher Alain, "authentic pacifist, antimilitarist, certainly, but Jacobin and loyal to his principle which is to obey the law, even a stupid one." [85] Here, Alain, presented as Crito, will thus join the artillery in 1944! Ultimate explanation for the literary and political activism of this group tutored by the First World War will rest on events.

But what is troubling once we seek an explanation is that the same school ties, those same lessons of war and peace should find radically opposing political expression. Let us focus for the moment on those school ties surrounding Déat and his cohorts at *L'Oeuvre*. In many ways, Déat represents the typical *normalien* of the left presented by historiographers of the school such as Bourgin. For Déat, in contrast to Brasillach and the marginal Action Française crowd, was personally linked to every major institutional trend. Throughout the war years, which delayed his entrance into Ulm, he corresponded with Dreyfusard Paul Dupuy, secretary in charge of the school. Through the socialist-aligned sociologist Célestin Bouglé (who was later to head the school until his removal during Vichy) Déat met the Halévy brothers as well as the influential school of sociology headed by Marcel Mauss.[86] The networks and cultural milieu in which he participated, however, are second to his readings. He read Simmel, Tönnies, Husserl, and German phenomenology as well as Scheler, Troeltsch, and finally Heidegger and existentialism and called this last an important "track" for him as it allowed him to discover that "unbridgeable distance between the notion and the concrete reality." [87]

Déat wrote for *normalien* Lévy-Bruhl's *Revue Philosophique* reviewing the books of a no less important *normalien* and Sorbonne professor, Léon Brunschvicq. Déat remained in the school after his *débouchement*, refusing to accept his first post and becoming secretary to Bouglé's

Centre du Documentation Sociale housed at the school. Déat passed to the *palais* of Ulm as *archicube* (those *normaliens* preparing theses), and shared this *palais* as well as the small refectory reserved for *archicubes* with Marcel Prenant, a naturalist who applied Marxist Leninism to zoology, and Emile Mireaux, future education minister during Vichy who would follow the path toward the technocratic elite led by radical A. François Poncet.[88] Most important, Déat served as second librarian to Lucien Herr, at the Ulm library which all *normaliens* agree played the formative role in their *normalien* experience.

As a socialist deputy, Déat continued a school tradition and participated with other leading *normaliens* and intellectuals in the "New School for Peace" of Louise Weiss; Edouard Herriot, Louis Eisenmann, future academician Paul Hazard, Léon Blum, Jules Romains all participated along with leading non-*normalien* intellectuals André Gide, Drieu, Henri and Bertrand de Jouvenel, Henri de Man, Emmanuel Berl, Friedrich Sieburg.[89]

Yet we would be wrong to see in Déat's story a univocal linkage to the left and its institutions. He is also tied to important rightist figures, not the least Georges Valois, head of the Faisceau and friend of Hubert Bourgin, who is his editor.[90] One might wonder if there is any coherence to Déat's political sojourn but for the old school tie. There is evidence for such an appraisal in his "Mémoires Politiques." The one continuity of Déat's life would appear to be unbreakable camaraderie. Déat is as much a bearer of the word as he is the head of a political movement—the Rassemblement Nationale Populaire— and indeed, has been contrasted with Doriot, who is seen as a "man of power" to Déat's "man of speech"; "the metallurgist who could have been head of the Communist party" against "the *normalien* who could have been head of the sfio."[91] Even their political visions can be reduced to this disjuncture between action and the word; Doriot believed in a putsch, while Déat crafted a project for the *parti unique*. The opposition between the man of action and the man of the word is reiterated in Déat's own appraisal of Doriot: "Doriot has all sorts of good qualities, but not those of a good journalist."[92]

We can witness the strength of the old school tie in *L'Oeuvre* and in the warm memories of the journal that Déat recounts in his memoirs. Déat exempts his comrades from towing a strong pro-Vichy line. Jean Piot, whom Déat calls his *"camarade pour toujours,"* writes about what he wishes; Déat will never give him direct orders. His cohort at ENS, André Guérin, is also integrated into the journal as head of a literary department. When Piot steps down from *L'Oeuvre*, he will be replaced by another *normalien*, René Chateau.[93]

The Ecole Normale Supérieure and the Scene of Writing

Part of the explanation of Déat's fondness for *L'Oeuvre* must be that it returns him to his primal scene of writing. His literary beginnings, like those of many of his leftist cohorts at Ulm, were delayed until after the start of either a career in higher education or a detour into politics. In Déat's case, we witness a double delay until the late thirties when he churns out between fifteen and twenty articles per month in *L'Oeuvre* and *République Quotidienne* while teaching at the Lycée Louis-le-Grand.[94] The March 4, 1939, provocative headline, "Mourir pour Danzig," that so captured the zeitgeist of Munich is recuperated in the posters announcing the relancing of *L'Oeuvre*; one is invited to read those authors "who did not wish to die for Danzig."[95]

However, all answers are necessarily incomplete, and Déat underscores this in a reflection in his "Mémoires Politiques" that could easily serve to describe the state of tension between his two sides: "But the two faces of France are as incompatible as two philosophical systems, as two religions; they prolong that war between Jean-Jacques Rousseau and de Bonald, between Voltaire and Joseph de Maistre. *At the same time, there is a profound affinity between these two sides that testifies to their kinship [consanguinité] and condemns them to a permanent war*" (italics mine).[96]

It is this cosanguinity, this blood brotherhood, which underscores the *normalien* fraternity, that is the ultimate locus of any full explanation of literary/political praxis of the thirties and forties. Kinship gives coherence to these sometimes "enemy brothers" who, however much they differ from one another, still bear some resemblance to their parents. Let us now turn to a recuperation of the *normalien* family in the journal *Je Suis Partout*. If *L'Oeuvre* demonstrated the viability of *normalien* friendship (surviving Déat's death—his literary executor is *normalien* lifelong socialist Georges Lefranc), *Je Suis Partout* illustrates its organizing structural principle, that of the *équipe*.

NORMALIZING DISCOURSE: THE CASE OF *JE SUIS PARTOUT*

It has been argued that Doriot's Parti Populaire Francaise (hereafter PPF) contributed to a homogenization of the extreme right.[97] In other words, the PPF was the far right "*normalisé*" and the journal *Je Suis Partout* was a miniature ("*en abîme*") of this tendency. It boasted the participation of an ex-Camelot du Roi turned PPF (Claude Jeantet), and a former secretary of *normalien* Jaurès' communist daily *Humanité* (Camille Fégy) turned PPF, yet there were notable exceptions to this pattern of normalizing extremes in the figures of its *normalien* contributors: Brasillach, Pierre Gaxotte, Maurice Bardèche, Thierry Maulnier, André Bellessort, Henri Guillemin, Jean Giraudoux. *Je Suis Partout*, the journal of the extreme right, is described by historians in that rhetorical trope of extremes: *hyperbole*. It is the most popular journal with the biggest diffusion and most consistently wide readership. Between 1930 and 1940, *JSP*'s readership grew from 45,000 to 100,000 readers. It was also seen by Ory to be the most brilliant, showing with "maximum clarity" the progressive shift from orthodox Maurrasianism (and its nationalist Germanophobia) to the internationalist fascism of the forties.[98] As we will see in our next chapter, it also boasted the most death sentences of any journal at the postwar purge trials.

Let us now examine the relation between *Je Suis Partout* and the Fayard journals it so ably characterizes. For Fayard was marked by their openness to foreign countries as opposed to the francocentrism of the Action Française journals.[99] And Pierre Gaxotte, *normalien* mentor to Brasillach's generation, provides the link between both circles. Indeed, Fayard can trace its own origin to an old school tie made in Lycée Louis-le-Grand (scene of the meeting between Gaxotte and Brasillach) between Arthème Fayard the second and Léon Daudet.[100] Fayard introduced himself to Léon's father Alphonse Daudet and convinced him to publish with Fayard. Arthème Fayard, French nationalist and rightist, had already launched two other journals before the successful *Je Suis Partout: Candide* (a literary and Parisian weekly, founded in 1924) and *Ric et Rac* (a family journal with a cartoon format, begun in 1927). If Arthème Fayard was a man of action, his son Jean pursued an easy literary life, with minor political activities—an insignificant collaboration on the *Action Française*—as well as a period of militance (1934) with Colonel de la Rocque's Volontaires Nationales. After Jean Fayard's literary success *Mal d'Amour* he directed some of his father's more literary publications (e.g., the cinema column of *Candide*, humorous editorials in *Ric et Rac*). Arthème Fayard thus left his history series under the direction of a young *normalien*, Pierre Gaxotte. Gaxotte's tenure was noteworthy for pro-German arguments.[101]

Candide was the contemporary of the "Grandes Etudes Historiques" series edited by Gaxotte, and it met with a similar success. *Candide* also served as the model for a whole host of cultural *hebdos* and is most often compared with Carbuccia's *Gringoire*. *Gringoire* was opposed to *Candide* as mass was to elite. In other words, *Gringoire* didn't "flinch before vulgarity," and *Candide* more closely resembled its leftist Gallimard competitor *Marianne* in its tone and approach. Arthème Fayard had one golden rule for this journal: "Not one single boring article." And literature was the sacred cow. Each issue contained "two short

The Ecole Normale Supérieure and the Scene of Writing

stories, an extract from a novel, a new article or biography (a popular genre illustrated by André Maurois), and two literary pages written by men of often opposing political opinions but who communicated the same devotion to Literature with a capital *L*."[102] It was not difficult to imagine the appeal of such a milieu for Brasillach, who first wrote for *Candide* in 1931.

In many ways *Je Suis Partout* could be *the* model expression of the *normalien* experience, its direct translation from the world of pedagogy to that of publishing. Moreover, it united four generations of rightist *normaliens* from André Bellessort (1880s), Jean Giraudoux (1904), Pierre Gaxotte (1914), to Robert Brasillach (1928). In personnel, as well as in structure (the *équipe*, or soviet cooperative) and attitude, it underlined the institutional discourse of the Ecole Normale (as revealed in Chapters 3 and 4) more closely than did any other journal. And it is with Pierre Gaxotte, described with all the reverence due a *normalien* patriarch, that any discussion of *JSP* must begin.

Gaxotte's itinerary is typical. Like many *normaliens*, he is the son of a republican with radical socialist inclinations. Gaxotte comes to Paris for his studies where he meets and is befriended by Arthème Fayard. Despite the differences of age (but with similarities of origin: both men who are so tied into the business of literary signatures, as author and editor, begin their lives as sons of notaries) they become great friends. Gaxotte, however, will follow the typical career route of his generation—he will begin as a lycée professor and go to work for Fayard only after several years of teaching. By the time *Je Suis Partout* is launched in 1930, he is already a celebrated author of a volume on the French Revolution.[103]

Yet what distinguishes Gaxotte are the intriguing anomalies he presents. He embodies many of the paradoxes of *JSP* in his person. Although Gaxotte is among the oldest of the inner circle of *JSP*, he will be the one to reject the right-left polarity in the name of youth: "Right? Left? . . . So many words henceforth without significance for the great party of the elite of the young generation."[104] Although Gaxotte is of the same war generation as Déat, he is singularly unaffected by it due to his nonparticipation in the war for reasons of health. In addition, the criticisms (or appraisal, depending upon one's outlook) one can make of Gaxotte go for *JSP* as well. Just as the journal was characterized by negative formulations, as it lacked a coherent ideology, so too Gaxotte's criticism was negative in character. Whether the focus was on deficits or other issues, Gaxotte was more comfortable in underlining the lack rather than in proposing positive measures.[105]

If Gaxotte was regarded by the *JSP équipe* alternately (and with great affection) as "*pape*," "führer," and "caudillo," [106] indeed, as a form of "theoretical patrimony," another *normalien*, Jean Giraudoux, was also heralded as supplying the requisite aesthetic legacy. Giraudoux was the author most interviewed by the *JSP* team, and his theatrical oeuvre was unanimously celebrated.[107] Thierry Maulnier could see in his *Electra* as well as in his *Guerre de Troie* a truly contemporary theater, while others could read his essays such as *Pleins Pouvoirs* as echoing the editorial pages of their own weekly. For Giraudoux proposed strikingly similar remedies for France's ills: major public work projects, urbanism, pronatalism, and immigration controlled by racial criteria. This last aspect was not without its explicit anti-Semitism. Fabre Luce writes in his memoirs that Giraudoux partook of fascism without knowing it. But, Giraudoux was most in line with this journal in his antiradical position. Giraudoux held the politician responsible for France's downfall and considered French democracy to be less a regime than a religion, a view that coincided with that of Gaxotte.

If Jean Giraudoux provided the link to a modernist aesthetic, André Bellessort provided the continuity of tradition. Bellessort served as book critic for ten years, beginning in 1932 and continuing until his death in 1942.[108] Bellessort is the archetypical academic: a *normalien*, the son of a *collège* principal, and the grandson of a teacher. Bellessort was most famous as the professor of the *hypokhâgne* at Lycée Louis-le-Grand during Brasillach's and Thierry Maulnier's literary formation. Robert Brasillach remembers his teacher: "But we know upon arrival at Louis-le-Grand that we were going to enter the class of André Bellessort, who taught Latin and French in *hypokhâgne*. There were many stories about him, that were not exactly true, but which gave him a particular physiognomy . . . It was recounted that in the year preceding ours, the Academy preferred M. Célestin Jonnart to Charles Maurras; André Bellessort came to class, scowled (his thick eyebrows forming a *V*), opened his briefcase, and proclaimed: 'Messieurs, the Académie Française has just elected M. Jonnart. I will read you some Charles Maurras.' "[109]

Brasillach admired Bellessort's ability to upset "inspector generals and ready-made ideas." Bellessort could submit to Maurras's seduction all the while remaining squarely within the conservative right; he could walk the fine line between the nationalism of the Action Française and that of the conservative right.[110]

If *JSP* shared a continuity of personnel with the ENS, the similarities extended to the very structure of the journal. The journal was subject to only two principles: autonomy and friendship. One could say the same for Ulm. Let us outline the symmetry between *JSP* and the

ENS as one means of explaining the disproportionately high number of *normalien* contributors to this extremist journal. Why did so many *normaliens* find this journal a home?

Like Ulm, *JSP* was regulated by a principle of autonomy. Brasillach writes of the ENS: "There were no rules. It was an establishment without either obligation or sanction." [111] Similarly, a principle of autonomy regulated the journal: autonomy of the editors in relation to the administration and autonomy of the contributors in regard to each other. This was all due to the perversity of paradox: following successive reshufflings in the aftermath of the election of *normalien* Blum's Popular Front government and following the death of Arthème Fayard, the Librairie Fayard transferred the title of *JSP* to its editors. This transfer resulted in a form of cooperative, which was dubbed by its members "our friendly 'soviet.'" [112]

What characterizes *JSP* characterizes the ENS: uniqueness. Just as the reality of the ENS might well reside in the tensions surrounding its "normality," that is, the implicit tension between "*normale*" and "*supérieure*," *JSP* refused to be a journal "like any other." Both *JSP* and the ENS are constituted in that discontinuity or breach between the exception and the rule. "In a capitalist country, presided over by a socialist government, the only organ of the press directed by a 'soviet' happened to be, paradoxically, a far right weekly . . ." [113] And the collective around *JSP* celebrated this perversity. "It's the 'team,' the 'band,' the 'gang,' the 'soviet,' as they liked to call themselves. It's *Je Suis Partout*." [114] This journal followed a principle of no internal constraints: Each of its young authors could write exactly what pleased them. All important decisions were made together in informal meetings.

It should be clear that the members of this *"bande"* are united by a bond other than that of journalistic professionalism. Just as we have seen that the ENS is not just any school but a "family," secret society, and closed shop, so too *JSP* celebrates the only tie that binds: friendship. Massis finds that only friendship ties him to Brasillach. [115] The journal creates rituals of friendship akin to those of Ulm: joyous dinners are organized by Laubreau which, like the celebratory excesses of the *canular*, end in song. [116] Friendship is also cemented by the many trips to attend conferences: Spain, Germany, Belgium; these diverse travel destinations don't disperse the *JSP* intimacy, rather they function as we have seen with their *normalien* analogue, the Bourses Lavisse, to create a community. [117] One does not talk of political positions or ideological or philosophical difference when speaking of *JSP*, as we have seen in the case of the ENS ("where differences such as communism, existentialism . . . are only first names"); one speaks of a community of temperament.[118] And this temperament is one that is exempt from any type of authoritarianism. Even when Brasillach is made editor-in-chief, he serves as a technical figurehead only; the political or ideological line of the journal doesn't change. Indeed, the spirit of the *équipe* is so strong that no real *maître* can emerge. "No member of the team, no outside personality is followed as a true '*Maître.*' "[119] We have seen in Chapter 4 the reluctance of many rightist *normaliens* to invoke a *maître*.[120] A figurehead such as Gaxotte may be a rallying point so that the team isn't threatened by the decomposition of heterodoxy, but he is not a commanding leader, either *maître* or *chef*. Moreover, what Brasillach writes of Gaxotte could be easily said of the sentiments of *anciens élèves* toward their school as well: "This unity between such diverse temperaments, such diverse origins could not exist without the admiration and . . . affection that we had for Pierre Gaxotte."[121]

But *JSP* shares other affinities with the Ecole Normale besides notions of friendship and team playing. Gaxotte and Giraudoux share an indispensible *normalien* style and language, in addition to a common notion of elites. Gaxotte evinces a contempt for the masses that we have seen in an earlier chapter on language and authority was typical. Gaxotte also retained a definite *normalien* allure, which is remembered by Fayard: "Gaxotte's style is of a Lorraine already dampened by nearby Champagne, softened by Paris. He kept the taste of pranks and a verbal agility from the rue d'Ulm which blossomed easily in *Je Suis Partout* where it found its polemical outlet."[122] Giraudoux also personified the beautiful language and intellectual qualities deemed rightist but that could be more accurately described as *normalien*.

It would appear that much of the attraction of *JSP* for the *normaliens* in our sample can be interpreted in light of shared institutional values: friendship, team spirit, language, style. One might say that the breakdown of the *JSP équipe* has an analogous explanation. Brasillach was to break off from the more rabid "ultras" of the PPF. Again, it would be erroneous to situate this split around a coherent political difference. Rather, this rift assumes meaning only in reference to the notion of the *équipe*. For the logic of the *équipe*, band, gang, or soviet is necessarily disrupted by the follow-the-leader sentiments involved in adherence to Doriot's PPF. Doriot seduces as a leader ("*chef*"), and the structure of this relation transforms *camaraderie*. In stubbornly resisting the appeals of the ultras of the PPF, Brasillach defends the principles of *normalien* camaraderie—as we will see in our next chapter, to the death.

One could possibly distinguish among this variety of literary and

The Ecole Normale Supérieure and the Scene of Writing

political praxes in relation to adherence to a part of the *normalien* legacy. What would separate Brasillach from *normalien* collaborationists such as Gillouin or technocrats such as Pucheu is this refusal of a *maître:* either Pétain (Gillouin as *"l'homme du Maréchal"*) or Doriot (in the case of Pucheu). Even Thierry Maulnier's swing toward a variant of Mounier's personalism can be similarly explained with reference to the *normalien* canon and its valuation of aristocratic reflection. What is fascinating is the inexplicability of political alignment in relation to any clearly defined binaries or typology, yet at the same time all difference, all variation can be recuperated in line with *normalien* myths and institutionalized discourse. Certain generalizations can be made; there are salient generational differences and ideological divergences between *L'Oeuvre* and Déat's radical socialist origins on the one hand, and the marginal youth journals around the Action Française and Brasillach's nascent internationalist fascism in the pages of *Je Suis Partout* on the other. Yet both positions can themselves be "normalized": around the love of friendship and the love for the word. Both Brasillach and Déat are men of words and underline the inextricable relation between politics and writing: "Success will come to movements which will demolish the Bastille after having done all the work of the Encyclopedists or seize the Winter Palace after having written *Capital*." [123]

7 THE POSTWAR TRIALS

WORDS AND DEEDS

> *Where an oeuvre had the duty of creating immortality, it now attains the right to kill, to become the murderer of its own author.*
> —M. Foucault, "What Is an Author?"

> *Pierre Rivière was the subject of the memoir in a dual sense: It was he who remembered, remorselessly remembered it all, and it was he whose memoir summoned the crime . . . He contrived the engineering of the narrative/murder as both projectile and target, and he was propelled by the working of the mechanism into the real murder . . . he was the author of it all in a dual sense:* author of the crime and author of the text . . . *Rivière, there is little doubt, accomplished his crime at the level of a certain discursive practice . . .* in the inextricable unity of his parricide and his text he really played the game of law . . .
> —M. Foucault, *I, Pierre Rivière, having slaughtered my mother, my sister, and my brother . . .*

The *normalien* Michel Foucault was not the only one to treat the authors of texts as the authors of crimes.[1] For Robert Brasillach, like Pierre Rivière, (the eighteenth-century parricide so admirably described by Foucault) was also doubly subject to his sentence: one, written by him, the other imposed by the courts in the postwar purge trials of intellectuals. Indeed, it is only in reference to these two sentences that a logic of the postwar trials unfolds. In the trial (and execution) of exceptional *normalien* Brasillach, one witnesses the rule of law and discourse, a meeting of a literary signature and legal authority. And the confrontation between this signature and law has been misunderstood by the conventional wisdom concerning political trials. For the question of Brasillach's guilt or innocence does not turn on the traditional relationship between intentionality, his text, and his deed. In other words: "The text did not express a desire, which was then expressed in action. Desire, text and action were indissolubly linked because they were shaped, made possible, therefore, in a sense, *produced* by a particular discursive practice . . ."[2]

We will name this discursive practice the Ecole Normale Supérieure. We might argue that Robert Brasillach died because he was a *normalien*, because the Ecole Normale shaped his literary sentence as much as we have seen it shape his journalistic praxis around the journal *Je Suis Partout* (which formed the basis of his indictment and ultimate juridical sentence). We will see how Brasillach's *normalien* status continually erupts in the juridical process. It is placed at the head of his indictment and forms the structure of his defense as well. "He ran his defense like an *orale* for the *concours*," it was noted by all trial commentators. It also serves as the basis for appeal; letters from *normalien* cohorts invoke the *normalien* fraternity as a reason for clemency. It disrupts the trial of *turne*-mate Claude Jamet as well. Jamet is continually asked (by prison guards and bailiffs) if he really knows Brasillach ("there are such beautiful passages in *Notre Avant Guerre, n'est-ce pas?*"),[3] and Jamet's trial, it can be argued, was a victory of university methods over university discourse.[4]

We will see how clearly the discourse of the ENS emerges in the logic of the postwar trial sentencing. Robert Brasillach's and Claude Jamet's trials also read as a commentary on the educational system itself. Both trials are noteworthy in that they are trials of purely literary collaboration; neither Brasillach nor Jamet joined a political party. Moreover, we will see that opportunism plays a key role in the logic of the sentencing. Opportunism actually helps to reduce a sentence. Jamet's literary collaboration motivated by his desire to finally get his name in print is treated more leniently—by mere exclusion from the teaching profession—whereas Brasillach's unmotivated literary collaboration wins him a death sentence.

Indeed, I would be so bold as to say that those liberal commentators who bemoan a nation that can kill one of its poets miss the point. They are subject to a naive conception of the "author function"; authors are, for them, creative subjects who through divine inspiration produce a form of writing that society dubs an "oeuvre." Rather, we should view the author as a victim of his writing which is a social product of an institutional practice—in this case the Ecole Normale. Let us therefore displace the question of how France could kill its poets/authors and ask in its place how it could (and why it must) kill its *normaliens*? In such a reading one returns to the question of the educational process as a ritualization of speech which inaugurated our examination of the

Ecole Normale, and as such the trial of Brasillach is more of a summation than an aberration. For the postwar trials revealed in striking clarity the political importance of the bearers of the word, more important than the numbers of votes received by the parties affiliated with the journals they wrote for. And the strategic importance of the ENS as licensee and regulator of the university of discourse has been demonstrated.

Foucault sees an educational system as a "ritualization of speech, a means of qualifying speaking subjects, the constitution of a doctrinal group, however diffuse, a distribution and appropriation of discourse."[5] Moreover, society controls, regulates, redistributes, organizes, and selects a number of procedures which "produce" discourse as much as it protects discourse and the institutional arrangements that are its supports.[6] The trials serve as both a judgment on and protection of an educational system that ritualizes speech, which is why Brasillach's sentence could not be commuted. The role is analogous to that of the bourgeoisie in Marx's *Eighteenth Brumaire:* "that in order to save its purse it must forfeit the crown."[7] To insure its status, the Ecole Normale had to sacrifice Brasillach. This pattern emerges only when read against other trials of intellectuals of the right, and so we will examine the trials and legal underpinnings of the postwar sentencing to see how far this play between the literary and the juridical sentence will take us in interpreting a pattern that has been deemed arbitrary by American interpreters (Paxton) or unjust by contemporaneous French ones (Camus, Beauvoir), or left essentially uninterpreted (Lottman, Assouline) or unproblematized (Ory and Sirinelli) in recent historical treatments.

The Liberation and postwar trial period was marked by a violence of separations. Collaborationist writers and professionals were separated from noncollaborationists. The new France in the making separated itself from its recent Vichy past while publishers and publishing houses were separated (at least temporarily) from their assets. Yet at the same time, the judicial machinery which was the political agent of the separation radically questioned an even more solidly entrenched separation of words and deeds. For what made the French purge trials at all noteworthy as more than yet another variant of the phenomenon well described by Otto Kirchheimer[8] as the successor trial was the insistence that words were deeds and should be so tried. We will see a pattern of trial sentencing emerge that is not as arbitrary as it is tied to a notion of textuality and literary signature.

Moreover the notion of separation itself played a double-edged role in the trials. On the one hand, the model defense posited a continuity of deeply held beliefs during precisely those periods France so eagerly sought to separate—the *avant-guerre* and collaborationist Vichy—yet at the same time stressed the necessity of separating words from political action. It is a somewhat fitting irony that most commentators on the postwar purge trials have made a parallel gesture in which the words or text of the trial have been separated from their effects (i.e., sentences, outcomes). But if the postwar trials were not wholly successful in treating words as deeds, later interpreters' completely successful separation has indeed obscured the intellectual challenges posed by the trials. For there are three basic ways to view the postwar trials of French intellectuals: as a typical successor trial, as a horse race, or as a circulation of signatures.

Most fundamentally, the French postwar trials represent a variant of the trial by fiat of the successor regime delineated by Kirchheimer. A main difference between the French trials and the Nuremberg trials (or indeed other political trials such as the Eichmann trial) is that the protagonists of the courtroom drama are in this case intellectuals. Therefore, it should not come as a surprise to the reader of trial transcripts that the French trials will evoke the familiar problems of any trial in the court of the victors, namely the problem of retrospective justice, of a prejudicial court, and the argumentation of *tu quoque* and justifications of binding orders (or some variant, i.e., necessity).[9] These similarities with the juridical problems posed by other successor trials accompany a pattern of sentencing the appears extremely arbitrary and teaches a concomitantly ambivalent political lesson.

Just Writing

> *Le mot d'épuration était déjà assez penible en lui-même. La chose est devenue odieuse.*
> —Camus, *Combat*, 30 août 1945

Paxton tells us that not all of Vichy was purged with equal severity: "The patterns of leadership survival and discontinuity are in themselves a revealing lineament. Experts, businessmen, and bureaucrats survived almost intact; intellectuals and propagandists were much more heavily purged." Indeed "the fate of overtly fascist intellectuals and party leaders in occupied parts was even more final. Men of public platform, *their words* condemned them to suffer at the liberation."[10] De Gaulle told Justice Minister Teitgen that there were two categories who deserved no pity or commutation of a death sentence: army officers and talented writers.[11]

The apparent irony of the situation is best summarized (and dismissed) by Simone de Beauvoir. To many French intellectuals of the period, not only was unevenness of sanction not surprising, it could not even be used as an argument for the unfairness of the trials. As Beauvoir's reaction may well mark an extreme, intransigent position, I will quote from her journal at length:

> People have condemned the weeding out of collaborationists for dealing more severely with those who talked approvingly about the Atlantic wall than with those who built it. To me, it seems utterly unjust that economic collaboration should have been passed over, *but not* that Hitler's propagandists in this country should have been so severely dealt with. By trade, by vocation, I attach enormous importance to words . . . there are words as murderous as gas chambers . . .[12]

Camus may mark a more moderate stance—he refuses theoretically Mauriac's stand of solidarity with collaboration authors yet sentimentally signs petitions in the end.[13] He cites the iniquity that the same court that sentenced Albertini, a recruiter for the LVF, to five years of forced labor condemned *normalien* pacifist André Guérin, literary chronicler for *L'Oeuvre* during the war, to death. To illustrate the same point, one of Drumont's men, Gendriot, receives a sentence of four years' forced labor for giving his name to *Au Pilori*, while the other editors of that journal as well as its founder weren't even indicted. Yet this preliminary outline of prejudicial sanctioning serves to underscore the point that trials of intellectuals were both juridical and symbolic acts.

Bernard Vosges, writing in a fifties reconstruction of the trials, stresses the ideological priority of intellectuals, both during Vichy and during the trials. "The intellectuals were thus flattered as priests denouncing the new sacrileges; the trials of intellectuals were particularly useful because they evoked the sphere where it was most urgent to establish boundaries." (This metaphor of reformation—clerical or secular—was given a nationalistic twist in *Figaro* and a revolutionary one in *Combat*.)[14] Indeed, two aspects of the legislation itself share a peculiar affinity with this symbolic nature of the trials. All trial legislation rested on the postulate of a *false* signature: "The armistice, signed by Pétain, was signed by a usurper and was, as such, not endorsed [non avenu]."[15] We will later see a curious relationship between the importance of the signature and hence authority (or responsibility) in determinations of guilt.

On philosophic levels as well, we witness an interesting juridical shift from indictment for precise crimes to a vaguer notion of guilt. The ordinance of August 26, 1944, instituted retroactively a "crime contraventionel inédit *l'indignité nationale*," and its sanction, *"la dégradation nationale."* Its justification is that criminal activity under the Occupation could not always come under the existing strict legal codes: "Criminal activity of enemy collaboration did not always take on the appearance of individual facts susceptible of review under a precise penal qualification in the terms of a juridical rule subject to strict legal interpretation." One could be convicted of *l'indignité nationale* "even without breaking any existing law!" This new concept thus turns culpability into ontology, not legal fact. The legal shift from what one did to what one is will prove crucial in the trials of intellectuals.[16]

Indignité nationale, literally "unworthiness," denotes a state of fact rather than a crime. It accompanies all verdicts and was punished by a range of penalties which include stripping of professional status and civil rights. *Indignité nationale*, it should be noted, was a new concept, not a new sanction in legal practice. It differed from the existing collaboration which was a form of intelligence with the enemy: "In this way persons who had not committed a definable crime, but who had supported collaborationist movements, for example, would not have to be tried for the more serious crime of collusion with the enemy." This apparent leniency, however, does not obfuscate the fact that this was a retroactive penalty. This retroactivity was tolerated as the penalty was deemed less serious than that for intelligence with the enemy and was thus beneficial to the defendant.[17]

The June 22, 1944, ordinance required periodicals appearing during the Occupation with occupied authority to be suspended and placed under judiciary confinement. The September 30, 1944, ordinance forbade publication of all journals created after June 24, 1940, and ones that didn't stop after the armistice. Paxton underlines this point: in law, things went back to the never-never land of before midnight on June 16, 1940.[18] These laws paved the way for a more interesting turn. The May 5, 1945, ordinance now instituted proceedings against *"personnes morales"* (artificial persons) and *"personnes physiques"* (individuals). People were declared not guilty, and one invented an anonymous culpability of *things*—desks, machines, wastepaper baskets—"Thus . . . no journal could escape from the repressive apparatus."[19] We witness a combination of extreme legal centralization of all enterprises of writing during the *épuration* along with tortuous categorizing. This legislation enabled Grasset to receive a less severe sentence than his publishing house.[20] As a result of the May 5 ordinance there were 538 proceedings against the press in three years. Out of these, 115 journals were totally confiscated and 51 partially. This incredible arbitrariness and division of the publishing house is evinced in the Lyon court confiscation of 50 percent of a journal whose director was shot at the Liberation, yet the same court confiscated totally another journal whose directors were free from the least personal sanction. This reaches an extreme in the case of René Taittinger, owner of three journals: one journal is acquitted, one merits partial confiscation, while the other journal merits total confiscation![21] The law of March 21, 1946, completes this process by giving goods of former journals to the state. Robert Aron concurs in the view that the juridical formulations of 1944–46 were extremely severe: "Rarely have such authoritarian provisions been instituted by a regime founded under the sign of liberty."[22] It was not sufficient to suspend journals; their disappearance had to be ensured. We witness a statement at a banquet for the *Federation Nationale de la Presse:* "it was necessary that they be buried in the communal grave of our national disgraces."[23]

And if the courts took care of the machinery of the publishing houses—their assets and material goods—intellectuals contributed in this erasure by various blacklists. In September 1945, the Comité National d'Ecrivains published its first blacklist, citing among others Brasillach, Benoist Méchin, Pierre Béarn, Abel Bonnard, Georges Blond, Henri Bordeaux, Henri Béraud, Céline, Alphonse de Chateaubriant, Jacques Chardonne, Drieu, André Demaison, André Fraigneau, Paul Fort, Fabre Luce, Giono, Marcel Jouhandeau, Bernard Grasset, Sacha Guitry, La Varende, Maurras, Montherlant, Paul Morand. On October 20, Pierre Andreu, Edmund Jaloux, Henri Massis, and André Salmon, among others, were added. Not only writers but artists were boycotted: Othon Friesz, Maillol, Oudot, Vlaminck, Despiau, Dunoyer de Segonzac, Derain. And then there are some names who are later rehabilitated: Morand, Paul Fort, Bordeaux.[24]

The role of *Combat* can not be underestimated. The 100,000 copies distributed between five and six o'clock within the perimeter of the *grands boulevards,* the Seine, Opéra, and Réaumur Sébastopol sold out in one and one-half hours. Aron sees the first blacklists as figurative dynamite ("dix tonnes de dynamite devaient faire sauter tout le quartier du Luxembourg").[25] Somewhat more irreverently, the pundit Jean Galtier Boissière saw the blacklists as a sort of society column in which the names of prominent persons were daily displayed. And people did turn to *Figaro's* daily lists under the subheading: arrests and purging.[26]

The *épuration* created divisions among the resistants. If there was concurrence of opinion at all, it was a general dissatisfaction with the way it was conducted. Two extremes were Mauriac (and Paulhan—

although, ironically, he helped to create the blacklists)[27] and communist resisters who demanded harsh sentencing. Camus, in *Combat*, argued for a middle ground. Simone de Beauvoir concurs with Camus in this recognition of the futility of vengeance, yet "certain men have no place in the world we are trying to build."[28] If Beauvoir approved the CNE decision and did not want to see her name alongside names of those who had urged the death of resistants and Jews, Camus posed the problem in terms of loyalty: loyalty to the families of those denounced and killed, loyalty to a system of beliefs. Beauvoir's intransigence can be seen in her refusal to sign Brasillach's petition. "The signers declared that as writers they show solidarity with him and ask for mercy from the court."[29] In no way did Beauvoir feel solidarity with Brasillach. But the blacklists of forbidden signatures later evoked a protest of countersignatures—in petitions for clemency for convicted writers. Agitation reached an extreme in Paris, especially before Brasillach's execution, after which Luchaire was the only journalist not to escape execution. (Cousteau and Rebatet of *Je Suis Partout* escaped execution in this way.)

If any banal generalizations can be made from this first cursory glance at the trials they are: (1) Severity was greatest in the early period (1944–45). There is interesting corroborative evidence in Fresnes prison; meant to be a model prison of one prisoner per cell, by winter 1944/45 it numbered three, four, and five per cell:[30] (2) Acquittals were more common in the provinces than in Paris: (3) Financial backers in general fared better than authors. We see a slight difference in sentencing by age in relative but not absolute terms. After all, a sentence of three years for an octogenarian can not be underestimated. Affiliation with elite institutions such as the Académie Française didn't affect the severity of sanction although in the case of Maurras his chair was filled only after his death. Other chairs left vacant were reelected immediately (including those of Abel Bonnard and Abel Hermant, inspiring satirists to wonder, With such Abels, who were the Cains?)[31]

We now turn from a diachronic analysis of the trials (i.e., evolution of enabling legislation, preliminary statistics) to a more synchronic analysis. Normative criteria may be established by the following caricature of a limit case: journalistic direction of a totally pro-German line. Few cases were, alas, this clear; we can expect a gray area extending from articles defending Germany, through articles sharing a German "point of view," collaboration with German authorized journals, direction of an institution that Germans visited (e.g., the Opéra), books liked by Germans, travel to Germany, attendance at musical evenings at the German Institute, friendships with Germans, to the "simple continuation of one's job." We will later see how most of these criteria were met in the case of Céline; however, it can be argued that the biggest factor in Céline's light sentence was that he waited it out before returning to France.

The case of Céline marks a certain extreme which will prove crucial for later literary history. The goal of revisionist literary history has been to admit active political participation of collaborationist intellectuals while at the same time stressing the point that the only "real" literature produced during the Occupation was Resistance poetry. In such a way, all collaborationist authors are seen to be little more than literary marginals. At the same time, something must be done to recuperate the image of Céline who resists the caricature of footnote in literary history.[32]

The Céline affair will thus turn on the separation of textuality from literary activity. For, it can be coherently argued from the standpoint of literary activity, Céline didn't collaborate; he refused membership in the European Circle, and his lack of significant participation in radio and journalism equaled his previously violent antirepublicanism. Moreover, he didn't write anything anti-Semitic after 1937, and with the arrival of the Germans he completely lost interest in this theme. He never put his foot in the German Embassy or belonged to French-German organizations. Nor was he friends with Brinon or among the artists invited to Germany by Goebbels, nor was he awarded any special honors by Germany. His description of Abetz, too, does not read like a billet doux: "a scourge of mediocrity, a plaster of horrible vanity, a clown for the cacaclysm . . . there was only, in my opinion, one other person as disastrous as Abetz: Suzanne Abetz, his wife." Céline neither joined nor advocated the PPF, was not friends with Doriot, and surprisingly was not anti-Resistance.[33] It becomes quite plausible to consider his claim "I was probably the only French writer of reknown to remain strictly, jealously, fiercely a writer and nothing else with no compromises." Yet it could also be argued that *Bagatelles* and reeditions of *Ecole* expounded a dangerous mixture of anarchism and anti-Semitism which could give "valuable aid to the occupation by action, by spoken word, or through writing."

Bernard Payr, head of the Nazi "literature" office, expresses the ambivalence of the German authorities towards Céline. Though he noted that Céline's targets (Freemasons, communists, Jews) were also enemies of the Reich, he criticized Céline's "savage, filthy slang" and "brutal obscenities." Céline's pamphlet *Les Beaux Draps* was "made up of exclamatory prose and snippets of sentences adding up to hysterical outcries that cancel out the author's good intents."[34] So much for "correct racial notions"! However, Céline received only a minor sentence in absentia: seven years prison, the confiscation of goods, and *indignité nationale*. Literary activity did prove a critical element in determinations of guilt.

It should also be noted that the purge of intellectuals, writers, and publishers was not confined to the metropolis. One of Dominique Sordet's Interfrance journals, *Dépêche Algérienne*, its editor-in-chief, Pierre Louis Ganne, and its founders, MM. Robe and Perrier, were tried under the law of May 11, 1946.[35] This trial is noteworthy in that it applied the law directly to Algeria and presented one of the most transparent variants of the double-game rationale so common in political trials. The *Dépêche Algérienne* gave every appearance of being a collaborationist newspaper par excellence. It was argued that this was merely to deceive the enemy and dissuade it from occupying a North Africa apparently devoted to Vichy. However, another of their evening newspapers—*Dernières Nouvelles*, with the same editors and directors —showed their resistance spirit. The "double game," alas, did not work as Germany read only the *Dépêche Algérienne*; *Dernières Nouvelles* could have been used to trick the allies. The real point behind the *Dernières Nouvelles* was M. Robe's financial profit (726,436 francs net benefit in 1940). Ganne (Abetz's friend and luncheon companion at *Propaganda Abteilung*) proved maladroit at this double-game rationale, which we will see in many guises—Luchaire invoked an equally implausible justification, and Maurras romanticized and displaced his version onto a rewriting of the tale of Solomon. The strategy so well evolved by Arendt's Nazi inner migrant who had to appear outwardly even more like Nazis than Nazis in order to keep their secrets was just not believed in the presence of so much corroborating literary activity.[36] We will later see how the inner migrant or double game (or the analogue, "mitigated harms") rationale is not merely opportunistic but curiously reinvents the word/deed, thought/action, essence/ appearance separation at the heart of the trials.

The Robe and Perrier and Ganne trials also serve to underline the need for trials of literary institutions or networks—e.g., the need for a trial of Dominique Sordet's *Interfrance*.[37] The Affaire Grasset adumbrates some of these issues and is not as bankrupt ideologically as that of Robe and Perrier. The principle in this trial of a publishing house and an activist publisher was that the mere functioning of a publishing house established an agreement with the enemy. More specifically, Grasset's memo of July 13, 1940, expresses an attempt to unify "la chose écrite en France."[38] The trial rested on evidence in Grasset's correspondence: his letters to German author Sieburg and to Alphonse de Chateaubriant. In his correspondence he stressed the necessity for an agreement of "l'esprit" along with a frank acceptance of political censorship by the occupying powers.

If Grasset's collaboration was unambiguous, his correspondence also had an "all or nothing" quality about it; Grasset's letters "were almost always unfair, not because he lacked judgment, but out of a kind of perversity." Grasset's letter to Goebbels was noted in his trial. After apologizing for his inability to attend the Weimar conference due to health reasons (and sending André Fraigneau in his place), Grasset writes: "What happiness it is for me to be your publisher, and all the hope we base upon an ever closer Franco-German intellectual collaboration."[39] But these principles did not merely remain in his private correspondence—he also sent his opinions to be published in *Candide*. Grasset, as a journalist, wrote for Déat's *L'Oeuvre*, Doriot's *Cri du Peuple*, *Paris-Soir*, and *France au Travail*. His collected journalistic oeuvre was republished in his *A la Recherche de la France* series and contained *éloges* for Hitler, pro-German sentiments, appeals to remain deaf to Radio Londres and for France to merit the respect of its occupiers. If there are any doubts about the ideological purport of his *A la Recherche* series,[40] one can merely glance at the other titles, which read like a collaborationist hit parade: Drieu, Doriot, Suarez, Pierre Daye, Jacques Chardonne. (And *hors série:* Georges Blond, Lesca, and Sieburg). Grasset published Goebbels' "Du Kayserhof à la Chancellerie" and desired a collaborationist policy that was not only literary but economic. Yet with all this activity, Grasset received a minor sentence. This may be due to the late date of his trial or, one wonders, to the fact that he was a publisher-activist and not an intellectual-writer. Publishers were seen as businessmen and punished less severely than writers and journalists.

If Grasset marks an extreme position of an activist publisher, our next group of writers are more clearly literary ideologues. Paul Chack and Georges Suarez were among the first journalist-intellectuals to be tried and executed. In many ways they are opposite figures. Aron concurs in the view that Suarez was an unproblematical opportunist while Chack raises the more ponderous ideological questions of finding the logical extension of his anti-British beliefs in the expression of beliefs which brand him, equally, a traitor. He is thus a tragic figure: "Thus his activity as a writer, like that of many others, linked bygone days (when they conducted dreadful careers) and a tragic future (when they would die)."[41] Chack was executed on January 9, 1945, two months after Suarez (November 5, 1944).

One begins to see a pattern unfold, so well stated by Béraud as "everything against ideas, nothing against money."[42] This theme of *"mort pour ses idées"* will haunt our next group of intellectuals.[43] Unlike publisher-activists, these intellectuals were tried for their words, and the only marginal questions posed were if there was also economic gain.

Henri Béraud was tried on article 75 (intelligence with the enemy) on the basis of his articles for *Gringoire*. His continual hatred of parliamentary democracy, Freemasons, the English, and the Russian army matched an equally passionate hatred of de Gaulle and dissident French anticollaborationist behavior and rhetoric. Yet if the Germans had extended their hand, he would have spit on it.[44] The case of Béraud does have the makings of a literary potboiler—why does a man of letters, winner of the Goncourt Prize (1921), and anti-Dreyfusard of the left become the leading right-wing polemicist in 1934? Is Béraud the archetypical loser: always earning more money with his novels (but Germany seizes all his goods in February 1941); yet his articles contributed largely to the financial success of *Gringoire* (a success that he recognizes is due to the ideological consonance of *Gringoire* for the French public); blamed for the campaign against Salengro (when it was the director of *Gringoire* who was responsible); accused of playing Germany's game (yet never making it to the big time with Luchaire and his circle). In short, he was accused of doing what he had been doing for the past twenty years. In a literary twist, no defense witnesses were called and the defense, as also the prosecution, rested on texts—two letters: one from M. Tisserant citing a 1920 text to prove that Béraud's Anglophobia was prior to his entrance to *Gringoire* and prior to the war; the other testifying to Béraud's help in supporting Italian exiles.

Before the end of the Affaire Béraud, the Dreyfus Affair will be replayed—false evidence is submitted before the eyes of the jury without the defense's being warned. If Maurras' dictum was "It's the revenge of Dreyfus," Béraud's was the rewrite ("le procès Dreyfus, lui, a été revisé").[45] And, as poetic justice in this hard-luck story where the protagonist never gains, Béraud, not wanting to be pardoned by de Gaulle, finally is. And although he had proved his innocence to both Mauriac and Camus[46] in the debates at the trial, his end was appropriate to the potboiler: hemiplegic, he died in prison after making *pochettes* (small purses) for 21 francs a month.

Lucien Combelle, director of the *Révolution Nationale*, secretary at various times to both Drieu and André Gide, was, like Béraud, an intellectual seen to "deceive himself with conviction."[47] Cited also for his articles in *Gerbe*, his attendance at the Franco-German Institute (along with his friends Drieu, Montherlant, Chardonne, and Thérive), and his visits to Germany, he was indicted for intelligence with the enemy. Although the death penalty was demanded, Combelle received a light sentence of fifteen years of forced work, because of "attenuating circumstances." One wonders if this leniency was a direct result of Gide's intervention by letter in which he stated that although they disagreed on everything, "I have nothing but the highest regard for him."[48]

Pierre Antoine Cousteau, too, was seen to be a heretic but not a traitor. His trial was subsumed under the trial of *Je Suis Partout*, since the team spirit (*"l'équipe"*) was seen to reign there ("There were no specialists among the editors, the most complete agreement reigned on political matters!").[49] The journal itself came before the court as a moral entity. Because Alain Laubreau, Charles Lesca, and Henri Poulain had fled they were condemned in absentia, and the trial comprised only Cousteau, Rebatet, and Claude Jeantet.[50] It could be clearly established that the extreme positions of *JSP* had been held long before the war and were not born with the Occupation. If the editors wished "a short and disastrous war," it was because that was "the only hope for France." This was, in fact, the second trial for the journal *JSP*. It had been tried in June 1940 for antinationalism and later allowed to appear in the occupied zone, where it continued until the last days of the Occupation. Its diffusion during the war years was 300,000 copies compared with 40,000 copies in 1939.[51]

Although it was the journal as a whole that was tried, the judge did distinguish between those who were in agreement with the political line and those who weren't. The court was therefore totally without pity for Rebatet; his many trips to Germany, his articles in favor of the Waffen SS, his favorable comparison of Hitler's execution of Lieutenants ("the night of the long knives") in a June 30, 1934, article with the epic vengeance of the *Tetralogue*, and his boasts that he was completely without "one drop of democratic blood" earned him a death sentence. For at the same time that *JSP* appeared to present an ideological united front, there were notable divergences. Aron cites the example of an economics editor who refused to praise the economic achievements of the Third Reich. Similarly, the court was more lenient with Cousteau, who (although a member of the Milice!) refused to publish in the German *Trait-d'Union*. Claude Jeantet, also, was absolved of his political affiliation with the PPF and Doriot, and of his service as editor-in-chief of the *Petit Parisien* because his articles did not reflect the vehement antidemocraticism of Rebatet.[52] A preliminary pattern does seem to emerge from the accounts of the trials and sentencing. It is that the literary product (signed articles) and institutional literary activity were seen as more significant than party membership or political affiliations.

We will now turn to four model political trials. Luchaire and Brasillach mark two extremes of the postwar purge trials of intellectuals. Brasillach and Jamet provide a *normalien* constrast, while Maurras's trial, albeit exceptional, may again be an exception that proves a rule.

If, as Kirchheimer states, the supreme rule of a political defense is the propagation of the doctrine, rather than the fate of the individual defendant, the trial of Robert Brasillach was a political trial par excellence.[53] Robert Brasillach's trial marks the extreme of intellectual integrity, elegant in its simplicity. "An alumn of the Ecole Normale Supérieure" (mentioned first in the indictment), he ran his defense as an oral exam (*orale de concours*).[54] Indeed, we see an affinity with Socrates' model lesson in the *Apology*. Again one wonders (with Kirchheimer) if the difference between a normal political defense and a nonpolitical one is that the order of priority is not that of obtaining a favorable court decision. In such a way, Brasillach recalls the Socrates of the *Crito*. However, this is not an attempt to romanticize the trial of Brasillach (an attempt almost canonical in the literature and abetted by the poems he wrote in Fresnes).[55] Brasillach's case is inextricably linked with the refrain "killed for his ideas,"[56] although one will see that the "*idées*" expressed in *JSP* had the very practical effect of denouncing Jews and resistants, and of advocating the introduction of the yellow star in France.

Whether one views Brasillach as a martyr or a criminal, one can agree with Aron on the classicism of his trial. The formal classicism of this trial of one of Racine's admirers allows fascist ideology to stand out in stark relief. No witnesses are called, nor are there extraneous appeals to those whom he has saved. "He wished to be judged on his ideas alone."[57] Brasillach's trial thus immediately underlines Arendt's analysis of the show trial: "A trial resembles a play in that both begin with the doer, not with the victim. A show trial needs even more urgently than an ordinary trial a limited and well-defined outline of what was done and how it was done. In the centre of the trial can be only the one who did—in this respect, he is like the hero in the play."[58] In the case of Brasillach, the show lasted for five hours—it began at 1 P.M. and at 6 P.M. he was condemned to death.

As befitting a "tragedy," the charge itself is solemn—Brasillach is tried on article 75, grand treason. It was obvious from the start that this was not a case of financial opportunism. *JSP* merely covered its costs before the war, and Brasillach's style of living was demonstrably modest and austere. He lived in a humble apartment at 5 rue Rataud, not far from the ENS, which he shared with his sister and brother-in-law, Maurice Bardèche. He never belonged to a political party. Even when he was on the staff of *Action Française* he was a purely literary collaborator. He always was reluctant to go beyond literary/textual participation to full activist political collaboration. This reluctance foreshadowed the later split in *JSP* between Robert Brasillach and the ultras—those with PPF or Milice membership who desired extremely active contact with Germany. If there was a consistency in Brasillach's lack of political activism, there was also a formal consistency in the level of his language—his was the language of adolescence (*chants de jeunesse*) expounding the same *avant-guerre* principles of friendship and communion of spirit going back to his days at Louis-le-Grand and ENS.[59]

His questionable activities were all of literary nature: he did attend the German Institute (along with Gallimard, Duhamel, and Giraudoux). Similarly, he did attend the Weimar Conference along with other French intellectuals (e.g., Abel Bonnard). Although editor of the *Rive Gauche* series, he argued that plenty of noncollaborationist works were sold, including those of Aragon and Triolet displayed prominently in the window. Yet the indictment of M. Reboul stated the link between literariness and political action more boldly: "Powerful prestige in a country such as ours so rich in such distinctions of this order has always placed uppermost the merits of the pen."[60] Although there is something naive in condemning intellectual treason as worse than economic or moral opportunism as it is a "sin born of pride,"[61] what does become painfully clear is the immediate passage from "pure letters" to the need for an audience. M. Reboul states that "he needed an audience, a public space, a political influence, and he was willing to do anything to conquer them." Reboul cites a letter of Cousteau, where Cousteau admits that without *JSP*, "we would just have been a small group of writers." The potential was multiplied by *JSP* and by the presence of Brasillach, who did have a literary reputation and following.

If the trials of literary collaborators were judgments of literary signatures, the case of Claude Jamet was perverse. He was first accused of being the director of the Rive Gauche bookstore due to a confusion of names with that of another Jamet—Henri. Jamet's trial bears many similarities to that of fellow *normalien* Brasillach. Like Brasillach, he chooses to defend himself and not to run his trial as a referendum on pacifism, Munich, or the Spanish Civil War. Jamet is sentenced not for isolated articles he wrote, such as "Bombing Parties" or "L'Heure *H*" but for his literary collaboration in the journal *Germinal* as late as 1944. "But don't you see, however, that precisely from the fact that you were able to write these articles, with your talent, that you brought them intellectual and moral support." [62] If his indictment is based on his writing talent, his defense will include those responsible for this talent: his *maître*, Alain, will write a letter in his behalf.

The ENS intruded in his trial in yet more subtle ways. His trial became the perfect example of Lanson's method of *explication de texte* (the target of *normalien* Peguy's wrath in *Argent Suite*). Jamet recounts: "But he [the prosecutor] also read my books, he had two of them in hand, and to my citations, he opposed other, well chosen ones. He had everything exhaustively researched and catalogued—oh, virtue of university methods. His 'homework' adhered equally to an indictment and a Sorbonne seminar. *He put all my crimes on index cards!* And I had to explain myself, defend myself, sentence by sentence." [63]

But the prosecutor was not the only one who did homework. Jamet prepared a little composition for his defense attorney, and he reviewed the defense with the discerning eye of both a literary critic and a teacher evaluating a "student teacher." (Moreover, his language reveals those figures of authoritative discourse we saw in a previous chapter invoking "loftiness".) "Excellent pleading by M. Maud. Well-chosen words without being grandiloquent; to the point; very effective. I noticed that he made excellent use of the little dissertation I wrote for him in Fresnes [prison]. He presented me as one of those Frenchmen that nothing could prepare for such a trial: disciple of Alain, in all ways an 'elite subject' . . . He compared me in passing to Romain Rolland, "above the masses." He situated the problem on a high plane [*à bonne hauteur*] . . ." [64] And if Brasillach prepared for his trial as for an *orale de concours*, Jamet awaited his sentence like a nervous candidate for the *agrégation* contemplating his test results.

It is obvious that both Jamet and Brasillach have internalized the norms of "Normal Sup." Jamet is, however, a weaker representative of the ENS. His critical defect is one that he readily admits: the woeful lack of *camaraderie*. Perhaps Jamet's lighter sentence can be attributed to this deviation from the norm. When *Au Pilori*'s critic castigated Jamet for his narcissism ("He's always talking about himself"), Jamet admits ruefully: "It's true . . . that I didn't have a sense of camaraderie . . . But how could I have acquired it? An only son, *externe* at my lycée, *externe* at the rue d'Ulm, married at the time of my military service, I never had to live in a group with other boys of my age." [65] Jamet is as cathected to the idea of publishing (seeing his name in print) as he is to his lack of camaraderie. Indeed this will motivate his literary collaboration. Jamet admits: "I won't deny that I was impatient . . . I was already thirty years old and I wanted finally to see a book of mine in print." [66]

If our two *normaliens* were characterized by a strong belief in what they wrote and an intellectual as well as political consistency, Jean Luchaire presents a stark contrast. If Jean Luchaire tried to stress continuity it might be formulated as follows: he was always an opportunist. Luchaire did stress continuity of a sort, but it was far from the intrinsic (or integral) continuity evoked by Brasillach. It was rather a continuity of *effect*—the effect of the war experience of 1914 meant that Luchaire would do anything to support pacifism. And if Brasillach believed in (and risked his life for) what he wrote, Luchaire presents a total reversal: "No one believed, no one even thought that people who wrote believed what they wrote. The French, who already doubt what their candidates promise them in election campaigns, are well aware that *between the discourse and the act there is an abyss,* that between the summary of a warrant and what one has done, there is a *nuance*." [67]

If Robert Brasillach was a classicist, Jean Luchaire was a realist. On the linguistic level it is interesting to note how his trial proceeded through the trope of metonymy, the trope of realism, external effect and desire, context and contiguity. Luchaire was tried under articles 7 and 2 of the November 28, 1944, ordinance in a trial that brought up every messy issue of external affiliation. Through friendship with Otto Abetz (whose wife had been Luchaire's secretary) Luchaire founded *Nouveau Temps*. However, it is clear that Franco-German rapprochement was not a longstanding ideological tenet of Luchaire's: "Franco-German rapprochement—this was both for a long while my ideal and for a short time my *dada* [pet subject]." [68]

Luchaire wrote an anti-Semitic piece (December 15, 1941). He was friends with other fascists, and signed with Darnand and Déat a plan for national *redressement* (recovery). He received Degrelle and had business with Goebbels. But it was largely through his presidency of the Corporation of the Press that Luchaire played a role that was to win him a death sentence. If *JSP* was largely economically solvent, such was not the case for *Nouveau Temps:* its circulation at 37,000 to 45,000 was weak. Moreover, of the two editions of *Nouveau Temps* (stock market and "political"), the *"bourse"* edition sold more copies. The weak reception of *NT* led to the need for German "subvention" at 25,000 to 700,000 francs per month. [69]

There was little dispute with the words of the indictment: "Among those who have betrayed through writing, treason was often inspired by fascism; with Luchaire it was inspired by venality and rotten-ness."[70] Luchaire's trial was one of perpetual dissimulation. (Metonymy is also the trope of displacement.) Therefore, it was not surprising that he advanced a version of the double-game rationale: "He sacrificed conjugal fidelity for the love of his country, and he had a sense of duty so maladapted, he was so *cornélian*, that he pushed heroism so far as choosing his mistress from among the most ravishing movie actresses!"[71] He just wasn't believed: "Philanthropist backstage, he was on the stage of public opinion a daily collaborator . . ."[72] Although there is any irony in Luchaire's denial, "one doesn't send sincere guys to the execution post!"[73]

And if Brasillach was a classicist, and Luchaire a realist, Maurras was a romantic. His trial was a mixture of ideological and factual rebuttals, not as "pure" as Brasillach's in that he did have letters in his defense and was tried along with his colleague, Maurice Pujo, in a Lyon court.[74] It was also a relatively long trial: four days. Much of the debate focused on the aptness of article 75 for what appeared as a mass of little accessory facts "such as denunciations more or less followed by effects."[75] His dossier of six hundred pages took more than three months to establish; his articles were the source of the prosecution's case. Maurras's poverty was an extenuating circumstance; he could not be compared to profiteers like Béraud, Suarez, or Stéphane Lausanne. Yet it was the effects of his articles and not his intentions that mattered. Maurras's piece on the Worms family's pro-Gaullist propaganda leads to deportation. His article on the "Jewish menace" leads to the fatal beating of Roger Worms by the Milice ("an unfortunate accident").[76] Yet Maurras's case is interesting in that his literary collaboration was used to bolster the legal government. He denounced all those he saw as insurgents against the legal government, and if he supported the Milice, it was not through ideological conviction, but because Darnand convinced him the Milice was a *"force d'ordre française."*[77] His antidemocraticism thus took on the forms of anti-Gaullism, anti-Maquis, and anti-Resistance.

Yet it was not a question of pro-Pétainism per se: "Did Maurras, having suddenly changed his mind, wish to favor Germany, or was he just convinced that Pétain was the only man who had in his hands the pieces and elements for necessary discussion?"[78] Maurras's trial is replete with the *topos* of loyalty and dedication. Maurras plays the part of a loyal dog: "And Maurras, who loves his country as a bitch loves her puppies and growls as soon as one comes near them . . ."[79] Thus he participated in French court martials because he reasoned it was still better than being caught and tried by Germans. Maurras combined the loyalty of a dog with the wisdom of Solomon. He retells the fable of Solomon approached by two mothers who dispute the claim for the child. Solomon's proposal to cut the child in two brings forward the real mother who says, " 'Give him to the other. But don't harm him'—such was Maurras' patriotism." [80]

Maurras continually distanced himself from literary collaborators such as Brasillach and Luchaire, seeing his role as that of advocate of Pétain and French patriot. He distanced himself from Sordet, Georges Claude, and Déat. Believing there was no way to have an honorable journal in Paris, he boasted that "one would never find a disgraced signature in *Action Française*." There was a pathos of monotone: "France, nothing but France . . . France, this meant Pétain." [81] It is, finally, articles propounding Pétainist dogma in an effort to "save France," and not the sum of Maurras's works, most of which were forbidden by the Occupation authorities, that provided the basis for the indictment. And if it was argued that "intentions matter little, it is the facts which count," much of the attendant discussion centered precisely on the question of intentionality. The death penalty was requested, but the image of two deluded old men who had not gained materially led to a reduced sentence.

Maurras's trial underlines an important problematic endemic to the purge trial, that of historicity. At this distance, it is difficult to see anyone who opposed de Gaulle as anything but a traitor. *Sans doute*, today, even Maurras would have an easy time distinguishing the truth: "without doubt, today it is much too easy to judge. *L'expérience a réussi*." [82] Or, as Talleyrand so aptly put it, "Treason is a matter of dates." [83]

Just Performing

> *Public service becomes a game, a kind of parimutuel where*
> *everyone is forced to bet on the winning horse.*
> —Merleau-Ponty

Yet, is there something that these trials tell us about intellectuals? Is there something constitutive about the arbitrariness? The trials have been seen in terms of a "necessary contingency" by critics as diverse as Merleau-Ponty and Maurice Bardèche. [84] In such a reading, the trials become little more than an immense parimutual, where each tries to pick the winning horse. For the postwar purge trials do resemble a horse race, but not merely in the superficial arbitrariness of their outcomes. They resemble a horse race in their very structure, in the structure of the bet.

In a recent article in *Social Praxis*, Agnes Heller reformulates Mannheim's concept of intellectuals as a class. She agrees in their inherent "classlessness" (belonging to neither the proletarian nor the capitalist class) but disagrees with Mannheim that this classlessness does not afford any particular access to thought. The validity and truth of their objective always is dependent upon its reception, especially its reception by nonintellectuals. Nor can we look to the content of their beliefs in order to construct a class view or interest, as intellectuals represent all types of worldviews. Moreover, these worldviews have less and less to do with shared mores. (We have seen how in the case of French intellectuals, many attended the same schools, frequented similar social and publishing circles, in short, shared a similar intellectual formation.) Heller states clearly that "life experience itself becomes ideologically constituted *post factum*. Posterior to what? *The bet*. Intellectuals bet on a worldview, they bet on the present, they bet on a class, on a group, an elite, an organization—they bet on the future—on all possible or impossible futures."[85] This bet is a creed —in the way Goldmann describes Pascal's bet on God or in the way Heller formulates Lukác's "bet" on the proletariat. This relationship between "creed" and intellectual praxis has in France been focused on the debate around "clericalism" from Julien Benda to the work of Régis Debray.[86] According to Heller "no cultural undertaking is, however, possible without a creed."

Indeed, the notion of the *bet* (or the model of betting) is an appropriate representation of both intellectual activity and the logic of the postwar trials. For "the bet" in its very linguistic structure exemplifies one of Austin's performative "speech acts." Austin's concept of speech act describes the situation where "the uttering is, or is part of, the doing of the action, which again would not normally be saying something."[87] It is not by accident that Austin's discussion of performatives in *How to Do Things with Words* begins with a discussion of jurists: "it is worth pointing out how many of the acts which concern the jurist are or include the utterance of performatives."[88]

Moreover, "performatives" offer a category to transcend or reformulate that very separation of words and deeds at the heart of the postwar trials. Austin explicitly chooses the example of betting (like that of marrying) which can be described as saying certain words, rather than performing a different, inward and spiritual action of which these words are merely the outward and audible sign. This is contrary to the prior assumption that to say something is to state something which can later be evaluated by claims of truth or falsity—to be true or false is characteristic of a statement, not of truth or falsity—to be true or false is characteristic of a statement, not of a performative. One does not speak of a false bet or a false christening.[89] In the case of performatives, the uttering of the words is usually *a* or even *the* leading incident in the performance of the act. Yet certain conditions must be satisfied. If we take Austin's example of betting, the bet must be accepted by the taker (who usually does something, i.e., says "DONE"). Moreover, one can't announce one's bet when the race is over![90] There is indeed one way to reconcile the separation of words and deeds in the postwar trial and that is to see the literary production which was the basis of the indictment not as mere "words" but as "speech acts." Robert Brasillach's slogan ("Mort pour ses idées") would thus have to be rewritten—"Dead for his speech acts." No displaced piety here: Good discourse is simply, for Austin, discourse that works.[91]

Perhaps it would be more instructive not to repair or rejoin the schism between words and deeds with the category of performatives but rather to view the trials from the vantage point of the *symptomatic* separation of word and deed. For, there is nothing bizarre about this separation. Structuralists from Saussure on have underlined the abyss between the signifier and what it signifies, the word and the act it describes. Yet the refusal of the postwar "liberation" trials to respect this distinction between words and deeds marks an interesting detour from the juridical developments described by Foucault. Like much of Foucault's work, *Discipline and Punish* centers on a developing abstraction or alienation, this time within punishment.[92] This begins with the juridical separation between the body and the soul. Where once there was the extreme literality of punishment acted out on the offender's body (i.e., cutting off a thief's hand), attention is now focused on the soul as a juridical object of punishment. We witness a process of increasing abstraction to more "remote" forms of detention and rehabilitation (which will then be generalized to other institutions, such as the schools.) Abstraction and separation proceed. The body bifurcated from its soul can be further divided: thought is separated from action, hence, words from deeds, and by extension, reading from writing. But most important, binary oppositions ensue in which one term has value (i.e., it counts).

Jameson, in his work *The Political Unconscious*, outlines a historic reexamination of the binary opposition itself. He sees the binary opposition as a "form without content which nonetheless ultimately confers signification on the various types of content . . . which it organizes." Indeed we will see how not "metaphysics but ethics is the informing ideology of the binary opposition." The work of Derrida ably demonstrates the canonical binary oppositions: the opposition of "speech and writing, presence and absence, norm and deviation, center and periphery, experience and supplementarity, male and female. Derrida has shown how all these axes function to ratify the centrality of a dominant term by the means of the marginalization of an excluded or inessential one." [93]

If we take, along with Jameson, the ethical interpretation of the binary opposition, the positive and negative terms are ultimately those categories of good and evil, and the master text, that of Nietzsche (*Beyond Good and Evil*). If we turn to an analysis of the trials through the notion of the binary opposition, we have a dichotomy between activity and passivity, as well as that between good and evil. Yet what is characterized as activity is not totally what one expects. It is usually physical activity that is a criterion for judicial and moral responsibility. Literary writers would thus be more passive political actors than the Milice; readers (ideological consumers) of journals would be seen to be less active than those who wrote for them. We witness a progression from the remoteness of physical activity to the determination of juridical guilt, a process also noted by Arendt in the Eichmann trial: guilt was seen to increase as one got further away from the act itself. [94] There is an irony in the passive-active dichotomy, and the role it plays in a curious moral economy keeps cutting through the trials. For example, in Béraud's case, the question of a large "diffusion" was used to establish his guilt as an ideologue. Diffusion was important not only to show influence, but also dialectically; a small diffusion would show the need for government "subvention." Yet, as Béraud noted, large diffusion meant that people bought those journals, that ideological message, and were also complicitous. One wonders if one use of the binary opposition is to contain guilt to at least one easily delineated segment of the population that can be purged symbolically.

Yet, putting aside questions of possible bad faith, if we reconsider the notions of passivity and activity we realize that there is not so much a movement away from physical activity as there is the creation of another active term—that of textuality. We might, like Jameson, find Greimas' semiotic rectangle an interesting heuristic device to model the system of ideological closure and to articulate the workings of the binary oppositions throughout the trials. In such a way we can construct an outline of political attitudes and sentences. Greimas' semiotic rectangle is "the representation of a binary opposition or of two contraries S and $-S$, along with the simple negations or contradictories of both terms ($-\overline{S}$ and $\overline{S}$); significant slots are constituted by vari-

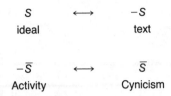

Figure 5. Greimas' Semiotic Rectangle

ous possible combinations of these terms, most notably the "complex" term (or ideal synthesis of two contraries) and the "neutral" term (or ideal synthesis of the two subcontraries).[95]

The antinomy in this case is between the ideal and the text. The contraries would be between "ideal" and "cynicism" (or greed or opportunism) and "activity" (political affiliations or literary activity not strictly bound up with the publication of journals in the occupied zone or in the Vichy region). By combining our categories, we can schematize the universe of possible political stances by literary intellectuals or activists: It is interesting that in Figure 6 our fourth category (the synthesis between activity and cynicism) is an intellectual absent from the trials because of suicide. Yet Drieu does act as a "foil" to Brasillach (and in some ways his "fatalist" stance is paradigmatic of those ultras of *Je Suis Partout*, Cousteau and Rebatet). Drieu's politi-

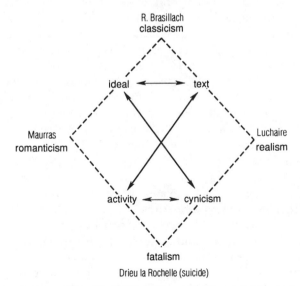

Figure 6. The Universe of Possible Political Stances by Literary Intellectuals or Activists

cal and psychological itinerary has been delineated by Desanti and Soucy, and summarized by Lottman.[96] I will cite only a few examples of his "fatalism," although his *Récit Secret* is full of more examples. Drieu had long been an activist; he had joined with Doriot and was among the first members of the PPF. He broke with it only to rejoin them later when it was beyond all his hopes and at a time when he urged his friend Lucien Combelle to join the PCF as a way of achieving their shared goals. Drieu was friends not only with Abetz, but with Gerhard Heller, who supplied him with a Swiss passport (which he did not use) to keep under his pillow in the hospital where he was recovering from his second suicide attempt. Drieu chose suicide as a matter of principle: "Yes, I had intelligence with the enemy. I brought French intelligence to the enemy. It's not my fault if this enemy wasn't intelligent. We played, I lost, I demand death."[97]

One could also insert the cases of two other *normaliens* whose experiences differ from the purely literary collaboration of Brasillach and Jamet in this diagram. I would situate Pierre Pucheu in the tension between the text and cynicism, along with Jean Luchaire, and Marcel Déat in the synthesis of activity and cynicism along with Drieu. Their respective endings are also apposite. Déat, like Drieu, assumes a fatalist attitude after Pucheu's summary trial and execution in Algiers and flees, first to Sigmaringen and later to Turin where he seeks refuge in Catholic mysticism.[98] (Drieu's flight—suicide—was more literal and swifter, but not more final.)

The case of Pucheu should be explained at greater length although we do have parallel executions of intellectuals who are as important for their networks as for their signatures and who, most important, are not idealist ideologues. Pucheu's cynicism, as recounted by Déat, rivals that of Luchaire. "I followed Pucheu from the corner of my eye since the Ecole Normale, since the time when he joined the *Bulletin Quotidienne de la Société d'Etudes et d'Informations Economiques* to finally earn a little money and be able to dress well."[99]

Déat remembers Pucheu's triumphant return as vividly as he remembers the clothes he wore on that occasion: a beautiful beige suit and yellow shoes. Pucheu explains his outfit: "I have sold myself to the capitalists, but at least I can dress well."[100] Déat presents Pucheu's political evolution as an allegory of his wardrobe ("From that time, he continued to dress better and better") until finally Pucheu cultivated the allure "of a young American boss." Sartorial considerations aside, Pucheu does exemplify a typical *normalien* career pattern. Influenced by alumn A. François Poncet and Mireaux (who was a minister in

Vichy), Pucheu ended his career at Ulm with a *débouchement* to the Comité des Forges. At least a dozen of his colleagues will make this journey in the direction of major industry—and they are not only "*scientifiques*." Students in the literary sections, such as Pucheu, will follow this path. Pucheu becomes a minister of industrial production and a minister of the interieur during Vichy. This will take him to Africa, a charade of a trial (condemned in advance and then shot), and his death.[101] And so another typical (albeit performative and technocratic rather than aesthetic and literary) *normalien* trajectory will lead to death.

Yet one should underline that it is not cynicism which motivates a death sentence. Rather it is interesting to note that severe sentencing will be around the textuality axis, it mattering little if, as in the case of Brasillach, one is ideologically pure or, as with Luchaire, is entirely bereft of principles.

If the binary opposition between words and deeds provides a point of departure for an analysis of the trials other than the canonical "yet another instance of the political repression of an elite by the successor regime," it might be interesting to review certain model trials. What were some of the binary oppositions at work in the trials? There was, to begin, a separation between speech and writing. The trials sought to reproduce the scene of writing. The oral reading of texts written by the accused, in his presence, finally reconciled the age-old separation of writing from speech. Moreover, this shift to speech restored the utterance as an act, validating the claim that ideas can be actions and serving to ground the trials if not in justice, at least in logic.

The trials of Brasillach and Maurras will now mark two extremes: in the case of Brasillach the relevant binary opposition will be between "signing" and "seeing" (vision is the crucial sense); and with Maurras, it will be between "signing" and "hearing" (with the emphasis on "voice").

The trial of Brasillach can be read as a circulation of signatures. The circulation of signatures inaugurates the trial in the form of the names published by the CNE, while the content of the prosecution's case is dictated by the articles Brasillach wrote, articles which are read out loud, in his presence. His case is an insistence on the written[102] (as Maurras's will be on the priority of voice over writing). The flurry of signatures will now move to an appeal for clemency in the guise of petitions signed by notable writers. Those who couldn't sign like Simone de Beauvoir were forced to rely on compensatory senses— seeing and hearing.[103] Simone de Beauvoir couldn't bring herself to sign the petition but had to see the trial and had to listen to the radio on the day of his execution. (She writes that she "had" to go to the trial and literally could not tear herself away from the radio on the morning of his execution). Brasillach's literary production in Fresnes prison was also used to appeal for de Gaulle's clemency. Mauriac, one of the more impressive literary signatures, goes to see de Gaulle to argue in Brasillach's favor, and although de Gaulle agrees to the pardon, this is undone by a fantastic trompe l'oeil finale:[104] de Gaulle mistakenly thinks he sees Brasillach in a German uniform in a photo. There is more than a little irony that this case that depended so much upon the visual (i.e., the written word) should be undone by the very aporia between looking and seeing.

The case of Maurras is, perhaps, even more perverse as Maurras's deafness proved critical for the judicial machinery. Yet we witness a trial language which repeatedly makes reference to his "remarkable voice," a compliment he can, unfortunately, not hear, but could read each day in the court transcripts. In a peculiar displacement, it is the voice of Maurras that becomes the "direct translation" of his thought.[105] Maurras's shattering voice is continually compared with his codefendant's tranquil voice. His deafness leads to a reversal of roles in the courtroom. He is given all night and morning to read the indictment, which leads him to become an accuser, such as the spectacle of reading a pamphlet against Claudel demonstrates.[106] And if the prosecution's case rested on articles he wrote and the journal he kept in Lyons, his defense was none other than the oral affirmation of his signature: "but I am Charles Maurras."[107] Maurras is an exemplar of total orality: "he speaks without notes."[108] He is not just a "brain" but a "sensibility." M. Goncet's defense speech consists of a text whose alliteration and repetition demand to be read out loud: "Maurras, poor Maurras, magnificent Maurras, Maurras the patriot, Maurras the great French and Latin mind, Maurras the academician, Maurras the great thinker, Maurras the writer, Maurras the poet, all this—nothing."[109] Maurras himself is obsessed with his name. "At my age, life means little. Honor: I defy that you tarnish mine." The court transcript continually cites his cries, and his trial ends on a cry: "it's the revenge of Dreyfus." The question of sentencing, too, will turn on his deafness—for how does one punish a double captive, captive of his thought and of his own deafness: "for him there can be only one punishment: deprive him of ink and paper."[110]

The lesson is clear: the insistence of the written leads to certain death; the priority of the spoken will lead to the end of writing.

Perhaps the best illustration of the interconnections between the "literary signature" and death is an anecdote of Rebatet's: while he was in the courtroom awaiting sentencing, the bailiff Boudry, head of those guarding Rebatet et al., showed them their photos and asked for their autographs. But as they got ready to sign, they were stopped: "rather, later on, if you don't mind, when you will be . . . you understand . . . did you know, he added with enthusiasm, I already have Laval, Paquis, Darnand, Bucard, Luchaire in my collection. All those shot!" After hearing the verdict, Rebatet signs his appeal. "I must sign also the photos of our excellent bailiff, Boudry." [111]

CONCLUSION

P.S. A POSTSTRUCTURALIST

POSTSCRIPT

Of course, as it is said, the letter killeth while the spirit giveth life. We can't help but agree, having had to pay homage elsewhere to a noble victim of the error of seeking the spirit in the letter, but we should like to know, also, how the spirit could live without the letter.
—Jacques Lacan, "The Insistence of the Letter in the Unconscious"

We began our examination of the ENS with the figure of Lakanal, and it is with the figure of Rebatet signing his photo after receiving a death sentence for his collaborationist writing that we conclude our narrative development of a literary signature. We have traced the origin of the *normalien* signature from a violation of spelling (Lakanal choosing to spell his name with a *c* to signal his republicanism) through its institutionalization (via the codes of elite discourse) to the moments of its circulation and judgment. Nor are these discrete events. For we have seen that the circulation of signatures obtained even at the time of the judgment of these signatures. Rebatet represents the ultimate conclusion in the logical development of this signature as he recuperates the notions of both violation and signature that inaugurated this book. Moreover, in the shift from Lakanal to Rebatet we witness a chiasmic reversal. Lakanal votes for the regicide and changes the spelling of his name to herald this death; Rebatet's signature achieves value only as corroboration of the sovereign's power to punish. In receiving a death sentence his signature acquires value for the bailiff, and he is allowed to sign his picture. This play between representations and this reversal are consonant with the practice of deconstructive reading. Mehlman writes of a "return reversal" in his *Legacies of Anti-Semitism in France*. In deconstructive readings, the history of writing is a history of repetition. But it is repetition with a difference. The postwar trials did not just neutralize the errant *normalien*, but in the sentencing according to a literary signature simultaneously guaranteed that signature and reinvested the ENS with its authority as a regulator and licensee of discourse.

In conclusion, I would like to succumb to the logic of reversal. Our analysis of the Ecole Normale has been an attempt to remedy a double absence:

1. *Empirically* to reinscribe the presence of the right within the school;
2. *Theoretically* to contribute to an absence of what has been elsewhere described as a "history of the act of writing."

Régis Debray believes that the *"pulsion graphique"* (urge to write) is a *"pulsion de vie"* (life impulse).[1] If we concur with one of Robert Brasillach's most astute commentators that: "Robert Brasillach had less a biography than a destiny,"[2] we are tempted to reverse Debray's formulation. The impulse to write is thus a death wish.

NOTES

WORKS CONSULTED

INDEX

NOTES

Caveat Lector

1. Roland Barthes, *Mythologies* (New York: Hill and Wang, 1972).

2. Régis Debray, *Critique of Political Reason* (London: Verso, 1983).

3. Michel Foucault, "Intellectuals and Power," *Language, Counter-Memory, Practice* (Ithaca: Cornell UP, 1977).

4. Edward W. Said, "The Problem of Textuality: Two Exemplary Positions," *Aesthetics Today* (New York: NAL, 1980).

5. Stanley Aronowitz and Henry Giroux, "Radical Education and Transformative Intellectuals," *Canadian Journal of Social and Political Theory* 9, no. 3 (Fall 1986). Michèle Le Doeuff, "La Philosophie Renseignée," in Christian Delacampagne, ed., *Philosopher* (Paris: Fayard, 1980); Roland Barthes, "Writers, Intellectuals, Teachers," *Image, Music, Text* (New York: Hill and Wang, 1977); Pierre Bourdieu, *Homo Academicus* (Paris: Minuit, 1985); Régis Debray, *Teachers, Writers, Celebrities* (London: New Left Books, 1981); Jacques Derrida, "The Principle of Reason: The University in the Eyes of Its Pupils," *Diacritics* 13 (1983): 3–19. See also Jacques Derrida, "Où Commence et Comment Finit un Corps Enseignant," in Dominique Grisoni, ed., *Politiques de la Philosophie* (Paris: Grasset, 1976).

6. Marc Chénetier, "Gods, Princes, and Scribes," *October* 24 (1983): 110.

7. Paul de Man, "Reading and History," *The Resistance to Theory* (Minneapolis: U of Minnesota P, 1986), 56.

8. Said, "Problem of Textuality," 116, 105.

9. Jacques Derrida, "But, beyond . . . (Open Letter to Anne McClintock and Rob Nixon)," *Critical Inquiry* 13, no. 1 (Autumn 1986): 168.

1. Introduction

1. "L'Ecole Normale Supérieure," *Larousse du Vingtième Siècle*, Vol. 3 (1930), 39.

2. "Lakanal," *Larousse du Vingtième Siècle*, Vol. 4 1931: 305–6.

3. The word *faisceau* also signifies the right-wing, proto-fascist group of Valois which attracted some *normalien* students, such as Bourgin.

4. Jean-François Sirinelli, *Génération Intellectuelle* (Paris: Fayard, 1988), 23–24.

5. Robert Brasillach, *Une Génération dans l'Orage* (Paris: Plon, 1955), 57.

6. Ibid., 29.

7. Philippe Ariès cited in Ezra Suleiman, *Elites in French Society* (Princeton: Princeton UP, 1978), 42. See also Pierre Bourdieu's excellent discussion of the creation of a nobility in *Noblesse d'Etat* (Paris: Minuit, 1989).

8. Suleiman, *Elites in French Society*, 37.

9. Jean Guéhenno, _Journal d'un Homme de Quarante Ans_ (Paris: Grasset, 1934), 114.

10. Brasillach, _Génération dans l'Orage_, 58.

11. Ibid.

12. Ibid., 59.

13. Ibid., 60.

14. Ibid.

15. Erving Goffman, _Asylums_ (Garden City: Anchor, 1961), 26.

16. Marcel Déat, "Mémoires Politiques," Vol. 1, MSS Papiers Déat, Bibliothèque Nationale, Paris, France. See also Sirinelli, _Génération Intellectuelle_, 32.

17. Brasillach, _Génération dans l'Orage_, 60.

18. Ibid.

19. Alan Sheridan, _Michel Foucault: The Will to Truth_ (London: Tavistock, 1980), 3.

20. Jeffrey Mehlman, _Legacies of Anti-Semitism in France_ (Minneapolis: U of Minnesota P, 1983), 84. For another theoretical approach to this study of rightist authors during this period, see Susan Rubin Suleiman, _Authoritarian Fictions: The Ideological Novel as a Literary Genre_ (New York: Columbia UP, 1983). Suleiman's work is based on the theorists of "narratology" such as Gérard Genette and Tzvetan Todorov (both _normaliens_), as well as Roland Barthes and A. J. Greimas. Mehlman's book, on the other hand, is influenced by the Freud of _Beyond the Pleasure Principle_ and shares a profound affinity with most of poststructuralist thought.

21. Mehlman, _Legacies_, 84.

22. Ibid., 3–4.

23. Barbara Johnson, introduction to _Dissemination_ by Jacques Derrida (Chicago: U of Chicago P, 1981), xiii.

24. Pierre Bourdieu, _Ce Que Parler Veut Dire_ (Paris: Fayard, 1982), 207–26. Bourdieu compares the rhetoric of Althusser and Heidegger and shows that the "discourse of importance" knows no ideological bounds.

25. Roland Barthes, _The Pleasure of the Text_, trans. Richard Miller (New York: Hill and Wang, 1975), 40–41.

26. Bourdieu, _Ce Que Parler Veut Dire_, 179. "La mise en forme est, par soi, une mise en garde: elle dit par sa hauteur, la distance souveraine à toutes les déterminations . . . et tout spécialement, bien sûr, aux déterminations irremplaçable d'un penseur à la banalité d'une classe (sociale)."

2. What's Left?

1. Sigmund Freud, _Moses and Monotheism_, trans. Katherine Jones (New York: Vintage, 1967), 15.

2. Ibid., 65.

3. Ibid., 6.

4. J. L. Loubet del Bayle, _Les Nonconformistes des Années Trente_, (Paris: Seuil, 1969), 57–58.

5. Barbara Johnson, introduction and trans., *Dissemination* by Jacques Derrida (Chicago: U of Chicago P, 1981), ix.

6. Freud, *Moses and Monotheism*, 20.

7. Johnson, *Dissemination*, xiv.

8. Ibid.

9. Samuel Weber, *Institution and Interpretation* (Minneapolis: U of Minnesota P, 1987), 155.

10. Johnson, *Dissemination*, xiv, xv.

11. Régis Debray, *The Critique of Political Reason*, trans. David Macey (London: Verso, 1983), 2.

12. Jacques Derrida, *Writing and Difference*, trans. Alan Bass (Chicago: U of Chicago P, 1978), 285.

13. Jacques Derrida, *Of Grammatology*, trans. Gayatri Chakravorty Spivak (Baltimore: Johns Hopkins UP, 1976), 83.

14. Michel Foucault, *Power/Knowledge*, trans. and ed. Colin Gordon (New York: Pantheon, 1980); Pierre Bourdieu, *Ce Que Parler Veut Dire* (Paris: Fayard, 1982).

15. Roland Barthes, *The Pleasure of the Text*, trans. Richard Miller (New York: Hill and Wang, 1975), 50.

16. Debray, *Critique of Political Reason*, 157–58.

17. Michel Foucault, "What is an author?" *Language, Counter-Memory, Practice*, trans. and ed. Donald Bouchard (Ithaca: Cornell UP, 1977), 122, 123.

18. Jacques Derrida, "Où Commence et Comment Finit un Corps Enseignant," in Dominique Grisoni, ed., *Politiques de la Philosophie* (Paris: Grasset, 1976), 82–83.

19. Derrida, "Où Commence," 71.

20. See also Pierre Bourdieu, *Homo Academicus*, trans. Peter Collier (Stanford: Stanford UP, 1988), 105, 109, 118–19.

21. Fredric Jameson, *The Political Unconscious* (Ithaca: Cornell UP, 1981), 114.

22. Marc Chénetier, "Gods, Princes and Scribes," *October* 24 (Spring 1983): 107.

23. Régis Debray, *Le Scribe* (Paris: Grasset, 1980), 163.

24. Ibid., 26–27.

25. Ibid., 31. See also the volume of Marthe Robert, *La Tyrannie de l'Imprimé* (Paris: Grasset, 1984).

26. Chénetier, "Gods, Princes," 109.

27. Debray, *Scribe*, 245.

28. Michel Foucault, *Discipline and Punish*, trans. Alan Sheridan (New York: Vintage, 1979), 189.

29. Roland Barthes, "To Write: An Intransitive Verb?" in *The Structuralists: From Marx to Lévi-Strauss*, ed. and trans. Ferdinande De George and Richard T. De George (Garden City: Anchor, 1972), 165.

30. Jacques Derrida, "The Principle of Reason: The University in the Eyes of Its Pupils," *Diacritics* 13 (Fall 1983): 3.

31. Derrida, "Principle of Reason," 5.

32. Derrida, *Grammatology*, 44.

33. James Siegel, "Academic Work: The View from Cornell," *Diacritics* (Spring 1983): 68.

34. Ibid., 75.

35. The ENS throughout this period might be considered to be an "empty signifier," as no teachers resided at the school, and there was no fixed curriculum that differed from that of the University of Paris. See our Introduction for a further discussion.

36. Derrida, "Où Commence," 60.

37. Ibid., 76. The text reads as follows: "cette structure retardaire de l'enseignement peut toujours être intérrogée comme répétition . . . Il procède de la structure sémiotique de l'enseignement . . . l'enseignement délivre des signes, le corps enseignant produit . . . des enseignes, plus précisément des *signifiants supposant le savoir d'un signifié préalable*" (italics mine).

38. See our discussion in Chapter 5, "Language and Authority."

39. Derrida, "Principle of Reason," 17, 19.

40. Derrida, *Grammatology*, 141–57.

41. Derrida, "Principle of Reason," 19.

42. Derrida, *Writing and Difference*, 75.

43. Ibid.

3. Le Cru et l'Ecrit

1. For two excellent and complementary physical geographies of the ENS, see Paul Dupuy, *Sa Vie Résumée par Lui-même* (Paris: Bropard et Taupin, 1951), and Robert Brasillach, *Notre Avant Guerre* (Paris: Plon, 1941).

2. Alain Peyrefitte, introduction to *Rue d'Ulm* (Paris: Flammarion, 1963). Copyright © Flammarion, Paris, 1977.

3. Compare Peyrefitte's introduction: "Destinée à recruiter des professeurs A. Thibaudet's description of university life: "On boit une tradition . . . ces portes de la culture . . . devenu liquide, ambre, savant et chaud . . ." *La République des Professeurs* (Geneva: Slatkine, 1979), 43. Similarly: "Le bloc de gauche sortait éclatante de la cuve" describes the three *normaliens* on the night of November 11. Thibaudet also laments that there is no place in the provincial press for a Daudet or a Maurras *du cru* (13, 14, 23). In addition, Bourdieu's recent analysis of adjectives used in teachers' appreciations of students reveals an affinity for viniculture. See *Noblesse d'Etat* (Paris: Minuit, 1989), 42–43.

4. Bourdieu translates *anciens élèves* (see *Noblesse d'Etat*), literally, alumni or former students, as "old boys," which is more apt in a discussion of the emblematic function of *normalien* status.

5. Hubert Bourgin, *De Jaurès à Léon Blum: L'Ecole Normale et la Politique* (Paris: Fayard, 1938). Most recently, Jean François Sirinelli's definitive study of the ENS between the two world wars has reproduced this leftist, parliamentary focus. While he does detail the importance of right-wing movements in the Latin Quarter and of André Bellesort as a mentor for right-wing students at the Lycée Louis-le-Grand, his primary focus is on pacifist and leftist students

of Alain and their political trajectories. See Jean François Sirinelli, *Génération Intellectuelle* (Paris: Fayard, 1988).

6. Ezra Suleiman, *Elites in French Society* (Princeton: Princeton UP, 1978), 37–38.

7. Charles Lemert, "Literary Politics and the *Champ* of French Sociology," *Theory and Society* 10, no. 5 (September 1981): 750.

8. Suleiman, *Elites in French Society*, 37, 101.

9. Ibid., 131–33.

10. Ibid., 644.

11. Régis Debray, *Le Pouvoir Intellectuel en France* (Paris: Ramsay, 1979), 92–93.

12. *Le Procès de Robert Brasillach* (Paris: Flammarion, 1946), 174.

13. Régis Debray, *Teachers, Writers, Celebrities*, trans. David Macey (London: New Left Books, 1981) 34.

14. René Rémond, *Les Droites en France* (Paris: Aubier, 1982), 398.

15. Robert Soucy, *Fascist Intellectual: Drieu La Rochelle* (Berkeley: U of California P, 1979); Herbert Lottman, *La Rive Gauche* (Paris: Seuil, 1981), and Drieu La Rochelle, *Récit Secret* (Paris: Gallimard, 1951).

16. Debray, *Teachers, Writers, Celebrities*, 50.

17. On the logic of the supplement see Jacques Derrida, *Of Grammatology*, trans. Gayatri Chakravorty Spivak (Baltimore: Johns Hopkins UP, 1976), 141–64.

18. Pierre Bourdieu, *La Reproduction* (Paris: Minuit, 1970), 152.

19. Renée Balibar echoes Bourdieu's formulation in *Les Français Fictifs* (Paris: Hachette, 1974), 212. "Cette attitude didactique . . . qui serait à la fois doctoral et spontané, érudit et libre, autrement dit à la fois *parlé comme un livre et écrit comme on parle*, c'est l'attitude idéale pour l'élite cultivée . . . du professeur de cagne dispensateur éminent de la culture générale, c'est à dire, transmetteur de l'idéologie dominante."

20. Lemert, "Literary Politics," 646.

21. Pierre Bourdieu, "Les Rites d'Institution," *Actes de la Recherche en Sciences Sociales* 43 (June 1982): 58.

22. Pierre Bourdieu, *Questions de Sociologie* (Paris: Minuit, 1980). In "Haute Couture et Haute Culture" Bourdieu raises an analogical problem to that of Suleiman in *Elites in French Society*, that of transformation and continuity: "Comment transformer en institution durable l'émergence unique qui introduit la discontinuité dans un univers." The question "Comment remplacer Jésus ou comment remplacer Picasso?" never arises as it is inconceivable. Yet it is possible to ask "Remplacer Chanel?" It is this problem of a *"griffe,"* both its consecration and its transubstantiation, that concerns us in a discussion of Normale.

23. Bourdieu, "Rites d'Institution," 60.

24. Pierre Bourdieu, *Distinction*, trans. Richard Nice (Cambridge: Harvard UP, 1984), 31, 142. See also *Noblesse d'Etat*, 396, 101–39 (La Production d'une Noblesse).

25. Bourdieu, *Distinction*, 25.

26. Pierre Bourdieu, *Homo Academicus*, trans. Peter Collier (Stanford: Stanford UP, 1988), 320 (footnote 11).

27. Ibid., 222.

28. Ibid., 152.

29. For a fuller empirical study see Diane Rubenstein, "What's Left: The Ecole Normale Supérieure and the Right," PhD diss., Yale University, 1985, and Sirinelli, *Génération Intellectuelle*.

30. Georges Lefranc, a lifelong socialist, was nevertheless censured after the liberation, for collaboration. He was charged for the articles he wrote: for his purely journalistic activity and not for any "political" (i.e., party) affiliations. For a full account of the "Affaire Lefranc," see Sirinelli, *Génération Intellectuelle*, 574–85.

31. Archives Nationales (AN) 61 AJ 171.

32. See Pascal Ory's discussion of *"la gauche collaborationiste"* in his *Les Collaborateurs* (Paris: Seuil, 1976). Jamet's desire to see his first book published is documented in his *Fifi le Roi* (Paris: Editions de l'Elan, 1947), 248–49. Interview with Claude Jamet, June 1982, Paris.

33. AN 61 AJ 166.

34. Ory, *Collaborateurs*, 142, 109.

35. Interview with Thierry Maulnier, December 1982, Versailles, and Maurice Bardèche, May 1982, Paris.

36. Interview with Henri Quéffelec, June 1983, Paris, and Maurice Bardèche May 1982, Paris.

37. Interview with Maurice Bardèche, May 1982, Paris, France. Other famous *externes* include Jacques Soustelle, the *cacique* (number one student on the *concours d'entrée*). The question of *externes* at the school was a hotly debated one; see AN 61 AJ 166. The average number of *externes* per year was cited as seven students. AN 61 AJ 249–56.

38. Claude Jamet, *Notre Front Populaire 1934–1939* (Paris: Table Ronde, 1977), 14; interview with Claude Jamet, Juné 1982, Paris.

39. Thibaudet, *République des Professeurs*, 43.

40. AN 61 AJ 104.

41. Jean François Sirinelli, "Quand Aron etait à gauche de Sartre," *Le Monde Dimanche*, 17 January 1982, 12–13. Sirinelli writes that the future champion of "engagement" revealed a total lack of interest in politics during his years at Normale. He also reveals Sartre's *estudantine* literary production and how it prefigured later works such as *La Nausée*. It would be interesting to compare lycée works of both leftist and rightist *normaliens*—e.g., Sartre's contribution to *La Revue sans Titre* and Brasillach et al to *Fulgur:* both figure inept lycée professors as protagonists; yet *Fulgur* experiments with many facets of the surrealistic aesthetic (automatic writing, puns, the *"surnaturel"* in everyday life). *Fulgur* was written at Louis-Le-Grand and was reprinted as a summer feuilleton in the *Journal de Yonne*. A bound copy is available for consultation at the family archives of Maurice Bardèche and Suzanne Brasillach Bardèche.

42. Pascal Ory, *Nizan: Destin d'un Révolté* (Paris: Ramsay, 1980). Sartre's pref-

ace to *Aden, Arabie* as well as Merleau-Ponty's introduction to *Signs* alludes to this "fascist" period of Nizan. Ory and Sartre situate it as yet another expression of Nizan's violent extremism. Merleau-Ponty's interpretation is more magnanimous, linking Nizan's "suffering" with his "dandyism" (i.e., wearing the uniform ["*cockage*"] of Valois). Interview with Pascal Ory, July 1982, Paris.

43. *L'Oeuvre* was a paper of the radical left. For a discussion of the relation between the ENS and *L'Oeuvre* see Chapter 6. Papiers Déat, Bibliothèque Nationale (BN); *Histoire Générale de la Presse Française*, 3: 562. For the earlier generation of *normaliens*, see student records AN 61 AJ 14, 17–22, 25.

44. AN 61 AJ 171. The *concours d'entrée* of 1920 marked a nadir. It is difficult to establish whether this is a result of poorer recruitment after the reforms or a result of disturbances during the war years. See also 61 AJ 161, 162.

45. Press clippings on the problems of recruitment, AN 61 AJ 171, 161, 166.

46. Many *normaliens* have written with nostalgia of their years at the Ecole. Recent memoirs include Raymond Aron, *Le Spectateur Engagé* (Paris: Julliard, 1981). In addition, former alumni who have written include Claude Jamet, Henri Quéffelec, and Jean Guéhenno. Robert Brasillach's *Notre Avant Guerre* is perhaps the best love poem written to the school. Not everyone has been so positive. Romain Rolland's *Le Cloître de la Rue d'Ulm* is a more dispassionate appraisal of the Ecole. But the *antimémoire par excellence* remains Nizan's *Aden Arabie*: "I was twenty. I will let no one say it is the best time of life."

47. AN 61 AJ 243, 247, 250–57. Pierre-Marie Dioudonnat, *Je Suis Partout* (Paris: Table Ronde, 1973), 238–39.

48. Jean François Sirinelli, "Khâgneux et Normaliens des Années Vingt: Contribution à l'Histoire des Intellectuels Français," *Bulletin de la Société d'Histoire Moderne* 21 (1983): 11. See also Alain Girard, *La Réussite Sociale en France* (Paris: PUF, 1961), and Pierre Bourdieu and Jean-Claude Passeron, *Les Héritiers* (Paris: Minuit, 1964).

49. Dioudonnat, *Je Suis Partout*, 29.

50. Peyrefitte, *République des Professeurs*, 103. The full text of Simon appears in his response to the reception of Georges Izard to the Académie Française. *Discours de Réception de Me. Georges Izard à l'Académie Française et Réponse de M. Pierre Henri Simon* (Paris: Gallimard, 1972), 57.

51. Jacques Soustelle was the only *normalien* interviewed not to agree with P. H. Simon's pronouncement. He was also the only one interviewed who did not attend a Parisian lycée. Interview with Soustelle, August 1984, Paris. AN 61 AJ 255–58.

52. Brasillach, *Notre Avant Guerre*, 31: "C'est dans le cour de Louis-le-Grand qu'à commencé mon amitié pour l'Action Française."

53. AN 61 AJ 250–56.

54. Interview with Georges Lefranc, July 1984, Courseules-sur-Mer, France. AN 61 AJ 166.

55. AN 61 AJ 166, 188, 251, 254–57.

56. AN 61 AJ 194.

57. See my "Intellectuals of the *Nouvelle Revue Française*, 1940–1944," unpub-

lished manuscript. Among those who failed an important examination: Paul Morand (*baccalauréat*), Giraudoux and Brasillach (*agrégation*), Mauriac (philosophy exam), Roger Martin du Gard, Montherlant, and Jouhandeau (*licence*). Sartre and Henri Guillemin failed their first attempts at the *agrégation*. Giraudoux, a brilliant student of German, fails his German *agrégation* exam (with a score of two out of thirty points!). Drieu fails his exam at the Ecole des Sciences Politiques, and Julien Benda is refused entrance to the Ecole Polytechnique.

58. George L. Mosse, *Toward the Final Solution* (Harper & Row: New York, 1978).

59. Bourdieu, *Reproduction*, 199–200 n. 35.

60. AN 61 AJ 104.

61. Bourdieu, *Reproduction*, 168.

62. AN 61 AJ 188, 255.

63. Brasillach, *Notre Avant Guerre*, 84; on the choice of thesis advisor and thesis topic in general, see Bourdieu, *Homo Academicus*, 93.

64. AN 61 AJ 188.

65. AN 61 AJ 188, 255.

66. John Talbott, *The Politics of Educational Reform in France* (Princeton: Princeton UP, 1959), 16–17. AN 61 AJ 202, 203.

67. AN 61 AJ 202, 203, 250–56.

68. Brasillach, *Notre Avant Guerre*, 87.

69. AN 61 AJ 255. For a full discussion, see Sirinelli, *Génération Intellectuelle*, 497–536.

70. AN 61 AJ 194.

71. AN 61 AJ 206, 207, 203.

72. AN 61 AJ 206, 207.

73. AN 61 AJ 104.

74. Balibar, *Français Fictifs*, 174: Balibar's thesis is that *Pierre* "est la reproduction fictive d'un travail universitaire," mirroring the findings of the *Année Psychologique* (1898) study on the first childhood memories. Freud also used this study in his discussion of childhood memory and memory screens in chapter 4 of *The Psychopathology of Everday Life*. But *Pierre* also parallels the form of a famous lycée homework assignment: "Le description d'objet" (182–86). It is, however, Péguy's *Note Conjointe* that most reflects a certain *normalien* mode: "Même abritée sous les scolarismes, l'écriture de la *Note Conjointe* révèle un peu trop l'ENS et manque un peu trop de modestie culturelle. Elle offre un nombre excessif de mots de passe à l'élite de l'élite cultivée."

75. Etiemble was in the Office of War Information; Giraudoux was a "*conseiller d'ambassade*"; Gillouin was "*chef adjoint du cabinet du president*."

76. AN 61 AJ 104.

77. AN 61 AJ 203.

78. AN 61 AJ 203, 255.

79. Bourdieu, "Rites d'Institution," 84.

80. Peyrefitte, *République des Professeurs*, 5.

81. Compare this with Roland Barthes, *Fragments d'un Discours Amoureux* (Paris: Seuil, 1977), 25–28, 36 n. 5, 41, 84–94, 101.

82. Bourdieu, "Rites d'Institution," 84; see also *Noblesse d'Etat*, 140–62.

83. AN 61 AJ 161.

84. Peyrefitte, *République des Professeurs*, 313.

85. Erving Goffman, *Asylums* (Garden City: Anchor, 1961), 59. See also Bourdieu, *Noblesse d'Etat*, 104.

86. Peyrefitte, *République des Professeurs*, 103–5.

87. Ibid., 14.

88. AN 61 AJ 104.

89. Peyrefitte, *République des Professeurs*, 61–62, 409, 49–50. Compare these recollections with those in the Archives de l'Ecole: AN 61 AJ 207, 161, 104.

90. The *canular* is the official initiation rite. For a history of the *canular*, see Roger Joxe, "Contribution à l'Histoire du Canular," *Bulletin de la Société des Amis de l'ENS* (June 1952): 27–29.

91. Goffman, *Asylums*, 12, 26.

92. Ibid., 22.

93. See Bourdieu, *Noblesse d'Etat*, 152–53.

94. For this viewpoint we look to the work of Georges Canguilhem (promotion 1924). (Interview with Canguilhem, January 1989, Paris.) Especially, see his *Le Normal et le Pathologique* (Paris: PUF, 1984).

95. AN 61 AJ 104; Peyrefitte, *République des Professeurs*, 98–99.

96. AN 61 AJ 104. On the *brimades* see also Bourdieu, *Noblesse d'Etat* 153 n. 23.

97. Bourdieu, *Reproduction*, 22.

98. Sigmund Freud, *The Sexual Enlightenment of Children* (New York: Collier, 1963). See also Bourdieu, *Noblesse d'Etat*, 148, 141.

99. Charles Andler, *La Vie de Lucien Herr*, n.d., 84.

100. Bourdieu, "Rites d'Institution," 60.

101. Peyrefitte, *République des Professeurs*, 411, 14.

102. Bourdieu, "Rites d'Institution," 59.

103. Peyrefitte, *République des Professeurs*, 14.

104. Bourdieu, "Rites d'Institution," 61.

105. Bourdieu, *Reproduction* 47, 48.

106. Girard, *Réussite Sociale*, 49.

107. Simon, Discours de *Réception*, 57.

108. Bourdieu, *Distinction*, 170.

109. Ibid., 24, and *Homo Academicus*, 93.

110. Bourdieu, *Homo Academicus*, 206.

111. Bourdieu, *Distinction*, 47, and *Noblesse d'Etat*, 447.

112. Bourdieu, *Distinction*, 71, 99.

113. Ibid., 101.

114. Ibid., 107.

115. Ibid., 466, 470, 474.

116. Peyrefitte, *République des Professeurs*, 389–96.

117. Goffman, *Asylum*, 53.

118. Bourdieu, *Noblesse d'Etat*, 387.

119. Peyrefitte, *République des Professeurs*, 14, 397.

120. Ibid., 118–19.
121. Bourdieu, *Distinction*, 466.
122. Ibid., 31, and *Homo Academicus*, 206.
123. Bourdieu, *Noblesse d'Etat*, 387, 447.
124. Peyrefitte, *République des Professeurs*, 407–9.
125. Bourdieu, "Rites d'Institution," 62; *Reproduction*, 155.
126. Peyrefitte, *République des Professeurs*, 5.
127. "Notes Radiophoniques," AN 61 AJ 104.
128. Daniel Sibony, *Le Groupe Inconscient* (Paris: Bourgois, 1980), 79.
129. Bourdieu, *Reproduction*, 80, 158.
130. Peyrefitte, *République des Professeurs*, 60.
131. Bourdieu, *Reproduction*, 158.
132. Balibar, *Français Fictifs*, 182–86.
133. Bourdieu, "Rites d'Institution," 63.
134. *Proces de Robert Brasillach*, 119. Interview with Jacques Isorni, July 1982, Paris.

4. The Return of the Repressed

1. Pierre Bourdieu, *Ce Que Parler Veut Dire* (Paris: Fayard, 1982); Michel Foucault, *Discipline and Punish*, trans. Alan Sheridan (New York: Vintage, 1979) and *Power/Knowledge*, trans. and ed. Colin Gordon (New York: Pantheon, 1980).
2. Paul Dupuy was a noted anarchist and Dreyfusard who served as director of the ENS. Paul Dupuy, *Sa Vie Résumée par Lui-même* (Paris: Bropard et Taupin, 1951).
3. Ezra Suleiman, *Elites in French Society* (Princeton: Princeton UP, 1978), 37.
4. Archives Nationales (AN) F7 1308.
5. Lucien Rebatet, *Les Décombres* (Paris: Pauvert, 1976), 19.
6. Bertrand de Jouvenel, *Voyageur dans le Siècle* (Paris: Laffont, 1979), 285–307.
7. Pierre Bourdieu, *Distinction* (Cambridge: Harvard UP 1984), chap. 1.
8. Interview with Maurice Bardèche (May and June 1982, Paris); Thierry Maulnier (December 1982, Versailles); Henri Quéffelec (June 1983, Paris); Jacques Derrida (April 1983, New Haven); Claude Jamet (June 1982, Paris); Jamet did admit to a *maître* as did Pierre Andreu (June 1982, Paris). Andreu's little book *Mon Maître Sorel* was intended as a parody of the genre.
9. Claude Jamet, *Notre Front Populaire* (Paris: Table Ronde, 1977), 1: "A gauche—c'est à dire en position de résistance 'contre les pouvoirs.' "
10. Hubert Bourgin, *De Jaurès à Léon Blum: L'Ecole Normale et la Politique* (Paris: Fayard, 1938), 150.
11. Paris, France, Bibliothèque Historique de la Ville de Paris (BH), Ochs Collection (Ochs) on the Dreyfus Affair, Folio D1222, Register (R) 7:1039.
12. *Journal du Saône et Loire*, 26 Dec 1984, BH Ochs D1222 R 7:1039.
13. *Libre Parole*, 1 Nov 1894, BH.

14. *Libre Parole*, 18 Aug 1906, BH.

15. Ochs Folio 9 (29 Jan 1895), BH.

16. Interview with Maurice Bardèche, June 1982, Paris.

17. Pierre Drieu La Rochelle, *Récit Secret* (Paris: Gallimard, 1951). See also Robert Soucy, *Fascist Intellectual: Drieu La Rochelle* (Berkeley: U of California P, 1979). Interviews with Jean Drieu La Rochelle (June and November 1982, Paris); Robert Soucy (July 1982, Paris); Pierre Andreu (June 1982, Paris).

18. Drieu La Rochelle, *Fragment de Memoires*, preface on the "parti unique" by Robert O. Paxton: "Il est curieux que l'ancien combattant Drieu, qui a consacré certaines de ses plus belles pages aux effets à la Légion dans ce *Fragment*." *Fragment de Mémoires* (Paris: Gallimard, 1982), 29.

19. Drieu La Rochelle, *Sur les Ecrivains* (Paris: Gaillimard, 1982), 172, 173, 215.

20. Soucy, *Fascist Intellectual*, 217.

21. Drieu, *Fragment*, 17.

22. Drieu, *Fragment*, 18.

23. AN F7 13241: 2 February 1931.

24. *Dépêche Algérienne* 11 June 1935, AN F7 13241.

25. AN F7 13208.

26. J. L. Borges, "Le Livre comme Mythe," *Débat* 22 (November 1983): 123.

27. AN 61 AJ 91.

28. AN 61 AJ 104.

29. Dupuy, *Sa Vie Résumée*, 90.

30. Henri Massis, "Filitation," *La Table Ronde* 155 (November 1960): 90.

31. Maurice Merleau-Ponty, *Signs* (Evanston: Northwestern UP, 1964), 26.

32. Ibid.

33. Marcel Déat, "Mémoires Politiques," Papiers Déat, Bibliothèque Nationale (BN), Paris.

34. Pascal Ory, *Nizan: Le Destin d'un Révolté* (Paris: Ramsay, 1980), 187. Interview with Pascal Ory, July 1982, Paris.

35. Ory 184.

36. See the student evaluations of Brasillach, Etiemble, Simone Weil, Henri Quéffelec, AN 61 AJ 255–56, and remarks on the *concours d'entrée*, AN 61 AJ 171.

37. Henri de Montherlant, *L'Equinoxe de Septembre, Le Solstice de Juin* (Paris: Gallimard, 1976), 111–25.

38. AN 61 AJ 161.

39. Montherlant, *Equinoxe de Septembre*, 185, 196.

40. Pierre Henri Simon, *Procès du Héros: Montherlant, Drieu La Rochelle, Jean Prévost* (Paris: Seuil, 1950).

41. René Gillouin, *Man's Hangman Is Man*, trans. Dorothy D. Lachman (Mundelein, Ill.: Island Press, 1957), 27.

42. Interview with Claude Jamet, June 1982, Paris, and Pierre Bourdieu, "Les Rites d'Institution," *Actes de la Recherche en Sciences Sociales* 43 (1982): 58–63.

43. J. Austin, *How to Do Things with Words* (Cambridge: Harvard UP, 1975).

44. For some biographic data on Alain Tourraine see Hervé Hamon and Patrick Rotman, *Les Intellocrates* (Paris: Ramsay, 1981).

45. AN 61 AJ 91 and Alain Peyrefitte, *Rue d'Ulm* (Paris: Flammarion, 1963), 409.

46. Ibid., 60.

47. Bourgin, *De Jaurès à Léon Blum*, 233.

48. Ibid., 148.

49. AN 61 AJ 104 2b.

50. *Gringoire*, March 24, 1933, 14.

51. Bourgin, *De Jaurès à Léon Blum*, 237. Compare with Ochs Folio 9, 5 January 1895: "Voici une jolie série de rimes que m'adresse un de nos lecteurs: . . . 'et qu'il possède à son actif / des faillites—c'est lucratif / grâce à son esprit inventif . . .'" The "il" refers to Jews.

52. P. H. Simon, *Discours de Reception de Me. Georges Izard à l'Académie Française* (Paris: Gallimard, 1972), 7.

53. Emile Durkheim, *Moral Education*, trans. Everett K. Wilson (New York: Free Press of Glencoe, 1961), xii.

54. Ibid., xxii.

55. Emile Durkheim, *The Evolution of Educational Thought*, trans. Peter Collins (London: Routledge, 1977).

56. Ibid., 158, 122. On the fascist body, see also George L. Mosse, *Nationalism and Sexuality* (Madison: U of Wisconsin P, 1985), chaps. 2 and 8.

57. "Notes Radiophoniques," Papiers Bouglé, AN 61 AJ 104.

58. AN 61 AJ 161.

59. AN 61 AJ 107.

60. Claude Jamet, *Fifi le Roi* (Paris: Editions de l'Elan, 1947), 205–8. Interview with Claude Jamet, June 1982, Paris.

61. Suleiman, *Elites in French Society*, 97.

62. *Table Ronde* 155 (November 1960): 64.

63. *Comoedia*, 23 August 1942.

64. Albert Bayet, "L'Ami de Herr," in Dupuy, 97–98.

65. Dupuy, *Sa Vie Résumée*; 97–98.

66. Michel Winock, *Edouard Drumont et Cie: Antisemitisme et Fascisme en France* (Paris: Seuil, 1982), 174.

67. F. T. Marinetti and Fillìa, *La Cuisine Futuriste*, trans. Nathalie Heinich (Paris: Metailié, 1982) 43, 23.

68. Dupuy, *Sa Vie Résumée*, 98.

69. Bourgin, *De Jaurès à Léon Blum*, 134–35. See also Mosse on the elevation of (*normalien*) friendships into a cult (*Nationalism and Sexuality*, 174–75).

70. Soucy, *Fascist Intellectual*, 205, 261.

71. Ibid., 206.

72. Dupuy, *Sa Vie Résumée*, 23.

73. Roland Barthes, *Fragments d'un Discours Amoureux* (Paris: Seuil, 1977), 101.

74. Jaurès to Salomon, 23 May 1844. AN 61 AJ 104 2b.

75. Peyrefitte, *Rue d'Ulm*, 181.

76. Alan Sheridan, *Michel Foucault: The Will to Truth* (London: Tavistock, 1980), 5.

77. Foucault, *Power/Knowledge*, 94.

78. AN 61 AJ 96. It is interesting to note that Bouglé in the same series of papers relates science to "nation" and to anti-Semitism, looking at the case of Germany. "C'est au nom de cette science-religion que la troisième Reich prétend étendre sa main." Or, "Veut-on voir à quelle construction idéologique conduit sa prétendue science? C'est ce même crédo que l'on retrouve chez Rosenbert comme chez Hitler, lui-même, et chez Darwin comme chez Goebbels . . ."

79. Sigmund Freud, *The Sexual Enlightenment of Children* (New York: Collier, 1978), 43. The mother is "Certissima."

80. Frederic Grover, *Drieu La Rochelle and the Fiction of Testimony* (Berkeley: U of California P, 1958), 42; R. B. Leal, *Decadence in Love* (St. Lucia: U of Queensland P, 1973), 26–29; Robert Payne, *A Portrait of André Malraux* (New York: Prentice Hall, 1970), 6.

81. Emile Littré, *Dictionnaire de la Langue Française* (Paris: Gallimard, 1957), s.v. "nation."

82. Paul Robert, *Dictionnaire Alphabétique et Analogique de la Langue Française*, s.v. *"nation."*

83. Ibid.

84. Littré, *Dictionnaire*, s.v. *"patrie"*; Robert, *Dictionnaire*, s.v. *"patrie."*

85. *Brockhaus Wahrig Deutsches Worterbuch*, s.v. *"Volk/volkisch."*

86. Ibid., s.v. *"vaterlandisch."*

87. Pierre Bourdieu, *La Reproduction* (Paris: Minuit, 1970), 136, 152–3.

88. Borges, "Livre comme Mythe," 119. "Curieusement, tous les grands maîtres de l'humanité ont donné un enseignement oral."

89. Bourdieu, *Reproduction*, 152.

90. AN 61 AJ 207. For the reproduction of academic taxonomies in the language of *normalien* obituaries, see also Pierre Bourdieu, *Homo Academicus* (Stanford: Stanford UP, 1988), pp. 217–224.

91. AN 61 AJ 206:1915.

92. AN 61 AJ 91.

93. Interview with Maurice Bardèche, June 1982, Paris.

94. AN F7 13209.

95. AN F7 13232.

96. AN F7 19241 (Pamphlet dated August 1935).

97. AN F7 13241 (Pamphlet dated 13 March 1930).

98. AN F7 13241 *L'Oeil de Paris.*

99. *Comoedia* 28 June 1941. *Service Inutile* had an interesting postwar history; it served as the basis for the CNE's condemnation of Montherlant.

100. AN 61 AJ 207.

101. Drieu La Rochelle, "Mussolini contre la Machine," *Les Derniers Jours*

(Paris: J. Michel Place, 1979), 11–12; Walter Benjamin, "The Work of Art in the Age of Mechanical Reproduction," _Illuminations_, trans. Harry Zohn, ed. Hannah Arendt (New York: Schocken, 1969). See also the recent volume of Alice Y. Kaplan, _Reproductions of Banality_ (Minneapolis: U of Minnesota P, 1986).

5. Language and Authority

1. Claude Jamet, _Fifi le Roi_ (Paris: Editions de l'Elan, 1947) 207.
2. Maurice Merleau-Ponty, _Sense and Nonsense_, trans. Hubert Dreyfus and Patricia Allen Dreyfus (Evanston: Northwestern UP, 1964) 99.
3. Robert Soucy, _Fascist Intellectual: Drieu La Rochelle_ (Berkeley: U of California P, 1979), 17.
4. Soucy, _Fascist Intellectual_, 19.
5. Ibid., 12.
6. Ibid., 5.
7. Ibid., 13.
8. Merleau-Ponty, _Sense and Nonsense_, 100–109.
9. Soucy, _Fascist Intellectual_, 5.
10. Maurice Merleau-Ponty, _Signs_, trans. Richard C. McCleary (Evanston: Northwestern UP, 1964), 319.
11. Ibid., 319.
12. Raymond Aron, _The Opium of the Intellectuals_, trans. Terence Kilmartin (New York: Norton, 1962).
13. Soucy, _Fascist Intellectual_, 5.
14. Jamet, _Fifi le Roi_, 179.
15. Raoul Girardet, "Notes sur l'esprit d'un fascisme français 1934–1939," _Revue Française de Science Politique_ 5 (January–March 1955): 531–32.
16. Maurice Bardèche, _Qu'est-ce que le Fascisme?_ (Paris: Plon, 1939).
17. Girardet, "Notes sur l'esprit d'un fascisme français," 531–32.
18. Simone Weil, _First and Last Notebooks_ trans. Ries (London: Oxford UP, 1970), 362.
19. Pascal Ory, _Paul Nizan: Le Destin d'un Révolté_ (Paris: Ramsay, 1980), 144.
20. Soucy, _Fascist Intellectual_, 9.
21. Raymond Aron, _Le Spectateur Engagé_ (Paris: Julliard, 1981).
22. Fredric Jameson, _Fables of Aggression: Wyndam Lewis, Modernist as Fascist_ (Berkeley: U of California P, 1979).
23. Pierre Bourdieu, _Ce Que Parler Veut Dire_ (Paris: Fayard, 1982), 176.
24. Ibid., 171.
25. Ibid., 193.
26. Ibid., 194.
27. Ibid., 176.
28. René Gillouin, _Man's Hangman Is Man_, trans. Dorothy D. Lachman (Mundelein: Island Press, 1957), 80.
29. Bourdieu, _Ce Que Parler Veut Dire_, 168.

30. Ibid., 33, 35.

31. Ibid., 39.

32. Ibid., 73 n.11.

33. Ibid., 68.

34. Ibid., 111.

35. Ibid., 23–24.

36. Archives Nationales (AN) 61 AJ 104.

37. *Discours de Réception d'Alain Peyrefitte à l'Académie Française et Réponse de Claude Lévi-Strauss* (Paris: Gallimard, 1977), 63, 68–69.

38. Roland Barthes, *The Pleasure of the Text* (New York: Hill and Wang, 1975), 50–51.

39. Bourdieu, *Ce Que Parler Veut Dire*, 171–72.

40. Robert Brasillach, *Portraits* (Paris: Plon, 1957), 201.

41. Jamet, *Fifi le Roi*, 292.

42. AN 61 AJ 207.

43. Alain Peyrefitte, *Rue d'Ulm* (Paris: Flammarion, 1963), 401.

44. AN 61 AJ 91.

45. AN 61 AJ 161.

46. AN 61 AJ 104.

47. AN 61 AJ 207.

48. AN 61 AJ 206.

49. Léon Blum, preface *Souvenirs du Vicomte de Courpière par un Témoin*, by Abel Hermant (Paris: Louis Michaud, n.d.), vii–ix.

50. Paul Dupuy, *Sa Vie Résumée par Lui-même* (Paris: Bropard et Taupin, 1951), 8.

51. Peyrefitte, *Rue d'Ulm*, 313.

52. Ibid., 179–81.

53. Bourdieu, *Ce Que Parler Veut Dire*, 175.

54. Sigmund Freud, *The Interpretation of Dreams* trans. James Strachey (New York: Avon, 1965), 338–339, 330–331, 477–479.

55. For all definitions in this paragraph see the *Petit Robert* (1981).

56. Robert Brasillach, *Une Genération dans l'Orage* (Paris: Plon, 1941), 61.

57. Peyrefitte, *Rue d'Ulm*, 119.

58. René Gillouin, *Aristarchie ou la Recherche d'un Gouvernement* (Geneva: Editions du Chevailé, 1946), 9, 33.

59. Gillouin, *Man's Hangman*, 56.

60. Fredric Jameson, *The Political Unconscious* (Ithaca: Cornell UP, 1981), 254.

61. Denis Hollier, "I've Done My Act: An Exercise in Gravity," *Representations* 4 (Fall 1983):88.

62. Gillouin, *Man's Hangman*, 51, 79.

63. Gillouin, *Aristarchie*, 33.

64. Hollier, "I've Done My Act," 99.

65. Gillouin, *Man's Hangman*, 49–58, 61–72.

66. Barthes, *Pleasure of the Text*, 40.

67. AN 61 AJ 104.

68. Jamet, *Fifi le Roi*, 207.

69. Peyrefitte, *Rue d'Ulm*, 408.

70. AN 61 AJ 104.

71. Jameson, *Political Unconscious*, 114–15.

72. Bourdieu, *Ce Que Parler Veut Dire*, 184.

73. Ibid.; Jacques Derrida, "The Double Session," *Dissemination*, trans. Barbara Johnson (Chicago: U of Chicago P, 1981).

74. Hubert Bourgin, *De Jaurès à Leon Blum: L'Ecole Normale et la Politique* (Paris: Fayard, 1938), 134.

75. Peyrefitte, *Rue d'Ulm*, 410, 235, 401.

76. AN 61 AJ 188, 254, 255.

77. Pierre Henri Simon, *Procès du Héros: Montherlant, Drieu La Rochelle, Jean Prévost* (Paris: Seuil, 1950), 179–80.

78. Brasillach, *Portraits*, 198.

79. Simon, *Procès du Héros*, 181.

80. Bourgin, *De Jaurès à Léon Blum*, 134.

81. Jean Guéhenno, *Carnets d'un Vieil Ecrivain* (Paris: Grasset, 1971), 132. One of the reasons for Claude Jamet's censorship postwar was that he took Guéhenno's place after Guéhenno was removed from his lycée post during Vichy.

82. Jean Guéhenno, *Journal d'un Homme de Quarante Ans* (Paris: Grasset, 1934), 119.

83. Simon, *Procès du Héros*, 181, 156.

84. *Reception Peyrefitte*, 102–3.

85. Bourdieu, *Ce Que Parler Veut Dire*, 176.

86. Jamet, *Fifi le Roi*, 251.

87. AN 61 AJ 161.

88. *Discours de Réception de Me. Georges Izard à l'Académie Française et Réponse de M. Pierre Henri Simon* (Paris: Gallimard, 1972), 23.

89. Gillouin, *Man's Hangman*, 78.

90. Bourdieu, *Ce Que Parler Veut Dire*, 177.

91. Gillouin, *Man's Hangman*, 58.

92. AN 61 AJ 207.

93. Guéhenno, *Journal*, 108–9. Guéhenno writes quite passionately of his days at ENS in a book entitled *Changer la Vie*. In *Carnets* (172) he recalls writing *Changer la Vie*: "Je n'ai retrouvé les passions qu'en revenant à ma jeunesse et en publiant un petit livre, *Changer la Vie*."

6. The Ecole Normale Supérieure and the Scene of Writing

1. Régis Debray, *Teachers, Writers, Celebrities*, trans. David Macey (London: New Left Books, 1981), 143. There are many versions of this story. Abetz is said to have asserted: "There are three powers in France: communism, the big banks, and the *NRF*." Although the anecdote varies, the *NRF* is in each

version. See Pierre Assouline, *Gaston Gallimard* (San Diego: Harcourt Brace Jovanovich, 1988), 227.

2. Debray, *Teachers, Writers, Celebrities*, 33.

3. Ibid., 99.

4. *Petit Robert* (1981), s.v. *"edifice."*

5. Ibid.

6. Debray, *Teachers, Writers, Celebrities*; *Le Scribe*(Paris: Grasset); *Critique of Political Reason*, trans. David Macey (London: New Left Books, 1983). All three works have been reviewed by Marc Chenetier, "Gods, Princes, and Scribes" *October* 24 (1983): 103–15.

7. "The concept is not to my liking. I find it shocking and repulsive."

8. Chénetier, "Gods, Princes, and Scribes," 105.

9. Ibid., 107.

10. Jacques Derrida, *Of Grammatology*, trans. Gayatri Chakravorty Spivak (Baltimore: Johns Hopkins UP, 1976), 92.

11. Ibid., 92.

12. Ibid., 93.

13. Debray, *Teachers, Writers, Celebrities*, 137.

14. Ibid., 10, 137.

15. Ibid., 50–51.

16. Ibid., 50. On intellectuals and the Dreyfus Affair, see Pascal Ory and Jean François Sirinelli, *Les Intellectuels en France de l'Affaire Dreyfus à Nos Jours* (Paris: Armand Colin, 1986). Roland Barthes discusses the difference between teaching and writing in "Writers, Intellectuals, Teachers," *The Rustle of Language*, trans. Richard Howard (New York: Hill and Wang, 1986).

17. Debray, *Teachers, Writers, Celebrities*, 59.

18. Ibid., 54.

19. Ibid.

20. Ibid.

21. Ibid., 55.

22. "Abel Hermant," *Larousse du Vingtieme Siècle*, Supplement 1953.

23. Debray, *Teachers, Writers, Celebrities*, 56.

24. *Petit Robert* (1981), s.v. *"pépinière."*

25. Ibid., s.v. *"pépin."*

26. Pierre Bourdieu, *La Reproduction* (Paris: Minuit, 1970), 152.

27. Debray, *Teachers, Writers, Celebrities*, 137; *Petit Robert* (1981), s.v. *"auteur."*

28. Pierre Andreu, *Le Rouge et le Blanc* (Paris: Table Ronde, 1977), 47. Interview with Pierre Andreu, June 1982, Paris. See also Bourdieu, Reproduction, 91 n. 3: "Comme aiment à dire les correcteurs *'l'essentiel, c'est que ce soit bien écrit.'* Célestin Bouglé écrivait: 'Il est formellement entendu que, même pour la dissertation d'histoire, qui suppose un certain nombre de connaissances de fait, les correcteurs doivent apprécier *surtôut* les qualités de composition et d'exposition'" (italics mine).

29. Hervé Hamon and Patrick Rotman, *Les Intellocrates* (Paris: Ramsay, 1981), 47.

30. Ibid., 33.

31. Debray, *Teachers, Writers, Celebrities*, 65.

32. Ibid.

33. J.-P. Sartre, preface to *Aden, Arabie* by Paul Nizan, trans. Joan Pinkham (New York: Monthly Review, 1968).

34. Debray, *Teachers, Writers, Celebrities*, 65, 67.

35. Assouline, *Gaston Gallimard*, 102, 135. Assouline also notes other aspects of the Gallimard firm that are of interest: It is a locus of "Protestant Left Bank pseudohomosexuality" (133). Certain *normaliens* such as Brice Parain are in key positions of power (96–97). Assouline's portrait of Grasset is on pages 117–21. His description of Grasset's disturbing facial similarities to Hitler—the same haircut, mustache, and mannerisms—is extremely witty.

36. For information concerning the receipt of literary and academic prizes for *normaliens* see Archives Nationales 61 AJ 206–7. Leftist *normaliens* are noteworthy in their *absence*. For example, neither J.-P. Sartre nor Raymond Aron receives a prize in the thirties or forties. Aron's first listing is in 1959! Nizan does receive a prize in 1939 for his *Conspiration*, which is sarcastically commented upon by Brasillach in *Je Suis Partout* of December 9, 1938. Brasillach calls *La Conspiration* a "*Deracinés* marxiste: on y voit des conspirateurs d'operettes, ennuyeux intellectuels des banquiers juifs . . . Les opinions de M. Nizan ne concernent pas la littérature, dire-t-on?" By contrast, rightist students such as Brasillach, Bardèche, and Thierry Maulnier receive their prizes less than ten years after their graduation (1936, 1938, 1941, respectively, for the award of *lauréat* of the Académie Française).

37. Charles Kadushin, *The American Intellectual Elite* (Boston: Little, Brown, 1974).

38. Pierre-Marie Dioudonnat, *Je Suis Partout (1930–1944): Les Maurrassiens devant la Tentation Fasciste* (Paris: Table Ronde, 1973), 116. Brasillach worked there for the month of January 1930 at the invitation of Ferdinand Divoire. See also Anne Brassié, *Robert Brasillach* (Paris: Laffont, 1987), 79.

39. Dioudonnat, *Je Suis Partout*, 29, 33–38.

40. J. L. Loubet del Bayle, *Les Nonconformistes des Années Trente* (Paris: Seuil 1969), 88–89, 72, 242, 248–67.

41. Kadushin, *American Intellectual Elite*, 22.

42. Hamon and Rotman, *Intellocrates*, 26.

43. Barthes, *Sade, Fourier, Loyola*, trans. Richard Miller (New York: Hill and Wang, 1976), 3.

44. Herbert Lottman, *La Rive Gauche* (Paris: Seuil, 1981), 103.

45. René Girard, *Le Violence et le Sacré* (Paris: Pluriel, 1979), 98–100.

46. Alain Peyrefitte, *Rue d'Ulm* (Paris: Flammarion, 1963), 181.

47. Henri Guillemin to the author, July 1983. Interview with Georges Lefranc, July 1984, Courseules-sur-Mer, France. Lefranc describes Guillemin's participation in Sangier's Young Republicans.

48. Dioudonnat, *Je Suis Partout*, 226–29.

49. Kadushin, *American Intellectual Elite*, 46.

50. Debray, *Teachers, Writers, Celebrities*, 72.

51. Ibid., 67.

52. Ibid., 74.

53. Kadushin, *American Intellectual Elite*, 46.

54. Debray, *Teachers, Writers, Celebrities*, 72.

55. Loubet del Bayle, *Nonconformistes*, 58.

56. Ibid., 89.

57. Ibid., 43.

58. Ibid.

59. *Je Suis Partout*, January 1939; Loubet del Bayle, *Nonconformistes*, 52, 22, 41, 70, 128–130.

60. Loubet del Bayle, *Nonconformistes*, 246.

61. Ibid., 213–214.

62. Lottman, *Rive Gauche*, 138–39.

63. Ibid.

64. Interviews with Georges Lefranc, July 1984, Courseules-sur-Mer, France, and Jacques Soustelle, August 1984, Paris.

65. Loubet del Bayle, *Nonconformistes*, 88–89.

66. Pascal Ory, *Les Collaborateurs* (Paris: Seuil, 1976), 142, 109.

67. *Pamphlet* 18 (9 June 1933). Bibliothèque Historique de la Ville de Paris (BH).

68. "Les Formes Intermediares," *Pamphlet* 26 (11 August 1933), BH.

69. Interview with Pascal Ory, July 1982, Paris. Pascal Ory suggests a possible typology of authors. He distinguishes between the extreme right and the right, and between those who followed a normal career like Thierry Maulnier, Pierre Gaxotte, and Jacques Bainville (who although tempted by fascism remained in the rightist camp, stayed close to Vichy, and were not purged) and the various forms of the extreme right (fascist). Those with normal careers are separated from the extremists by traditional allegiances, such as nationalism. Chateaubriant and Drieu represent a parody of right-wing discourse. Céline represents an anarchist of the left; Drieu vacillates between Céline's elitism/individualism and Brasillach's adherence to the collectivity. Ory sees a form of self-punishment inherent in Drieu's adherence and continual deception.

70. Loubet del Bayle, *Nonconformistes*, 57–58.

71. Ibid., 64.

72. Ibid., 304, 296, 297; Maurice Blanchot to the author, 20 August 1983: "De *Combat* je me souviens peu. Je me rappelle cependant qu'étant tout à fait opposé à Brasillach, lui-même tout acquis au fascisme et à l'antisemitisme, j'avais mis comme condition à ma participation à cette revue l'assurance qu'il n'y collaborait pas. Au reste, la réciprocité etait vraie. Brasillach détestait *Combat*, parce que j'y avais pris part. L'opposition à Brasillach et à ce qu'il représentait a été une de mes constantes."

73. Loubet del Bayle, *Nonconformistes*, 61.

74. Interview with Maurice Bardèche, June 1982, Paris.

75. Loubet del Bayle, *Nonconformistes*, 61.

76. The role of the Count of Paris in *JSP* is speculated upon in Dioudonnat, *Je Suis Partout*, 111.

77. Loubet del Bayle, *Nonconformistes*, 55. See also Jeffrey Mehlman, "Blanchot at *Combat*," *Legacies of Anti-Semitism in France* (Minneapolis: U of Minnesota P, 1983), 9–12. Mehlman writes that in the years from 1936 to 1938, Blanchot appears as a seminal political thinker for his generation and less as a "littérateur with rightist learning." Indeed, Pierre Andreu in an interview (June 1982, Paris) acknowledges his debt to Blanchot, citing him as the person he felt closest to in those years. Blanchot becomes the standard bearer for a new generation, echoing Bernanos' critique of the "gutlessness of the French right, especially in regard to the Spanish Civil War." His 1936 piece "La Grand Passion des Modérés" echoes Bernanos' title "La Grand Peur des Bien Pensants," and its "subject is the alibi that the French right has found for its cowardice in the 'simulacrum' of 'neutrality' . . . with respect to the Spanish Civil War." Mehlman correctly situates Blanchot's articles' dual posture: between a depiction of an "infernal, comic machine" and exhortations to violence. Two examples suffice to illustrate this depiction. On Spain: "Every day they comically invent new chefs, and, as soon as they think they detect an autocrat on the horizon, throw themselves deliriously at his feet. It's the latest thrill, Mussolini's bronze pout has them swooning. The monotone howls of Hitler leave them frightened and ravished . . . And now what luck to have Franco . . ." When we examine Blanchot on the Geneva pact, we see the prior logic for his espousal of terrorism as a way out of France's immobilizing contradictions and a way of reversing February 6, 1934: "All of our treaties are grafted on the Geneva pact. There is nothing more demanding and more feeble, more harmful and in appearance more necessary than the League of Nations. It seems equally impossible to leave it and to remain within it."

78. Loubet del Bayle, *Nonconformistes*, 275.

79. Marcel Déat, "Mémoires Politiques," 1:13, Papiers Déat, Bibliothèque Nationale (BN).

80. Among those who did not wish to die for Danzig was *normalien* Le Bail, classmate of Georges Lefranc: "On ne va tout de même pas faire la guerre pour 100,000 juifs polonaises." Ory, *Collaborateurs*, 32. Lottman presents a more ambiguous formulation of the problem posed in less virulent terms by Antoine de Saint-Exupéry: "Nous avons choisi la paix. Mais . . . nous avons mutilés des amis. Et sans doute, beaucoup de parmi nous étaient disposé à risquer leur vie pour les devoirs de l'amitié. Ceux-là connaissent une sorte de honte. Mais s'ils avaient sacrifié la paix, ils connaîtraient la même honte. Car ils aurait alors sacrifié l'homme; ils aurait accepté l'irremplaçable éboulement des *bibliothèques*, des cathédrales, des laboratoires . . ." (*Rive Gauche*, 173).

81. Andreu, *Rouge et le Blanc*, 29.

82. Hélène Déat recounts the flight in an unpublished manuscript dated 1955, Papiers Déat BN.

83. Ory, *Collaborateurs*, 142, 109.

84. Lottman, *Rive Gauche*, 173.

85. Déat, "Mémoires" Vol. 1, Chap. 2: 30.

86. Ibid., Vol. 1, chap. 6: 11.

87. Ibid., Vol. 1, chap. 5: 27–28.
88. Ibid., Vol. 1, chap. 5: 28.
89. Letters from Louise Weiss, Nouvelle Ecole de la Paix, BN naf 17814: 265, 260, 52.
90. Déat, "Mémoires," Vol. 1, chap. 9: 27.
91. Ory, *"Collaborateurs"*, 101.
92. Déat, "Mémoires," Vol. 2, chap. 4: 98.
93. Ibid., Vol. 2, chap. 3: 65.
94. Ibid., Vol. 2, chap. 17: 1.
95. Ibid., Vol. 2, chap. 3: 65.
96. Ibid., Vol. 1, chap. 2: 24.
97. Ory, *Collaborateurs*, 37.
98. Ibid., 21.
99. Dioudonnat tells how Gaxotte inaugurates the journal with a strikingly Germanophilic posture (14); cartoonist Ralph Soupault is typical of the cosmopolitan tastes of *JSP*, with his love of Marx Brothers films, jazz, Oscar Wilde, and Joseph Conrad novels (120–121). Indeed, in all ways *JSP* exemplifies the second type of fascism adumbrated by Dioudonnat: "Il est beaucoup plus ressenti que pensé . . . et ressenti comme un phénomène international par nature" (414).
100. Dioudonnat, *Je Suis Partout*, 115.
101. Ibid., 12–15.
102. Ibid., 15.
103. Ibid.
104. Ibid., 83.
105. Ibid.
106. Ibid., 124.
107. Ibid., 226–29.
108. Ibid., 37–38.
109. Robert Brasillach, *Une Génération dans l'Orage* (Paris: Plon, 1968), 21–22.
110. Dioudonnat, *Je Suis Partout*, 39.
111. Brasillach, *Génération dans l'Orage*, 58–59.
112. Dioudonnat, *Je Suis Partout*, 111–13.
113. Ibid., 122.
114. Ibid., 114–15.
115. Ibid., 127.
116. Ibid., 123.
117. Ibid., 124.
118. Ibid., 125.
119. Ibid., 127.
120. See our discussion of *maître* and *maître* admission in Chapter 4.
121. Dioudonnat, *Je Suis Partout*, 128.
122. Ibid., 32. Indeed, Gaxotte's style is described like the process of ripening cheese: "Humidifiée . . . amolli . . ."
123. Loubet del Bayle, *Nonconformistes*, 114.

7. The Postwar Trials

1. Michel Foucault, "What is an author?", *Language, Counter-Memory, Practice*, trans. and ed. Donald F. Bouchard (Ithaca: Cornell UP, 1977) 117.

2. Alan Sheridan, *Michel Foucault: The Will to Truth* (London: Tavistock, 1980), 133–34.

3. Claude Jamet, *Fifi le Roi* (Paris: Editions de l'Elan, 1947), 155: "On parle de Brasillach. M. le Greffier 'adore' la sensibilité de ce jeune *normalien;* enchanté de savoir que je le connais personnellement; il y a des choses si charmantes, n'est-ce pas, dans *Notre Avant Guerre.*"

4. Ibid., 247–249.

5. Sheridan, *Michel Foucault*, 127.

6. Ibid., 121. See also Roland Barthes, "The Death of the Author," *The Rustle of Language*, trans. Richard Howard (New York: Hill and Wang, 1986). On the ritualization of (university) speech see Pierre Bourdieu's *Homo Academicus* (Stanford: Stanford UP, 1988).

7. Karl Marx, *The Eighteenth Brumaire of Louis Napoleon*, in Saul K. Padover, ed. and trans., *Karl Marx on Revolution* (New York: McGraw-Hill, 1971), 280.

8. Otto Kirchheimer, *Political Justice* (Princeton: Princeton UP, 1961), 304–50.

9. Ibid., 327–37.

10. Robert O. Paxton, *Vichy France: Old Guard and New Order, 1940–1944* (New York: Norton, 1972), 334 and 345, respectively.

11. Herbert Lottman, *The Purge* (New York: Morrow, 1986), 158. See also Pierre Assouline, *L'Epuration des Intellectuels* (Brussels: Complexe, 1985).

12. Simone de Beauvoir, *Force of Circumstance* (New York: Putnam, 1965), 21–22. The "Atlantic Wall" and its builders was a frequent reference of intellectuals; see Assouline, *Epuration*, 123–24, for some examples.

13. Albert Camus, *Actuelles* (Paris: Gallimard, 1950), 78–81. On the Camus-Mauriac polemic, see Lottman's chapter "Justice and Charity," *Purge*, 142–49.

14. Bernard Vosges, *Défense de l'Occident* (Paris: Les Septs Couleurs, 1957) 58, 116. On the clerical-intellectual relationship, see Julien Benda's preface to the 1946 edition of *La Trahison des Clercs* (Paris: Grasset, 1977) and Régis Debray's *Le Scribe* (Paris: Grasset, 1980).

15. Vosges, *Défense*, 9.

16. Ibid., 5.

17. Lottman, *Purge*, 164–65, 41–42, 134.

18. Paxton, *Vichy France*, 330–31.

19. Vosges, *Défense*, 108.

20. Ibid. For the case of Bernard Grasset see also Hervé Hamon and Patrick Rotman, *Les Intellocrates* (Paris: Ramsay, 1981), 85–86; and Herbert Lottman, *La Rive Gauche* (Paris: Seuil, 1981), 222 and 242. See also Pascal Fouché, *L'Edition Française sous l'Occupation* (Paris: Bibliothèque de Littérature Française Contemporaine, 1987), 2:313 and 3:348, and Pierre Assouline, *Gaston Gallimard* (San Diego: Harcourt Brace Jovanovich, 1988), 316–20.

21. Vosges, *Défense*, 108. See also Robert Aron, *Histoire de l'Epuration* 1(Paris: Fayard, 1976), 144–145.

22. Aron, *Histoire de l'Epuration*, 241.

23. Ibid., 144–45.

24. Ibid., 241; Vosges, *Défense*, 119.

25. Aron, *Histoire de l'Epuration*, 130–31.

26. Lottman, *Purge*, 87, 78. For a full list of petition signers and for the text of the petition, see Assouline, *L'Epuration des Intellectuels*, 159.

27. Lottman, *Purge*, 297. The role of Jean Paulhan and his *"politique dégagée"* can not be underestimated and is the subject of the following research: Gerhard Heller, "Mon Maître Paulhan," *Un Allemand à Paris* (Paris: Seuil, 1981), 96–113; Pascal Mercier, "Les Ecrits de Jean Paulhan dans la Presse Clandestine: une résistance appliquée, dégagée?" *Actes du Colloque La Littérature Française sous l'Occupation*, Reims, France, October 1981.

28. Simone de Beauvoir, *La Force de l'Age* (Paris: Gallimard, 1960), 36–37.

29. Camus, *Actuelles*, 72–73. Other signatures included Claudel, Valéry, Mauriac, Duhamel, Henri Bordeaux, Prince et Duc de Broglie, Emile Henriot, Patrice de la Tour du Pin, Paulhan, Thierry Maulnier, Jean Schlumberger, Jean Anouilh, Roland Dorgèles, Jean Louis Barrault, Jean Cocteau, Max Favalleli, Marcel Aymé, Colette, Gabriel Marcel. André Gide refused to sign.

30. Vosges, *Défense*, 54. Famous denizens of Fresnes prison included Henri Massis, Pierre Benoit of the Académie Française, and Xavier de Magillon.

31. Lottman, *Rive Gauche*, 308. "Voyant de tels Abels, avait écrit Paulhan . . . on se demande ce que fait les Cains."

32. Recent work on Céline that touches on this issue of political "recuperation" includes Philippe Muray's excellent *Céline* (Paris: Seuil, 1981); François Gibault's introduction to *Céline, Romans III* (Paris: Mercure de France, 1981). See also "Voyage au bout de Céline," *Le Monde*, October 16, 1981, 20–21.

33. "L'Affaire Céline," *Cahiers de la Résistance*, Centre de Documentation Juive Contemporaine (CDJC) Paris, France, Document 1882: 5–79. Philippe Muray takes issue with this representation of Céline.

34. Assouline, *Gaston Gallimard*, 277.

35. "L'Affaire du *Dépêche Algérienne*", CDJC Document ccx 11–33, 35a,b.

36. Hannah Arendt, *Eichmann in Jerusalem: A Report on the Banality of Evil* (New York: Penguin, 1977), 128.

37. CDJC Document 1882. Dominique Sordet was affiliated with Maurras's Action Française as well as actively collaborating (politically) with Otto Abetz and Brinon. Other Interfrance journals included: *Marseille Matin, L'Eclair de Montpelier, La Republique de l'Isère, Le Courrier du Centre, L'Echo de la Loire, La Liberté du Sud-Ouest, L'Eclair de Brest, Journal de Rouen, Petit Parisien, Le Petit Courier d'Angers.*

38. "L'Affaire Grasset," CDJC Document 1882.

39. Assouline, *Gaston Gallimard*, 117, 22, 221. See also Fouché, *Edition Française*, for reproductions of Grasset's correspondence.

40. The full series included: Drieu, *Ne Plus Attendre*; Barthélémy, *Provinces*; Doriot, *Je Suis un Homme du Maréchal*; Suarez, *Pétain ou la Démocratie*; Bonnard, *Pensées dans l'Action*; Chardonne, *Voir la Figure*; Pierre Daye, *Guerre et Révolution*; (Lesca, *Quand Israel Se Venge*; Sieburg, *La Fleur d'Acier*; and Blond,

L'Angleterre en Guerre were published out of series.)

41. Aron, *Histoire de l'Epuration*, 342–43.

42. "Le Procès Beraud," *Crapouillot* 31–33. CDJC Document 3897. *Crapouillot* was published under the direction of Galtier Boissière.

43. Lucien Combelle, *Péché d'Orgueil* (Paris: Olivier Orban, 1978), 300–301. "une mort qui n'a pas été choisie, comme ce fut le cas pour Drieu et Fontenoy . . . Mort pour ses idées! Eh oui! Qui plus est: des idées de droite pour gens de gauche!"

44. *Crapouillot* 37. For public opinion data on the Beraud verdict, see Lottman, *Purge*, 144. See also Assouline, *Histoire de l'Epuration*, 26, 42–46.

45. *Crapouillot* 41.

46. Camus, *Actuelles*, 73.

47. Combelle, *Péché d'Orgeuil*, 329.

48. Ibid.

49. "Procès de l'Equipe *Je Suis Partout*," CDJC Document xlvii: 5.

50. This led to Henri Jeanson's renaming of the trial "Je suis parti."

51. "Procès de l'Equipe"; Régis Debray, *Le Pouvoir Intellectuel en France* (Paris: Ramsay, 1979), 92.

52. "Procès de l'Equipe."

53. Kirchheimer, *Political Justice*, 225.

54. *Le Procès de Robert Brasillach* (Paris: Flammarion, 1946), 9. Anne Brassié describes how Brasillach always prepared for exams by taking notes, and he did the same in his trial: *Robert Brasillach* (Paris: Laffont, 1987), 328.

55. *Procès de Brasillach*.

56. Combelle, *Péché d'Orgeuil*, 300.

57. *Procès de Brasillach*, 3.

58. Arendt, *Eichmann in Jerusalem*, 9.

59. P. A. Cousteau, *En ce Temps-là*, CDJC Document 6844:1. "En ce temps-là, j'étais à Louis-le-Grand. J'y faisais l'apprentissage de l'opposition de l'âge des boutons d'acné."

60. *Procès de Brasillach*, 124.

61. *Procès de Brasillach*, 146–47.

62. Jamet, *Fifi le Roi*, 242 (translation mine). Interview with Claude Jamet, June 1982, Paris.

63. Jamet, *Fifi le Roi*, 248 (translation mine).

64. Ibid., 250–51 (translation mine).

65. Ibid., 179, 250–51 (translation mine).

66. Ibid., 240.

67. For an elaboration of the trope of metonymy see Roman Jakobson, "Two Aspects of Language and Two Types of Aphasic Disturbances," in Jakobson and Morris Halle, *Fundamentals of Language* (The Hague, 1956), and Jacques Lacan "The Insistance of the Letter in the Unconscious," in Richard T. De George and Fernande M. De George, eds., *The Structuralists: From Marx to Lévi-Strauss* (Garden City: Anchor, 1972). *Les Procès de Collaboration: Brinon, Darnand, Luchaire* (Paris: Alban Michel, 1948), 610.

68. *Procès de Collaboration*, 379.

69. Ibid., 509.

70. Ibid., 526.

71. Ibid., 538.

72. Ibid., 542.

73. Ibid., 628–29.

74. *Le Procès Maurras*, Les Editions de Savoie, 80.

75. Ibid., 75.

76. Ibid., 47. See also 155: Maurras discounts the charge of anti-Semitism. "Mais il aime le juif aimable, le juif bien-né, le juif qui n'abuse pas de notre hospitalité."

77. Ibid., 25.

78. Ibid., 112.

79. Ibid., 134.

80. Ibid., 135.

81. Ibid., 41.

82. Ibid., 133.

83. Talleyrand is quoted in Lottman, *Purge*, 133.

84. Vosges, *Défense*, 13.

85. Agnes Heller, "Group Interest, Collective Consciousness, and the Role of the Intellectual in Lukács and Goldmann," *Social Praxis* 6 (1979): 186.

86. Debray, *Scribe*.

87. J. L. Austin, *How to Do Things with Words* (Cambridge: Harvard UP, 1975), 5.

88. Ibid., 19 (see also the discussion on p. 4).

89. Ibid., 19.

90. Ibid., 9. See also Austin's discussions of commissives (151–57) and exeratives (162) as specific forms of performatives.

91. Ibid., 151–57. On the deconstruction of thought as act, see Paul De Man, *Allegories of Reading* (New Haven: Yale UP, 1979), 129.

92. Michel Foucault, *Discipline and Punish*, trans. Alan Sheridan (New York: Vintage, 1979).

93. Fredric Jameson, *The Political Unconscious* (Ithaca: Cornell UP, 1981), 113–15.

94. Arendt, *Eichmann in Jerusalem*, 247.

95. Jameson, *Political Unconscious*, 166 n. 3.

96. Robert Soucy, *Fascist Intellectual: Drieu La Rochelle* (Berkeley: U of California P, 1979); Dominique Desanti, *Drieu ou le Séducteur Mystifié* (Paris: Flammarion, 1978).

97. Pascal Ory and Jean François Siranelli, *Les Intellectuels en France, de l'Affaire Dreyfus à Nos Jours* (Paris: Armand Colin, 1986), 137.

98. Marcel Déat, "Mémoires Politiques," Papiers Déat, Bibliothèque Nationale, Paris, France. See also Hélène Déat's recollection of the flight (written in 1955), Papiers Déat. Interview with Georges Lefranc, July 1984 Courseules-sur-Mer, France.

99. Déat, "Mémoires Politiques," Vol. 1, chap. 4: 107.

100. Ibid., 107.

101. Robert Aron, "Pucheu au Nom de la Raison d'Etat," *La Justice Sommaire de l'Été 44, Historia* (hors serie no. 41).

102. This discussion is grounded in two articles: Lacan's "Insistence of the Letter" (*supra*) and Derrida's "Signature, Evènement, Contexte," *Marges de la Philosophie* (Paris: Minuit, 1972), 390–93.

103. The prevalent specular relationship throughout the trial and the attendant theme of fascination can be seen in Beauvoir's *La Force de l'Age*.

104. *Procès Brasillach*, 51.

105. *Procès Maurras*, 16.

106. Ibid., 163. (See also p. 28.)

107. Ibid., 31. "J'ai ma vie, j'ai ma doctrine, j'ai mon avenir. Vous pouvez faire de moi ce que vous voudrez; mais je suis Charles Maurras."

108. Ibid., 57.

109. Ibid., 78.

110. Ibid., 73.

111. Lucien Rebatet, *Les Mémoires d'un Fasciste*, 2 vols. (Paris: Pauvert, 1976), 2: 231–32.

Conclusion

1. Regis Debray, *Le Scribe* (Paris: Grasset, 1980) 30.

2. Pierre-Marie Dioudonnat, *Je Suis Partout 1930–1944: Les Maurassiens devant la Tentation Fasciste* (Paris: Table Ronde, 1973), 115.

WORKS CONSULTED

Theoretical Background

Arendt, Hannah. *The Human Condition*. Chicago: U of Chicago P, 1958.

Balibar, Renée. *Les Français Fictifs*. Paris: Hachette, 1974.

Barthes, Roland. *Fragments d'un Discours Amoureux*. Paris: Seuil, 1977.

Barthes, Roland. *Mythologies*. Trans. Annette Lavers. New York: Hill and Wang, 1972.

Barthes, Roland. *The Pleasure of the Text*. Trans. Richard Miller. New York: Hill and Wang, 1975.

Barthes, Roland. *The Rustle of Language*. Trans. Richard Howard. New York: Hill and Wang, 1986.

Barthes, Roland. *Sade, Fourier, Loyola*. Trans. Richard Miller. New York: Hill and Wang, 1976.

Benjamin, Walter. *Illuminations*. Trans. Harry Zohn. New York: Schocken, 1969.

Besnier, Jean Michel. *La Polique de l'Impossible*. Paris: La Découverte, 1988.

Borges, Jorge Luis. "Le Livre comme Mythe." *Le Débat* 22 (1982): 118–26.

Bourdieu, Pierre. *Ce Que Parler Veut Dire*. Paris: Fayard, 1982.

Bourdieu, Pierre. "La Délégation et le Fétichisme Politique." *Actes de la Recherche en Sciences Sociales* 52–53 (1984): 49–55.

Bourdieu, Pierre. *Distinction*. Trans. Richard Nice. Cambridge: Harvard UP, 1984.

Bourdieu, Pierre. "Espace Social et Genèse des 'Classes,'" *Actes de la Recherche en Sciences Sociales* 52–53 (1984): 3–14.

Bourdieu, Pierre. *Homo Academicus*. Trans. Peter Collier. Stanford: Stanford UP, 1988.

Bourdieu, Pierre. *Noblesse d'Etat*. Paris: Editions de Minuit, 1989.

Bourdieu, Pierre. *Questions de Sociologie*. Paris: Editions de Minuit, 1980.

Bourdieu, Pierre. *La Reproduction*. Paris: Editions de Minuit, 1970.

Bourdieu, Pierre. "Les Rites d'Institution." *Actes de la Recherche en Sciences Sociales* 43 (1982): 58–63.

Bourdieu, Pierre, and Jean-Claude Passeron. *Les Héritiers*. Paris: Editions de Minuit, 1964.

Bürger, Peter. *Theory of the Avant-Garde*. Trans. Michael Shaw. Minneapolis: U of Minnesota P, 1984.

Chénetier, Marc. "Gods, Princes, and Scribes." *October* 24 (1983): 103–15.

Debray, Régis. *Critique of Political Reason*. Trans. David Macey. London: New Left Books, 1983.

Debray, Régis. *Le Pouvoir Intellectuel en France*. Paris: Ramsay, 1979.

Debray, Régis. *Le Scribe*. Paris: Grasset, 1980.

Works Consulted

Debray, Régis. *Teachers, Writers, Celebrities*. Trans. David Macey. London: New Left Books, 1981.

De George, Richard T., and Fernande M. De George, eds. *The Structuralists: From Marx to Lévi-Strauss*. Garden City: Anchor-Doubleday, 1972.

Derrida, Jacques. *Dissemination*. Trans. Barbara Johnson. Chicago: U of Chicago P, 1981.

Derrida, Jacques. *Of Grammatology*. Trans. Gayatri Chakravorty Spivak. Baltimore: Johns Hopkins UP, 1976.

Derrida, Jacques. *Margins of Philosophy*. Trans. Alan Bass. Chicago: U of Chicago P, 1982.

Derrida, Jacques. "The Principle of Reason: The University in the Eyes of Its Pupils." *Diacritics* 13 (1983): 3–19.

Derrida, Jacques. *Writing and Difference*. Trans. Alan Bass. Chicago: U of Chicago P, 1978.

Durkheim, Emile. *Education et Sociologie*. Paris: Presses Universitaires de France, 1966.

Durkheim, Emile. *The Evolution of Educational Thought*. Trans. Peter Collins. London: Routledge and Kegan Paul, 1977.

Durkheim, Emile. *Moral Education*. Trans. Everett K. Wilson and Herman Schnurer. New York: Free Press, 1961.

Durkheim, Emile. *Selected Writings*. Trans. and ed. Anthony Giddens. Cambridge, Eng.: University Press, 1972.

Durkheim, Emile. *Textes: Fonctions Sociales et Institutions*. Paris: Editions de Minuit, 1975.

Foucault, Michel. *Discipline and Punish*. Trans. Alan Sheridan. New York: Vintage-Random, 1979.

Foucault, Michel. *I, Pierre Rivière, Having Slaughtered My Mother, My Sister, and My Brother . . .* Trans. Frank Jellinek. Lincoln: U of Nebraska P, 1982.

Foucault, Michel. *Language, Counter-Memory, Practice*. Trans. Donald F. Bouchard and Sherry Simon. Ithaca: Cornell UP, 1977.

Foucault, Michel. *L'Ordre du Discours*. Paris: Gallimard, 1971.

Foucault, Michel. *Power/Knowledge*. Trans. Colin Gordon, Leo Marshall, John Mepham, and Kate Soper. New York: Pantheon, 1980.

Freud, Sigmund. *Group Psychology and the Analysis of the Ego*. Trans. James Strachey. New York: Norton, 1959.

Freud, Sigmund. *The Interpretation of Dreams*. Trans. James Strachey. New York: Avon, 1965.

Freud, Sigmund. *Moses and Monotheism*. Trans. Katherine Jones. New York: Vintage-Random, 1967.

Freud, Sigmund. *The Psychopathology of Everyday Life*. Trans. Alan Tyson. New York: Norton, 1960.

Freud, Sigmund. *The Sexual Enlightenment of Children*. Ed. Philip Rieff. New York: Collier, 1978.

Goffman, Erving. *Asylums*. Garden City: Anchor-Doubleday, 1961.

Grisoni, Dominique, ed. *Politiques de la Philosophie*. Paris: Grasset, 1976.

Guillemin, Alain. "Pouvoir de Représentation et Constitution de l'Identité Locale." *Actes de la Recherche en Sciences Sociales* 52–53 (1984): 15–18.

Hollander, Paul. *Political Pilgrims*. New York: Oxford UP, 1981.

Hollier, Denis. "I've Done My Act: An Exercise in Gravity." *Representations* 4 (1983): 88–100.

Horkheimer, Max, and Theodor W. Adorno. *Dialectic of Enlightenment*. Trans. John Cumming. New York: Seabury, 1972.

Jameson, Fredric. *The Political Unconscious*. Ithaca: Cornell UP, 1981.

Karady, Victor. "Les Professeurs de la République: Le Marché Scolaire, les Réformes Universitaires, et les Transformations de la Fonction Professorale à la Fin du 19e Siècle." *Actes de la Recherche en Sciences Sociales* 47–48 (1983): 90–112.

Lacan, Jacques. *Ecrits 1*. Paris: Seuil, 1966.

Lacoue-Labarthe, Philippe. *La Fiction du Politique (Heidegger, l'Art et la Politique)*. Strasbourg: Université de Strasbourg, 1987.

Lafarge, Claude. *La Valeur Littéraire*. Paris: Fayard, 1983.

Lévi-Strauss, Claude. *Le Cru et le Cuit*. Paris: Plon, 1964.

Lyotard, Jean-François. *Heidegger et "les Juifs."* Paris: Galilée, 1988.

Mannheim, Karl. *Ideology and Utopia*. Trans. Louis Wirth and Edward Shils. New York: Harvest-Harcourt, 1936.

Martin, Henri-Jean. "Pour une Histoire de la Lecture." *Le Débat* 22 (1982): 160–77.

Mehlman, Jeffrey. *Legacies of Anti-Semitism in France*. Minneapolis: U of Minnesota P, 1983.

Miller, Gérard. *Les Pousse-au-Jouir du Maréchal Pétain*. Paris: Seuil, 1975.

Pinto, Louis. "L'Ecole des Philosophes." *Actes de la Recherche en Sciences Sociales* 47–48 (1983): 21–36.

Prost, Antoine. *Eloge des Pédagogues*. Paris: Seuil, 1985.

Robert, Marthe. *La Tyrannie de l'Imprimé*. Paris: Grasset, 1984.

Sabelli, Fabrizio. "Le Rite d'Institution, Résistance et Domination." *Actes de la Recherche en Sciences Sociales* 43 (1982): 64–70.

Sibony, Daniel. *L'Amour Inconscient*. Paris: Grasset, 1983.

Sibony, Daniel. *Le Groupe Inconscient*. Paris: Christian Bourgois, 1980.

Sibony, Daniel. *La Haine du Désir*. Paris: Christian Bourgois, 1978.

Siegel, James. "Academic Work: The View from Cornell." *Diacritics* 11 (1981): 68–83.

Suleiman, Susan Rubin. *Authoritarian Fictions*. New York: Columbia UP, 1983.

Weber, Samuel. *Institution and Interpretation*. Minneapolis: U of Minnesota P, 1987.

Books by or about *Normaliens*

Aron, Raymond. *Mémoires*. Paris: Julliard, 1983.

Aron, Raymond. *The Opium of the Intellectuals*. Trans. Terence Kilmartin. New York: Norton, 1962.

Works Consulted

Aron, Raymond. *Le Spectateur Engagé*. Paris: Julliard, 1981.

Bardèche, Maurice. *Qu'est-ce que le Fascisme?* Paris: Plon, 1939.

Bloch, Maurice. *Strange Defeat: A Statement of Evidence Written in 1940*. Trans. Gerard Hopkins. New York: Norton, 1968.

Bourgin, Hubert. *L'Année Sociologique (1903–1904)*. *Première Partie: Mémoires Originaux*. Paris, n.d.

Bourgin, Hubert. *De Jaurès à Léon Blum: l'Ecole Normale et la Politique*. Paris: Fayard, 1938.

Brasillach, Robert. *Comme le Temps Passe*. Paris: Plon, 1937.

Brasillach, Robert. *Ecrits à Fresnes*. Paris: Plon, 1967.

Brasillach, Robert. *Une Génération dans l'Orage*. Paris: Plon, 1968.

Brasillach, Robert. *Journal d'un Homme Occupé*. Paris: Plon, n.d.

Brasillach, Robert. *Portraits*. Paris: Plon, 1957.

Brasillach, Robert. *Les Quatres Jeudis*. Paris: Les Septs Couleurs, 1943.

Brasillach, Robert. *Les Septs Couleurs*. Paris: Plon, 1939.

Brassié, Anne. *Robert Brasillach*. Paris: Laffont, 1987.

Canguilhem, Georges. *On the Normal and the Pathological*. Trans. Carolyn R. Fawcett. Dordrecht, Holland: Reidel, 1978.

Dupuy, Paul. *Sa Vie Resumée par Lui-même*. Paris: Bropard et Taupin, 1951.

Gillouin, René. *Man's Hangman Is Man*. Trans. Dorothy D. Lachman. Mundelein, Ill.: Island Press, 1957.

Ginsberg, Ariel. *Nizan*. Paris: Editions Universitaires, 1966.

Giraudoux, Jean. *Lettres*. Ed. Jacques Body. Paris: Klincksieck, 1975.

Giraudoux, Jean. *Souvenirs de Notre Jeunesse*. Geneva: La Palatine, 1948.

Guéhenno, Jean. *Carnets d'un Vieil Ecrivain*. Paris: Grasset, 1971.

Guéhenno, Jean. *Journal d'un homme de Quarante ans*. Paris: Grasset, 1934.

Hermant, Abel. *Souvenirs du Vicomte de Courpière par un Témoin*. Paris: Louis-Michaud, n.d.

Hermant, Abel. *Souvenirs de la Vie Frivole*. Paris: Hachette, 1933.

Hermant, Abel. *Souvenirs de la Vie Mondaine*. Paris: Plon, 1935.

Hermant, Abel. *Trains de Luxe*. Paris: Alphonse Lemerre, n.d.

Hollier, Denis. *The Politics of Prose*. Minneapolis: U of Minnesota P, 1986.

Inskip, D. *Jean Giraudoux: The Making of a Dramatist*. London: Oxford UP, 1957.

Isorni, Jacques, et al. *Le Procès de Robert Brasillach*. Paris: Flammarion, 1946.

Izard, Georges. *Discours de Réception de Me. Georges Izard à l'Académie Française et Réponse de M. Pierre-Henri Simon*. Paris: Gallimard, 1972.

Jamet, Claude. *Fifi le Roi*. Paris: Editions de l'Elan, 1947.

Jamet, Claude. *Notre Front Populaire, 1934–1939*. Paris: Table Ronde, 1977.

Jankélévitch, Vladimir. *Sources: Recueil*. Paris: Seuil, 1984.

Kaplan, Alice Yaeger. *Reproduction of Banality*. Minneapolis: U of Minnesota P, 1986.

LaCapra, Dominick. *A Preface to Sartre*. Ithaca: Cornell UP, 1978.

Maulnier, Thierry. *La Pensée Marxiste*. Paris: Fayard, 1948.

Merleau-Ponty, Maurice. *Sense and Nonsense*. Trans. Hubert L. Dreyfus and Patricia Allen Dreyfus. Evanston: Northwestern UP, 1964.

Merleau-Ponty, Maurice. *Signs*. Trans. Richard C. McCleary. Evanston: North-western UP, 1964.

Nizan, Paul. *La Conspiration*. Paris: Gallimard, 1938.

Nizan, Paul. *The Watchdogs: Philosophers and the Established Order*. Trans. Paul Fittingoff. New York: Monthly Review, 1971.

Ory, Pascal. *Nizan: Le Destin d'un Révolté*. Paris: Ramsay, 1980.

Pado, Dominique. *Maurras, Béraud, Brasillach*. Monaco: Editions O. Pathé, 1945.

Péguy, Charles. *Jeanne d'Arc*. Paris: Gallimard, 1948.

Péguy, Charles. *Oeuvres en Prose, 1898–1908*. Paris: Gallimard, 1959.

Peyrefitte, Alain. *Discours de Réception d'Alain Peyrefitte à l'Académie Française et Réponse de Claude Lévi-Strauss*. Paris: Gallimard, 1977.

Peyrefitte, Alain. *Rue d'Ulm: Chronique de la Vie Normalienne*. Paris: Jean Vigneaux, 1950.

Rouiz, Louis. *Pierre Poyet: le Chretien et l'Apotre*. Paris: P. Lethielleux, 1914.

Sartre, Jean-Paul. *Le Mur*. Paris: Gallimard, 1939.

Sartre, Jean-Paul. *Situations III*. Paris: Gallimard, 1949.

Sartre, Jean-Paul. *The Words*. Trans. Bernard Frechtman. 1964. Greenwich, Conn.: Fawcett, 1966.

Simon, Pierre-Henri. *Procès du Héros*. Paris: Seuil, 1950.

Sirinelli, Jean François. *Génération Intellectuelle*. Paris: Fayard, 1988.

Sirinelli, Jean François. "Khâgneux et Normaliens des Années Vingt: Contribution a l'Histoire des Intellectuels Français." *Bulletin de la Société d'Histoire Moderne* 21 (1983): 6–17.

Weil, Simone. *First and Last Notebooks*. Trans. Ries. London: Oxford UP, 1970.

Books by or about Cohorts of *Normaliens*

Andreu, Pierre. *Georges Sorel: Entre le Noir et le Rouge*. 1953. Paris: Syros, 1982.

Andreu, Pierre. "L'Idée Politique de la Jeunesse Intellectuelle de 1927 à la Guerre." *Revue des Travaux de l'Académie des Sciences Morales et Politiques*. 1957.

Andreu, Pierre. *Le Rouge et le Blanc, 1928–1944*. Paris: Table Ronde, 1977.

Ariès, Philippe. *Un Historien du Dimanche*. Paris: Seuil, 1980.

Benda, Julien. *La Trahison des Clercs*. 1927. Paris: Grasset, 1977.

Céline, F. *Cahiers Céline*. Vol. 1. Paris: Gallimard, 1976.

Céline, F. *Cahiers Céline*. Vol. 6. Paris: Gallimard, 1980.

Céline, F. *D'un Château à l'Autre*. Paris: Gallimard, 1957.

Combelle, Lucien. *Péché d'Orgueil*. Paris: Olivier Orban, 1978.

Desanti, Dominique. *Drieu ou le Séducteur Mystifié*. Paris: Flammarion, 1978.

Drieu La Rochelle, Pierre. *Les Chiens de Paille*. Paris: Gallimard, 1964.

Drieu La Rochelle, Pierre. *Etat Civil*. Paris: Gallimard, n.d.

Drieu La Rochelle, Pierre. *Le Feu Follet*. 1931. Paris: Gallimard, 1959.

Drieu La Rochelle, Pierre. *Fragment de Mémoires, 1940–41*. Paris: Gallimard, 1982.

Works Consulted

Drieu La Rochelle, Pierre. *Le Jeune Européen, suivi de Genève ou Moscou.* 1927 and 1928. Paris: Gallimard, 1978.

Drieu La Rochelle, Pierre. *Mesure de la France, suivi de Ecrits, 1939–1940.* Paris: Grasset, 1964.

Drieu La Rochelle, Pierre. *Notes pour Comprendre le Siècle.* Paris: Gallimard, 1941.

Drieu La Rochelle, Pierre. *Pierre Drieu la Rochelle: Textes de Drieu la Rochelle.* Ed. Marc Hanrez. Paris: Herne, 1982.

Drieu La Rochelle, Pierre. *Récit Secret.* Paris: Gallimard, 1951.

Drieu La Rochelle, Pierre. *Socialisme Fasciste.* Paris: Gallimard, 1964.

Drieu La Rochelle, Pierre. *Sur les Ecrivains.* 1964. Paris: Gallimard, 1982.

Drieu La Rochelle, Pierre, and Emmanuel Berl. *Les Derniers Jours: Cahier Politique et Littéraire.* 1927. Paris: Jean-Michel Place, 1979.

Estève, Michel. *Georges Bernanos: Un Triple Itinéraire.* Paris: Hachette, 1981.

Heidegger, Martin. "Le Rectorat 1933–1934. Faits et Réflexions." *Débat* 27 (1983): 73–89.

Heller, Gerhard. *Un Allemand à Paris, 1940–1944.* Paris: Seuil, 1981.

Isorni, Jacques. *Le Condamné de la Citadelle.* Paris: Flammarion, 1982.

Jouhandeau, Marcel. *Journal sous l'Occupation, suivi de La Courbe de Nos Angoisses.* Paris: Gallimard, 1980.

Jouvenel, Bertrand de. *Un Voyageur dans le Siècle: 1903–1945.* Paris: Laffont, 1979.

Jouvenel, Bertrand de. *La République des Camarades.* Paris: Grasset, 1914.

Jünger, Ernst. *Le Coeur Aventureux.* Trans. Henri Thomas. Paris: Gallimard, 1969.

Jünger, Ernst. *Premier Journal Parisien.* Trans. Henri Plard. Paris: Christian Bourgois, 1980.

Jünger, Ernst. *Second Journal Parisien.* Trans. Henri Plard. Paris: Christian Bourgois, 1980.

Marinetti, F. T., et Fillià. *La Cuisine Futuriste.* Trans. Nathalie Heinich. Paris: Métailié, 1982.

Maurras, Charles. *L'Avenir de L'Intelligence.* Paris: Flammarion, 1927.

Montherlant, Henri de. *L'Equinoxe de Septembre suivi de Le Solstice de Juin et de Mémoire.* Paris: Gallimard, 1976.

Muray, Philippe. *Céline.* Paris: Seuil, 1981.

Les Procès de Collaboration: F. de Brinon, Joseph Darnard, Jean Luchaire (Compte Rendu Sténographique). Paris: Albin Michel, 1948.

Rebatet, Lucien. *Les Mémoires d'un Fasciste I: Les Décombres, 1938–1940.* Paris: Pauvert, 1976.

Rebatet, Lucien. *Les Mémoires d'un Fasciste II: 1941–1947.* Paris: Pauvert, 1976.

Thibaudet, Alfred. *La République des Professeurs.* Geneva: Slatkine, 1979.

Thournoux, Raymond. *Le Royaume d'Otto.* Paris: Flammarion, 1982.

Works Consulted

Reference Works on France or Fascism

Amaury, Philippe. *De l'Introduction et de la Propagande d'Etat, les Deux Premiers Experiences d'un Ministre de l'Information en France*. Paris: Librairie Générale de Droit et de Jurisprudence. 1969.

Anglès, Auguste. *André Gide et le Premier Groupe de la NRF: 1890–1910*. Paris: Gallimard, 1978.

Arendt, Hannah. *Antisemitism: Part One of the Origins of Totalitarianism*. 1951. New York: Harcourt, 1968.

Arendt, Hannah. *Eichmann in Jerusalem: A Report on the Banality of Evil*. 1963. New York: Penguin, 1977.

Arendt, Hannah. *Totalitarianism: Part Three of the Origins of Totalitarianism*. 1951. New York: Harcourt, 1968.

Assouline, Pierre. *L'Epuration des Intellectuels*. Brussels: Complexe, 1985.

Assouline, Pierre. *Gaston Gallimard*. San Diego: Harcourt Brace Jovanovich, 1988.

Bataille, Georges. "La Structure Psychologique du Fascisme." *Oeuvres Complètes*. Vol. 2. Paris: Gallimard, 1970.

Boudon, Raymond. "The French University since 1968." *Comparative Politics* (1977): 89–118.

Caute, David. *Le Communisme et les Intellectuels Français: 1914–1966*. Paris: Gallimard, 1967.

Clark, Terry. *Prophets and Patrons: The French University and the Emergence of the Social Sciences*. Cambridge: Harvard UP, 1973.

Clouard, Henri. *Histoire de la Littérature Française*. Paris: Michel, 1949.

Cousteau, P. A. *En Ce Temps Là*. n.p.: La Librairie Française, n.d.

Farias, Victor. *Heidegger et le Nazisme*. Paris: Verdier, 1987.

Faye, Jean Pierre. *Langages Totalitaires*. Paris: Hermann, 1973.

Fouché, Pascal. *L'Edition Française sous l'Occupation, 1940–1944*. Paris: Bibliotheque de Littérature Française Contemporaine de l'Université de Paris VII, 1987.

Girard, Alain. *La Réussite Sociale en France*. Paris: Presses Universitaires, 1961.

Girardet, Raoul. "Notes sur l'Esprit d'un Fascisme Francaise." *Revue Française de Science Politique* 5 (1955).

Girardet, Raoul, ed. *La Crise Militaire Française, 1945–1962: Aspects Sociologiques et Idéologiques*. Paris: Armand Colin, 1964.

Grover, Frederic. *Drieu La Rochelle and the Fiction of Testimony*. Berkeley: U of California P, 1958.

Guissard, Lucian. *Emmanuel Mounier*. Paris: Editions Universitaires, 1962.

Hamon, Hervé, and Patrick Rotman. *Les Intellocrates: Expédition en Haute Intelligentsia*. Paris: Ramsay, 1981.

Hoffman, Stanley. *Decline or Renewal? France since the 1930s*. New York: Viking, 1974.

Joll, James. *Three Intellectuals in Power*. London: Pantheon Books, 1960.

Kadushin, Charles. *The American Intellectual Elite*. Boston: Little Brown, 1974.

Kirchheimer, Otto. *Political Justice: The Use of Legal Procedure for Political Ends.* Princeton: Princeton UP, 1961.

Kunnas, Tarmo. *Drieu, Brasillach, Céline et al.: Tentation Fasciste.* Paris: Les Septs Couleurs, 1971.

Lalou, René. *Contemporary French Literature.* New York: Knopf, 1924.

Laqueur, Walter, ed. *Fascism: A Reader's Guide.* Berkeley: University of California Press, 1976.

Leal, R. B. *Decadence in Love.* St. Lucia: U of Queensland P, 1973.

Lemert, Charles C. "Literary Politics and the *Champ* of French Sociology." *Theory and Society* 10 (1981): 645–69.

Lévy, Bernard-Henri. *L'Idéologie Française.* Paris: Grasset, 1981.

Lottman, Herbert R. *The Purge.* New York: William Morrow, 1986.

Lottman, Herbert R. *La Rive Gauche.* Trans. Marianne Veron. Paris: Seuil, 1981.

Loubet del Bayle, Jean-Louis. *Les Nonconformistes des Années Trente.* Paris: Seuil, 1969.

McCarthy, Patrick. *Céline.* London: Allen Lane, 1975.

Macciocchi, Maria-A., ed. *Eléments pour une Analyse du Fascisme.* 2 vols. Paris: Union Générale d'Editions, 1976.

Mazgaj, Paul. "The Young Sorelians and Decadence." *Journal of Contemporary History* 17 (1982): 179–299.

Mehlman, Jeffrey, ed. "Les Années Trente." Special French issue. *Modern Language Notes* 95, no. 4 (May 1980).

Mehlman, Jeffrey. "Blanchot à 'Combat': Littérateur et Terreur." *Tel Quel* 92 (1982): 48–65.

Michelin France Guide Rouge. Clermont-Ferrand: Michelin, 1983.

Moore, Harry T. *Twentieth Century French Literature to World War I.* Carbondale: Southern Illinois Press, 1966.

Mosse, George L. "The Mystical Origins of National Socialism." *Journal of the History of Ideas* (January 1961): 81–96.

Mosse, George L. *Nationalism and Sexuality.* Madison: U of Wisconsin P, 1985.

Mosse, George L. *Toward the Final Solution: A History of European Racism.* 1978. New York: Harper, 1980.

Noguères, Louis. *La Dernière Etape Sigmaringen.* Paris: Fayard, 1952.

Nolte, Ernst. *Three Faces of Fascism: Action Française, Italian Fascism, National Socialism.* Trans. Leila Vennewitz. 1965. New York: New American Library, 1969.

Novick, Peter. *The Resistance versus Vichy.* New York: Columbia UP, 1968.

O'Brien, Justin. *From the NRF.* New York: Farrar, Straus, 1958.

Ory, Pascal. *Les Collaborateurs, 1940–1945.* Paris: Seuil, 1976.

Ory, Pascal, and Jean François Sirinelli. *Les Intellectuels en France, de l'Affaire Dreyfus à Nos Jours.* Paris: Armand Colin, 1986.

Paxton, Robert O. *Vichy France: Old Guard and New Order.* 1972. New York: Norton, 1975.

Pélassy, Dominique. *Le Signe Nazi: L'Univers Symbolique d'une Dictature.* Paris: Fayard, 1983.

Le Petit Robert. Paris: Le Robert, 1981.

Picon, Gaeten. *Contemporary French Literature*. New York: F. Ungar, 1974.

Picon, Gaeten. *L'Usage de la Lecture*. Paris: Mercure de France, 1961.

Plumyène, J., and R. Lasierra. *Les Fascismes Français 1923–1963*. Paris, 1963.

Rémond, René. "Droite-Gauche: Division Réelle ou Construction de l'Esprit?" *Bulletin de la Société d'Histoire Moderne* 22 (1983): 7–15.

Rémond, René. *Les Droites en France*. Paris: Aubier Montaigne, 1982.

Rémond, René. "Université: une Loi en Trop?" *Débat* 25 (1983): 52–57.

Rousso, Henry. *Un Château en Allemagne: Sigmaringen 1944–1945*. Paris: Ramsay, 1980.

Rousso, Henry. *Pétain et la Fin de la Collaboration*. Brussels: Complexe, 1984.

Serant, Paul. *Le Romantisme Fasciste*. Paris: Fasquelle, 1959.

Soucy, Robert. *Fascist Intellectual: Drieu La Rochelle*. Berkeley: U of California P, 1979.

Soucy, Robert. "Romanticism and Realism in the Fascism of Drieu." *Journal of the History of Ideas* 31 (1970).

Sternhell, Zeev. *La Droite Révolutionnaire, 1885–1914: Les Origines Françaises du Facisme*. Paris: Seuil, 1978.

Sternhell, Zeev. *Ni Droite Ni Gauche: L'Idéologie Fasciste en France*. Paris: Seuil, 1983.

Suleiman, Ezra N. *Elites in French Society*. Princeton: Princeton UP, 1978.

Talbott, John E. *The Politics of Educational Reform in France*. Princeton: Princeton UP, 1959.

Thibaudet, Albert. *French Literature from 1795 to Our Era*. New York: Funk and Wagnalls, 1967.

Tucker, William. "Fascism and Individualism in the Political Thought of Drieu." *Journal of Politics* 27 (1965): 153–77.

Vivie, François-Xavier de, ed. "La Collaboration." *Historia*, hors serie no. 39 (1975): 1–160.

Vivie, François-Xavier de, ed. "L'Epuration." *Historia*, hors serie no. 41 (1975): 1–160.

Weber, Eugen. *The European Right*. Berkeley: U of California P, 1975.

Werth, A. *France 1940–1955*. London: Robert Hale, 1956.

Winock, Michel. *Édouard Drumont et Cie*. Paris: Seuil, 1982.

Winock, Michel. "Fascisme à la Française ou Fascisme Introuvable?" *Débat* 25 (1983): 35–44.

Wolf, Dieter. *Doriot*. Paris: Fayard, 1969.

Woolf, S. J. *European Fascism*. London: Morrison and Gibb, 1968.

Unpublished Sources

ARCHIVES NATIONALES, PARIS, FRANCE

61 AJ Series: "Les Fonds de l'ENS aux Archives Nationales"

61 AJ 12 Promotions 1882–1890
    13 Promotions 1891–1901
    14 Promotions 1902–1909

15 *Concours d'entrée* 1880–1890
16 *Concours d'entrée* 1901–1904
17 *Concours d'entrée* 1905–1915
27 Scores on oral exams
60 Disciplinary Council 1929–1931
91 "Questions politiques, sociales, pedagogiques 1932–1933"
94 ENS-Sèvres; Papiers Bouglé 1921–1933
95 Bouglé, Centre du Documentation Sociale
96 Papiers Bouglé 1934–1939
98 Papiers Bouglé
104 Papiers Bouglé
104 2b Chapters of a work on illustrious *normaliens*
105, 106 ENS during World War II
109 ENS after the Liberation
110–113 Papiers Dupuy 1906–1910
119 *Agrégation* Candidates list 1914–1919, 1925–1934
161 Recruitment, Press Clippings 1921–1923
162 ENS Teaching/Political Organization
166 Students (Letters) 1927–1929
175 Individual student dossiers, *Certificat de licence* 1925–1926
176 Student Teaching
188 Student Teaching; Reports on students 1922–1930 (Letters)
192 General Statistics
198 Military Affairs
199–201 Fellowships, Prizes
202 Travel, Foreign Fellowships, "*Détachés*"
203 *Débouchement*, Alumni abroad
204 *Archicubes* (Letters), Alumni
206, 207 Association Amicale des Anciens Elèves
243 Promotion 1914
247 Promotion 1919
250 Promotion 1922–1923
251 Promotion 1924
252 Promotion 1925
253 Promotion 1926
254 Promotion 1927
256 Promotion 1929
257 Promotion 1930
258 Promotion 1931

72 AJ Series: Recent Gifts

72 AJ 249 End of Vichy Government, Press clippings, Pétain's speeches, Pucheu
253 La Liste Otto, Press/Publishing 1942–1944
257 France during the Occupation, Milice, Public Opinion
258 Political parties, Ideological forces

259 Propaganda, Questionnaires
353 Epuration and the Press

F7 Series: "Etats des versements des ministères" Série F Police Générale

F7 13196 Manifestations Diverses, Camelots du Roi 1938
13199 Action Française 1928–1932 (AF)
13207 Action Française Press 1921–1932
13208 Fascist movements: *Nouveau Siècle*, Faisceau
13209 Francistes, Bucard, Valois, Diverse tracts 1925
13211 Faisceau
13232 Jeunesses Patriotes, Phalange Universitaire 1926–1932
13241 Dissidents of the AF 1930–1931
13245, 13246 Activities of fascists: Notes, Press reports 1925–1926
13247 Surveillance of French Fascists
13248 Propaganda 1924–1925
13956 Fascist propaganda and diverse press: *Le Sillon, La République*
13957 Dissidents of the AF, Press, Piot (1934) Taittinger (1936)

CENTRE DU DOCUMENTATION JUIVE CONTEMPORAINE (CDJC)
PARIS, FRANCE

Trials

DLVI-879, CCII-2, CCII-7 Otto Abetz
CXCVII 2/4 Maurice Bardèche, Apologie du crime for *Nuremberg ou la Terre Promise*
3897 Procès Béraud
7806 Béraud
5714 Brasillach/Maurras
8705 Brasillach
1582 Isorni on Brasillach's trial
7516 Céline
1882 Céline, Affaire Grasset
CCXII-33, 34, 35a, 35b Affaire du *Dépêche Algérienne*
3242 Drieu, censorship of, *Révolution Nationale*
XLVII Procès de l'équipe *Je Suis Partout*
CCXIV 37, 38 Claude Jeantet
XLVII-5 Claude Jeantet
1406 Luchaire
8431 Maurras
XLVII-5 Rebatet

Texts

CCXX Brasillach, introduction to a book of A. Rosenberg
1566 Céline, *Bagatelles pour un Massacre*
1561 Céline, *L'Ecole des Cadavres*
DLVI 79, 80 *Voir la Figure* series: Chardonne, Fernandez

Works Consulted

4581 Giraudoux, *Pleins Pouvoirs*
8498 Luchaire, *Une Génération Realiste*
6844 Cousteau, *En ce Temps là*

Journals

XLD 516, XID 8, XXVa-305, LXXV 145 *Au Pilori*
9129 *Cahiers Jaune (Le Grand Magazine Illustré de la Race)* 1943
7628 *L'Assaut*
DXXXIV-22 *Nouveau Temps* (Luchaire)
CCCLXXXIII-14 Dossiers on *Gringoire*
7632 *L'Emancipation Nationale* PPF (1936–1938)
1651, 1652, 1653 *Notre Combat: Hebdomadaire Politique, Littéraire, Satirique* 38
"L'Enigma Maurrassienne" vue par Rebatet et Fernandez

BIBLIOTHÈQUE HISTORIQUE DE LA VILLE DE PARIS (BH)
PARIS, FRANCE

Ochs Collection on the Dreyfus Affair

Ochs D1221, 1222, 1223, 1225, 1226 Press Clippings
D1588, 1590, 1591, 1592, 1584 *Libre Parole* (1899–1910)
D1215 *La Bastille*, journal antimaçonnique (1902–1905)
D1589 Procès Zola-Dreyfus-Esterhazy
D1583 Ligue Antisemite de France

Periodical Collections

Comoedia (Hebdomadaire des Spectacles, Concerts, Lettres, Beaux Arts) René Delange, ed. September 1941–June 1944
La Gerbe (Hebdomadaire de la Volonté Francaise) A. de Chateaubriant, ed. 1940–1944
Gringoire (Le Grand Hebdomadaire Parisien, Politique et Littéraire) H. de Carbuccia, ed. 1928–1929, 1933
Je Suis Partout (Le Grand Hebdomadaire de la Vie Mondiale) Charles Leca, ed. 1942–1944
Pamphlet A. Fabre Luce, Pierre Dominique, J. Prévost, eds. 1933

NEW YORK PUBLIC LIBRARY PERIODICAL COLLECTION

Candide (Grand Hebdomadaire Parisien et Littéraire) A. Fayard, ed. 1924–1940 (microfilm)
Je Suis Partout (Le Grand Hebdomadaire de la Vie Mondiale) R. Brasillach, ed. 1938–1939 (microfilm)

Letters to the Author

Philippe Ariès June 1983
Mme. Raoul Audibert 2 August 1984

Maurice Blanchot 20 August 1983
Henri Guillemin 25 June 1983, 10 July 1984
Georges Lefranc 8 July 1983, 8 July 1984
Bertrand de Jouvenel 25 July 1982
Claude Roy 13 July 1984
Pierre Vilar 18 July 1984

Interviews

Pierre Andreu June 1982 Paris
Etienne Balibar June 1980 Paris
Maurice Bardèche May and June 1982 Paris
Georges Canguilhem January 1989 Paris
Jacques Derrida April 1983 New Haven
Jean Drieu La Rochelle June and November 1982 Paris
Jacques Isorni July 1982 Paris
Claude Jamet June 1982 Paris
Georges Lefranc July 1984 Courseules-sur-Mer, France
Herbert Lottman November 1981 Versailles
Thierry Maulnier December 1982 Versailles
Pascal Ory July 1982 Paris
Henri Quéffelec June 1983 Paris
Jean François Sirinelli April 1980 and June 1982 Paris
Alain Girard Slama June 1983, Paris, and November 1982 Florence, Italy
Robert Soucy July 1982 Paris
Jacques Soustelle August 1984 Paris

Personal Papers

MAURICE BARDÈCHE PERSONAL ARCHIVES, PARIS

Robert Brasillach *Fulgur* (*Tribune de l'Yonne*, Sens, 5 April 1927–28 August 1927). Other authors: Antoinin Fabre, Pierre Frémy, Fred Semach, Jean Martin, Jacques Talagrand (Thierry Maulnier), Paul Gadenne, José Lupin, Roger Vailland.

BIBLIOTHÈQUE NATIONALE MANUSCRIPT COLLECTION

Marcel Déat, Papiers Déat, "Mémoires Politiques" (4 vol.) Georges Lefranc, executor

JEAN DRIEU LA ROCHELLE, PERSONAL ARCHIVES, PARIS

Pierre Drieu La Rochelle "Lettres Réçus," "Lettre à Charles Maurras," "Lettre à A. Artinian"

INDEX

Abetz, Otto, 145–46, 153, 160
Abetz, Suzanne, 145, 153
Académie Française, 40, 83, 85, 99, 105, 109, 133, 144, 186n36
Académie des Inscriptions, 40
Action Française, 57, 106, 131, 133; Brasillach and, 28, 35, 128, 136; Fayard journals and, 116; Maxence's journals, 124–25
Action Française, Brasillach and, 28, 41, 151; Gaxotte and, 108; Marcel Jouhandeau and, 112; Thierry Maulnier and, 124; forties reviews and, 125; Jean Fayard and, 131; Charles Maurras and, 155
Alain (Emile-Auguste Chartier), 31, 55, 97; Claude Jamet and, 32, 119, 152; leftist pacifism and, 35, 127–28; Fabrègues' journals and, 123–24
A la Recherche de la France (Grasset), 147
Althusser, Louis, 26, 49, 54, 170n24
Anciens élèves, 26–28, 51, 68, 98, 135, 172n4
Andler, Charles, 55, 67, 97–98, 105
Andreu, Pierre, 107, 122–23, 127, 143
Anouilh, Jean, 191n29
Anti-Semitism, 8, 116; Ecole Normale Supérieure and, 14, 55–56, 63–64, 181n78; *Combat* and 125–26, 187n72, 188n80; Céline and, 145; Maurras and, 154, 193n76
Appel, Paul, 74, 100
Aragon, Louis, 119, 121, 151
Arendt, Hannah, 81, 146, 150, 158
Ariès, Philippe, 5
Arland, Marcel, 108, 121
Aron, Raymond, 26, 32, 34, 37–39, 70, 78–79, 121, 186n36
Aron, Robert, 113, 115, 119, 121, 143, 147, 149–50
L'Assault, 110–11, 113
Assouline, Pierre, 108, 139, 186n35
Audibert, Raoult, 31, 37–38, 40, 70, 122
Au Pilori, 78, 126, 141, 152
L'Aurore, 105

Austin, J., 156–57, 193n90
Aymé, Marcel, 191n29

Bainville, Jacques, 71, 187n69
Balibar, Renée, 173n19, 176n74
Bardèche, Maurice, 1928 promotion of, 26, 31, 35; school career of, 37–41 *passim*; and depiction of fascism, 73, 79; publishing networks and, 109, 111, 121–25 *passim*, 131
Barrault, Jean Louis, 191n29
Barrès, Maurice, 33, 40, 55–57, 72, 74, 78, 82, 105
Barthes, Roland, 10, 17, 19, 21, 68, 84, 94, 103, 112
Bataille, Georges, 38–39
Beach, Sylvia, 116
Béarn, Pierre, 143
Beaufret, Jean, 31, 35, 37, 41, 70
Beauvoir, Simone de, 139, 141, 144, 161–62
Bellesort, André, 35, 55, 172n5; publishing networks and, 111, 124; *Je Suis Partout* and, 131–33
Benda, Julien, 77, 156, 176n57, 190n14
Benoit, Pierre, 191n30
Béraud, Henri, 32, 77, 143, 148, 154, 158
Berdiaff, Nicholas, 121
Bergson, Henri, 119
Berl, Emmanuel, 123–24, 129
Bernanos, George, 121, 123–24, 188n77
Bernstein, Basil, 82
Berr, Henri, 63
Berthod, Aimé, 27
Blanchot, Maurice, student career of, 38–39; publishing networks and, 113–25 *passim*; *Combat* and, 125, 126, 187n72, 188n77
Blanzat, Jean, 121
Bloch, J. R., 121
Bloch, Marc, 34, 37, 70
Blond, Georges, 122–23, 143, 147, 191n40
Bloy, Léon, 8
Blum, Léon, 12, 27, 54, 56, 86, 93, 129, 134

Index

Lying Down Together: Law, Metaphor, and Theology
Milner S. Ball

Shaping Written Knowledge: The Genre and Activity of the Experimental Article in Science
Charles Bazerman

Textual Dynamics of the Professions: Historical and Contemporary Studies of Writing in Professional Communities
Charles Bazerman and James Paradis

Politics and Ambiguity
William E. Connolly

Machiavelli and the History of Prudence
Eugene Garver

Language and Historical Representation: Getting the Story Crooked
Hans Kellner

The Rhetoric of Economics
Donald N. McCloskey

Therapeutic Discourse and Socratic Dialogue: A Cultural Critique
Tullio Maranhão

The Rhetoric of the Human Sciences: Language and Argument in Scholarship and Public Affairs
John S. Nelson, Allan Megill, and Donald N. McCloskey, eds.

What's Left? The Ecole Normale Supérieure and the Right
Diane Rubenstein

The Politics of Representation: Writing Practices in Biography, Photography, and Policy Analysis
Michael J. Shapiro

The Legacy of Kenneth Burke
Herbert Simons and Trevor Melia, editors

The Unspeakable: Discourse, Dialogue, and Rhetoric in the Postmodern World
Stephen A. Tyler

Heracles' Bow: Essays on the Rhetoric and the Poetics of the Law
James Boyd White